Shankara
and
Indian Philosophy

SUNY Series in Religious Studies
Harold Coward, editor

Shankara and Indian Philosophy

Natalia Isayeva

State University of New York Press

Published by
State University of New York Press, Albany

Printed in the United States of America

For information, address the State University of New York Press,
State University Plaza, Albany, NY 12246

Library of Congress Cataloging-in-Publication Data

Isayeva, Natalia, 1954—
Shankara and Indian Philosophy/Natalia Isayeva.
p. cm. ... (SUNY series in religious studies)
Includes bibliographical references and index.
ISBN 0-7914-1281-4 (alk. paper). ...ISBN 0-7914-1282-2 (pbk.: alk. paper)
1. Śaṅkarācārya. 2. Philosophy, Indic. I. Title. II. Series.
B133. S5I84 1993
181'. 482...dc20

91-44466
CIP

10 9 8 7 6 5 4 3 2 1

To the memory of my teacher—
Oktyabrina Volkova

Contents

CHAPTER I

Introduction

The history of mankind can boast not only of its times of fame and glory but also of quieter times with a different kind of heroism. People cherish not only the names of great warriors and politicians but also the memory of sages, poets and spiritual teachers. Some of them died in oblivion, only to become absolutely indispensable at some crucial turning point in the development of cultural or religious life. (One remembers how, half a century after his death, Sören Kierkegaard, the eccentric Protestant mystic was posthumously recognized as a founder of existentialist trends in religious and philosophic thought.) Others were luckier: they came to this world so opportunely that their teachings were destined to influence their surroundings, enthrall thousands of followers and stamp the epoch with their own image. Such were the founders of the world religions and also such figures as Francis d'Assisi and Martin Luther.

According to the religious tradition of India, a happy correspondence between the efforts of a sage or reformer and the response of his followers is explained rather simply: when the world once again becomes steeped in sin or ignorance and deviates too far from the true path of knowledge, the higher God—Viṣṇu or Śiva—is embodied again and enters the world to restore its moral order. We have heard of ten principle *avatāras*[1] of Viṣṇu, among

1. *Avatāra* (from Sanskrit root *ava-tṛ* or go down, descend, be manifested) means descent or manifestation of a God in a lower form, accessible to perception.

whom one may note Kṛṣṇa, who took part in the famous battle between the Pāṇḍavas and the Kauravas on the field of Kuru as a charioteer and spiritual guide of the hero Arjuna. Many orthodox Hindus still believe that one of *the avatāras* of Śiva was Śaṅkara, the philosopher and religious figure of the early mediaeval period.

Śaṅkara is an amazing figure and, to my mind, the most brilliant personality in the history of Indian thought. An outstanding religious philosopher and mystical poet, an orthodox theologian and a shrewd reformer, a founder of monasteries, an errant preacher and a brilliant polemist—this is not even a full enumeration of his achievements, known to contemporaries and, more than a thousand years later, to us as well. He is believed to have died at the age of 32, approximately the age of Christ, but during his lifetime he managed to compose more than 400 works of various genres and to travel throughout nearly all of South India, edifying disciples and disputing opponents. It is Śaṅkara's preaching and philosophic activity that, in the eyes of orthodox tradition, accounts for the ultimate ousting of Buddhism from India in about the eighth century AD, and the revival of Brahmanism. But what matters most is not even the scale of the task set before the philosopher. The teaching of Śaṅkara is an example of extreme, perhaps unprecedented intellectual courage: starting with the orthodox idea of the unity of all being, he did not shy away from tracing all its consequences.

Vedanta, a religious and philosophical school founded by Śaṅkara, was shaped later than other *darśanas*: it happened after India had passed through Buddhist temptation and was moving back towards the womb of Brahmanist religion. The very name of this system (*veda-anta*, literally, end of the Vedas) is interpreted either as a systematic summary of their main points or as a school having its immediate source in the final portions of the Vedas, that is, in the Upaniṣads.

According to the venerable tradition of coupling orthodox philosophical schools, Vedanta is usually grouped with Mīmāṃsā; hence its other name—Uttara-Mīmāṃsā, or later Mīmāṃsā. In contrast to Pūrva-Mīmāṃsā, or first Mīmāṃsā, which also declared its close connection with sacred scripture, Vedanta teaches not about ritual rules and laws, based primarily on the literal interpretation of Vedic texts, but about the integral sense of revelation. Philosophic trends within Vedanta vary greatly: starting with Śaṅkara's monistic school, passing through the system of Rāmānuja, where the world and souls are considered to be parts or attributes of eternal Brahman, and winding up in the theistic dualism of Madhva, where Brahman is opposed to nature and living beings.

The system of Śaṅkara is called Advaita-Vedanta, that is, non-dual Vedanta; its task is to teach about eternal Brahman as the higher and only reality. Here Brahman is not simply one from the standpoint of higher knowledge *(pāramārthikam),* nothing ever happened to it; all the multiplicity of the phenomenal world is unfolded through *māyā*, its own creative power. *Māyā* is a kind of screen or magic illusion but, at the same time, it is the reverse side of Brahman itself. Just as a rope in the hands of a juggler seems to turn into a snake, or just as a piece of shell can be taken for silver from a distance, the qualities of the universe, according to Advaita-Vedanta, are only temporarily superimposed on the unchanging foundation of being. Liberation from this cosmic illusion *(mokṣa)* is achieved only through the return to Brahman as true knowledge.

The European public became acquainted with the ideas of Advaita as early as the first part of the nineteenth century;[2] however, a solid base for research into Śaṅkara's

---

2. One might remember in this respect a Latin treatise written by F. H. Windischmann (*Sancara sive de theologumenis Vedanticorum*, Bonn, 1833); a monograph by G. C. Haughton (*The Exposition of the Vedānta Philosophy*, London, 1835); and a somewhat later critical work by T. Foulkes (*The Elements of the Vedāntic Philosophy*, Madras, 1860). There is also an interesting work by J. R. Ballantyne (*Christianity Contrasted with Hindu Philosophy*, Madras, 1860) in which Śaṅkara's teaching is seen in relation to the ideas of G. Berkeley.

system was not supplied until nearly the end of the century. In 1883, Paul Deussen, an outstanding German scholar (who was, incidentally, also a friend and biographer of Nietzsche), published a monograph in which the teaching of the Indian philosopher was investigated mainly in the light of classical German philosophy, primarily the system of Kant.[3] Four years later, he published a full German translation of Śaṅkara's principal work, his Commentary on the *Brahmasūtras*.[4] After this, works dealing with Śaṅkara and his teaching started to appear by the dozen. By now their number has grown so vast that it would be senseless to suggest even a tentative review of the main ideas put forward by different scholars. One can take into account only some of the works which are still relevant for present-day Indology.

The exploration of Vedanta by the German historian of philosophy F. Max Müllar followed more or less along the lines drafted by Deussen, but he was mainly looking for analogies between the systems of Śaṅkara and Plato (discussed in one of his most popular books *Three Lectures of Vedānta Philosophy*). A monograph on early Vedanta written by Max von Walleser dealt with the teaching of Śaṅkara and some of his predecessors.[5] In 1926 an interesting book appeared by a German historian of religion, Rudolf Otto, who compared the notions of Śaṅkara and Meister Eckhart, while describing pecularities of the mystical traditions of East and West.[6] By that time Vedanta,

3. P. Deussen, *Das System des Vedānta,* Leipzig, 1883.

4. P. Deussen, *Die Sūtra's des Vedānta, nebst dem vollständigen Kommentare des Śaṅkara,* Leipzig, 1887.

5. M. von Walleser, *Der ältere Vedānta,* Geschichte, Kritik and Lehre, Heidelberg, 1910.

6. R. Otto, *West-östliche Mystik,* Vergleich und Unterscheidung zur Wesendeutung, Gotha, 1926. Later I will be considering some of the ideas of this book, as well as its critical review published by Paul Hacker in connection with its new edition (1971).

presented chiefly by Śaṅkara's Advaita, became (along with Buddhism) a popular subject not only for scholarly research but also for fiction.[7]

---

7. Vedantic themes, taking their origin in the ideas of the Upaniṣads, appear inthe works of the American Transcendentalists—Emerson and Thoreau. Fiction writers of the end of the nineteenth and the beginning of the twentieth century derived their image of Vedanta mainly from the first volume of Arthur Schopenhauer's famous work *Die Welt als Wille und Vorstellung* (1819), in which the German philosopher bases his research not on Buddhist sources but clearly on the Upaniṣads. Most susceptible to the ideas of Vedanta among all the literary currents proved to be the poetry of Symbolism. One is reminded, for example, of the Russian Symbolists with their frequent image of *māyā*. A poem by Konstantin Balmont "Māyā" was written in 1899 and included in the poetical cycle *Indian Herbs*. Its epigraph is composed by one of the 'great sayings' of the Upaniṣads—*Tat tvam asi* (Thou art that), as well as a saying "who knows the essence transcends grief," attributed by the poet to Śrī-Śaṅkarācārya. One remembers the lines of Vyacheslav Ivanov: "O Transparence! make a smiling fairy tale / Of the visions of life / Make lucid the veil of *māyā*!" (1904). And there is a quatrain of Maximilian Voloshin: "Sadly I accept / Lingering of ancient snakes: / A slow *Māyā*/ Of hastening days." (1905). Playing with the name of his correspondent, Voloshin writes to M. Kudashova (future wife of R. Rollan) "I am accepting you so: / Earth's midday mirage, / An illusion, a deception—a *māyā*." And in the threefold poem of an Akmeist poet Nickolay Gumilev "Soul and body", which is part of his collection of verses *Fiery column*, one encounters a threefold division of human nature: it is composed of soul, body and some "demanding subject", embracing all the universe. Though at first glance this poem is devoid of Indian notions and terms, this third entity invisibly present in every human being is evidently correlated with the idea of *ātman*: "When from the height the word of God / Blazed like a Polar Star, / Asking: "Who are you, the Demander?/ The soul appeared before Me, and the body." And here is the answer given by the Self "I'm He who dreams, and depth is covering / His ineffable name, / While you are only a weak glimpse of a dream / That is unfolding at the bottom of His consciousness!" (1919). It is fairly clear that Vedantic images are assuming here the traits of a widely shared metaphor, almost a platitude; they should be considered essentially a tribute to an accepted cultural tradition. A deeper acquaintance with Indian philosophy is more characteristic of prose writers of the next generation—H. Hesse, T. Mann, R. Rollan, A. Huxley. But it should be admitted that in their writings as well as in those of our contemporaries J. Kerouac and J. Salinger, Vedantic notions cannot be practically separated from Buddhist or Indian motifs in general.

Starting from the first decades of this century, the Western public became acquainted with the works of Indian scholars who received their education not only in traditional Indian centers of learning but also in Western universities. These scholars interpreted the religious and philosophical systems of India in the context of world (primarily European) history of philosophy. One should mention here the fundamental many-volumed works by S. Dasgupta and S. Radhakrishnan, in which Vedanta occupies the most extensive as well as the most prominent place.[8] A more concise exposition of Indian philosophy can be found in the well-known monograph by M. Hiriyanna.[9]

Indian and Western historians of philosophy laid a foundation for the comparative analysis of Vedanta and other religious and philosophical schools of India. A fruitful comparison and investigation of the main notions of Śaṅkara's Advaita and Rāmānuja's Viśiṣṭa-Advaita can be found in the works of D.N. Srinivasacari,[10] O. Lacombe,[11] P.N. Srinivasachari[12] and other scholars. The problems of historical borrowings and typological affinities between Vedanta and Buddhism were raised in the works of H. von Glasenapp.[13] The orthodox Indian scholar T.M.P. Mahadevan published several books on Advaita and a work dealing with the ideas of Śaṅkara's prede-

---

8. S. Dasgupta, *A History of Indian Philosophy*, vols. 1-4, Cambridge, 1921-22; vol. 5, Cambridge, 1955. S. Radhakrishnan, *Indian Philosophy*, New York, 1951.

9. M. Hiriyanna, *Outlines of Indian Philosophy*, Bombay, 1976.

10. D. N. Srinivasacari, *Śaṅkara and Rāmānuja*, Madras, 1913.

11. O. Lacombe, *L'absolu selon le Vedānta*, Paris, 1937.

12. P. N. Srinivasachari, *Advaita and Viśiṣṭādvaita*, Bombay, 1961.

13. H. von Glasenapp, *Der Stufenweg zum Göttliche, Śaṅkaras Philosophie der All-Einheit*, Baden-Baden, 1948. H. von Glasenapp, *Vedānta und Buddhismus*, Wiesbaden, 1950.

cessor, Gauḍapāda; he also translated into English some works of Śaṅkara and other Advaitists.[14]

Probably the most noticeable trait, and one of the major shortcomings, of the first scholarly works on Śaṅkara is their enthusiastic superficiality of investigation. In the words of Paul Hacker, taken from his review of I. Vecchiotti's book on present-day Indian thinkers, "ist es gewiss ... Gewohnheit, Probleme, statt sie zu lösen, in schwebender Formulierung literarisch zu stilisieren" ("It is certainly ... the usual practice instead of solving the problems to stylize them literarily in misty formulae.")[15] Though this scathing remark applies mainly to the peculiarities of Radhakrishnan's literature style, which differs considerably from the more sombre and sober style of Śaṅkara, it also pertains to quite a number of critical essays on Advaita.

Among the historical works on Śaṅkara's teaching which resisted the temptation of too sweeping generalizations, one should note two books and numerous articles by P. Hacker,[16] as well as a precise and serious work by K. Satchidananda Murty.[17] In my opinion, they not only ensure the right direction of analysis but also substantiate the examination by a thorough analysis of original San-

---

14. T.M.P. Mahadevan, *The Philosophy of Advaita,* London, 1938. T.M.P. Mahadevan, *The Study of Advaita,* London, 1957. T.M.P. Mahadevan, *Gauḍapāda: A Study in Early Advaita,* Madras, 1952. T.M.P. Mahadevan, *The Hymns of Śaṅkara,* Madras, 1970.

15. P. Hacker, Review of Icilio Vecchiotti's *Pensatori dell'India contemporanea,* Roma, 1959, in *Zeitschrift der Deutschen Morgenländischen Gesellschaft,* no. 111, 1961, p. 373.

16. P. Hacker, "Untersuchungen über Texte des frühen Advaitavāda." *I. Die Schüler Śaṅkaras,* Meinz-Wiesbaden, 1951. P. Hacker, *Vivarta, Studien zur Geschichte der illusionistische Kosmologie und Erkenntnistheorie der Inder,* Meinz-Wiesbaden, 1953. P. Hacker, "Eigentümlichkeiten der Lehre und Terminologie Saṅkaras: Avidyā, Nāmarūpa, Māyā, Īśvara," *Zetschrift der Deutschen Morgenländischen Gesellschaft,* no. 100, 1950, pp. 246-86, etc.

17. K. Satchidananda Murty, *Revelation and Reason in Advaita-Vedanta,* London, 1959.

skrit texts and their categorical structure. I will often make use of these works in my own investigation of Advaita that follows.

Recently a new period of Vedantic studies has developers which is characterized by philological methods and specific textological devices. Many works have appeared dealing with the technical terms and notions of this religious school of thought, as well as with some of the actual texts. This trend looks most promising and may well become highly significant in the historical and philosophical analysis of Advaita. A close interweaving of philology and philosophy is characteristic of recent publications by Lambert Schmithausen,[18] Klaus Rüping,[19] Tillmann Vetter,[20] Wilhelm Halbfass[21] and other German and Austrian Indologists. New critical editions of Śaṅkara's works have appeared,[22] as well as numerous new translations.[23]

---

18. Lambert Schmithausen, "Maṇḍanamiśra's Vibhramavivekaḥ", *Mit einer Studies zur Entwicklung der Indischen Irrtumslehre,* Wien, 1965.

19. Klaus Rüping, *Studien zur Frühgeschichte der Vedanta-Philosophie, Part 1. Philologische Untersuchungen zu den Brahmasūtra-Kommentaren des Śaṅkara und des Bhāskara,* Wiesbaden, 1977.

20. Tillmann Vetter, *Studien zur Lehre und Entwicklung Śaṅkaras,* Wien, 1979.

21. Wilhelm Halbfass, *Studies in Kumārila and Śaṅkara,* Reinbek, 1983.

22. One of the most active scholars in this field is a professor of Indian philosophy from Tokyo University, Sengaku Mayeda, who recently published a new annotated edition of Śaṅkara's treatise *(Upadeśasāhasrī, Śaṅkara's Upadeśasāhasrī.* Critically edited with introduction and indices by Sengaku Mayeda, Tokyo, 1973.)

23. Among more recent translation of Śaṅkara's Commentary on *Brahmasūtra* one should mention an English translation of Swami Gambhīrānanda, closer to the original text than a famous classical version by G. Thibaut, *Brahma-Sūtras with Śaṅkara's Commentary,* translated by Swami Gambhīrānanda, New Delhi, 1968. Another fairly exact rendering is that of V.H. Date, though sometimes it seems too literal. V.H. Date, *Vedanta Explained, Śaṅkara's Commentary on the Brahmasūtra,* vols. I-II, New Delhi, 1973.

The Italian scholar Mario Piantelli wrote a biography of Śaṅkara in which he brought together the material of hagiographical sources and also analyzed extensive literary, historical and archaeological data on Śaṅkara's life.[24]

Even in Russia some recent work seems to be pointing in this direction. V. S. Kostyuchenko published *Classic Vedanta and Neo-Vedantism,* part of which is devoted to the analysis of the main notions of various schools of Vedanta.[25] V. G. Lysenko's work on Indian atomism includes a chapter on Śaṅkara's polemics with the Vaiśeṣikas.[26] The first excerpts from Śaṅkara's original texts were published in Russian by E. Zilberman and later, after his emigration, by myself.

The aim of this book is to examine the main notions of Śaṅkara's Advaita: his concept of the identity of *ātman* and Brahman, his unusual understanding of causality, his idea of *māyā,* etc. It goes without saying that at some points this goal presupposed an explicit interpretation of the inner logical connections inherent in Advaita. Such an interpretation unavoidably requires a certain arbitrariness: these inner connections and logical links are usually anything but self-evident, and Śaṅkara himself probably did not consciously lay them down in the foundation of his system. Indeed, the Advaitist regarded his own school of thought basically as a true reflection of the original teachings of the Vedas, where each notion was equally important, that is, theoretically independent. In my opinion, logical correspondences, outlined in this work, were brought about mostly by the needs of inner structure and the balanced architectonics of Advaita itself.

---

24. M. Piantelli, *Śaṅkara e la rinascita del brāhmanesimo,* Fossano, 1974.

25. V. S. Kostyuchenko, *Klassicheskaya Vedanta i neovadantizm,* Moskva, 1983.

26. V. G. Lysenko, *Indiyskaya filosofiya prirody; Atomizm shkoly vaisheshika,* Moskva, 1986.

All of this does not mean, however, that the historical development of Vedanta as well as its immediate roots and sources will be ignored. Some historical material is to be found mainly in the first two chapters of the book. The problem of historical analysis of Advaita is not as simple as it might seem at first sight. It compels the researcher to assume a definite attitude towards the problem of the influence of Buddhism and other religious and philosophical schools on Śaṅkara's teaching.

It is well known that one of Śaṅkara's closest teachers was Gauḍapāda, whose main work, *Māṇḍūkya-kārikā*, was undoubtedly composed under the direct impact of Buddhist ideas. Śaṅkara wrote a deferential commentary on the *Kārikā*; it was owing to the intermediary position of Gauḍapāda that there appeared in Śaṅkara's works the notion of different levels of reality, the concept of higher and lower truth, and even the idea of *māyā*, which was not clearly elaborated in the Upaniṣads. Many present-day scholars maintain that Advaita was formed through the decisive influence of earlier teachings and that its main notions were intentionally or unintentionally borrowed from earlier and contemporary systems, some of them even from heterodox ones.

It goes without saying that historically Advaita could not have taken its distinctive shape without the contribution and experience of its numerous predecessors. Śaṅkara was quite ready to acknowledge the connections of his own teaching with Pūrva-Mīmāṃsā, especially as regards its relations to the Vedas or to *pramāṇas*. Quite evident also is the conceptual affinity between Advaita, on the one hand, and Sāṃkhya and Yoga, on the other. And of course, Śaṅkara owes much of his inclination towards logical argumentation, as well as his interest in epistemological problems not only to the orthodox systems but primarily to Buddhism and Jainism.

Nevertheless, an attempt to understand Advaita's connections with other systems seems rather futile when it is made not to clarify historical influences but to single out 'borrowed' elements from this solid and complete system.

Polemizing against other teachings and defending his own school of thought, Śaṅkara often assimilated and integrated religious and philosophical concepts of his predecessors and opponents; but he bore full responsibility for the specific way in which these blocks were fitted into the balanced structure of Advaita, as well as for the part they were forced to play to maintain its new equilibrium. His task was to try to curb the activity of 'heretics', to put an end to mental instability in general and what was of no less importance—to set limits on ritual trends within a former Brahmanist unity, submitting it to a new kind of spiritual order. He became the author of a precise and internally consistent system, which later proved to be sufficiently tolerant to interpretations at the level of ordinary life, which marked the beginning of numerous trends and new schools—but which still played its part in the gradual restoring of a Brahmanic unity.

In this context an essential issue, as well as a particularly delicate one is Śaṅkara's relationship with Buddhism. Judging by the crucial position of Gauḍapāda, who presented a sort of intermediary between Mahāyāna and Vedanta, this problem cannot be solved by determining, so to speak, Buddhist fragments inside Advaita teaching.

Sometimes scholars seek a satisfactory solution by dividing Śaṅkara's work into several stages. Early Śaṅkara is virtually identified with Gauḍapāda and Buddhism, while his mature works, to their mind, testify to the growing of more traditional and objective or even realistic elements. This attitude is characteristic of S. Dasgupta and P. Hacker; the latter singles out yet another stage in the development of Śaṅkara's thought—his alleged attraction to Yoga, preceding even the Buddhist period.[27] This opin-

---

27. Cf. P. Hacker, "Śaṅkara der Yogin und Śaṅkara der Advaitin, Einige Beobachtungen." Beitrage zur Gelstesgeschichte Indiens. Festschrift für Ericn Frauwallner, Wien, 1968, pp. 119-48. In the work dealing specially with Śaṅkara's commentary on *Māṇḍūkya-kārikā* of Gauḍapāda, P. Hacker writes, "The only possible explanation of the inconsistency and confusion of Śaṅkara's argumentation is the hy-

ion became more or less prevalent among Western Indologists. In the words of F. Whaling, "Part of the story of Śaṅkara's own development is his own reaction against the undue Buddhist influence he felt he had received from Gauḍapāda ... While Śaṅkara applied Gauḍapāda's key to his interpretations, the very fact that his canvas was so much wider, and his task more varied, meant that he could not follow Gauḍapāda in every detail.[28]

In my opinion, this division of Śaṅkara's—rather brief, incidentally—activity into periods seems a bit strained. Differences in the contents (as well as style) of his works are not that great; his divergencies from Gauḍapāda and the Buddhists look far more significant. Finally, the notion of the gradual development of Śaṅkara's views from Buddhist inclinations towards conventional orthodoxy leaves without any satisfactory explanation the fact that all his life was devoted to a fierce struggle against the Buddhists and other heterodox opponents.

In general, the problem of the essence of Advaita and the scope of Buddhist influence on its formation continues to draw the attention of scholars interested in Śaṅkara's system. Though a wide variety of opinions has been presented, their very approach to the problem suggests a common presupposition to which I feel bound to raise an objection.

According to T.M.P. Mahadevan, an apparent similarity between Advaita and Buddhist Śūnyavāda was simply a tactical device of Śaṅkara, his means of overcoming an opponent, while pretending to take his side. He is speak-

---

pothesis that he tried his level best, but failed, to unite into a consistent whole elements of different traditions and some ideas of his own .... In his other commentaries the same confusion does not appear again. P. Hacker, "Notes on *Māṇḍūkyopaniṣad* and Śaṅkara's *Āgamaśāstravivaraṇa*", *India Maior,* Congratulation volume presented to J. Gonda, ed. J. Ensink and P. Gaeffke, Leiden, 1972, p. 129.

28. F. Whaling, "Śaṅkara and Buddhism", *Journal of Indian Philosophy,* Dordrecht, vol. 7, no. 1, March 1979, p. 23.

ing about Gauḍapāda but his words are meant to embrace the attitude of Gauḍapāda's disciple: "[T]he main aim of the teacher is to expound the philosophy of the Upaniṣads, and ... he does not deviate from his purpose even when he adopts the arguments of the Bauddha Idealists and dresses his thought in Buddhist terminology."[29] Summing up similar statements, characteristic of traditionally minded Indian scholars, S. Mudgal says that according to them, Śaṅkara "adopted practically all ... dialectic (of the Buddhists), their methodology, their arguments and analysis, their concepts, their terminologies and even their philosophy of the Absolute, gave all of them a Vedantic appearance, and demolished Buddhism ... Śaṅkara embraced Buddhism, but it was a fatal embrace.[30]

There is great support for the diametrically opposed point of view according to which Mahāyāna Buddhism and Advaita of Śaṅkara absolutely coincide in their main tenets. In the opinion of S. Radhakrishnan, C. Sharma and many other scholars, any differences found between these schools concern barely perceptible academic (that is, scholastic) matters and do not touch the core of the problem. In the words of Chandradhar Sharma, "Buddhism and Vedanta should not be viewed as two opposed systems but only as different stages in the development of the same central thought which starts with the Upaniṣads, finds its indirect support in Buddha, its elaboration in Mahāyāna Buddhism, its open revival in Gauḍapāda, which reaches its zenith in Śaṅkara and culminates in the Post-Śaṅkarites."[31]

On closer deliberation, the roots of similar statements can be found in the views of those passionate advocates of

---

29. T. M. P. Mahadevan, *Gauḍapāda: A Study in Early Advaita*, p. 219.

30. S. Mudgal, *Advaita of Śaṅkara: a Reappraisal, Impact of Buddhism and Sāṃkhya on Śaṅkara's Thought*, Delhi, 1975, p. 187.

31. C. Sharma, *A Critical Survey of Indian Philosophy*, London, 1960, p. 318.

Vedantic tradition who suspected even Śaṅkara himself of hidden sympathies for Buddhism. These views go back to Śaṅkara's junior contemporary, the Vedantist Bhāskara, who thought that Śaṅkara's notion of *māyā*, derived from Buddhism, was undermining the authority of Vedic religion. Later Rāmānuja was to call Śaṅkara a 'crypto-Buddhist' *(pracchanna-bauddha)*.[32] It is clear, however, that the matter boils down to a shift in emphasis. The aspects that aroused the indignation of strictly orthodox Vedantins are now extolled by their more liberally-minded successors. After a small cosmetic operation, after purifying Buddhism and Advaita of accidental or historically conditioned accretions, both systems can be safely regarded as an expression of one and the same eternal absolute truth. In the words of one of the leading historians of religion, "the differences between Śaṅkara and Mahāyāna doctrines are largely a matter of emphasis and background" rather than real essence.[33] The same notion prevails in the fundamental work of S. Radhakrishnan *Indian Philosophy*, the last chapter of which deals specifically with the unity of all systems.[34]

Finally, a modification of this thesis is presented by the notion of a deep and decisive influence of Buddhism upon renewed Brahmanism. When a scholar feels reluctant to deny the originality of Vedanta, he can find a solution, ascribing to Śaṅkara an attempt at reconciliation of two currents of thought: the Buddhist and the orthodox one (the latter starting with the Upaniṣads). According to S. Mudgal, for example, "the Advaita Vedanta seems to be an attempt on the part of Gauḍapāda and Śaṅkara, to recon-

---

32. The definition can be found in Rāmānuja's main work, his commentary on Bādarāyaṇa's *Brahmasūtra* (see *Śrībhāṣya*, II.II. 27).

33. Ninian Smart, *Doctrine and Argument in Indian Philosophy*, London, 1964, p. 104.

34. See S. Radhakrishnan, *Indian Philosophy*, vol. 2, New York, 1951.

cile the two currents of thought, Buddhist and Upaniṣadic. The two currents thus developed separately and independently, are opposed to one another, as the orthodox and heterodox, the thesis and its antithesis, and a synthesis was attempted by the Advaitin Śaṅkararācārya, in his *Two Tier Philosophy*.[35]

According to the extreme version of these notions, one cannot even maintain the thesis of mutual enrichment of both teachings within the Advaita framework. Talking about Buddhist impact on Advaita, S. Dasgupta, incidentally, flatly denies Śaṅkara's system any originality: "I am led to think that Śaṅkara's philosophy is largely a compound of Vijñānavāda and Śūnyavāda Buddhism with the Upaniṣad notion of the permanence of self superimposed.[36] In other words, some scholars try to create the impression that the new ideas, dialectics and other intellectual achievements of Buddhism were extracted by the Advaitist from the 'heretical' teaching of his opponents and hastily disguised with the help of conventionally safe orthodox phraseology—just so that their explosive potential could be rendered harmless and adapted to the existing religious and social order. The same conclusion is drawn by C. Eliot in a fundamental work devoted to the problem of interrelations between Buddhism and orthodox religion: "The debt of Śaṅkara to Buddhism is an interesting question. He indited polemics against it and contributed materially to its downfall, but yet if the success of creeds is to be measured by the permanence of ideas, there is some reason for thinking that the vanquished led the conqueror captive."[37]

Irrespective of whether a scholar acknowledges or denies a certain independence in Śaṅkara's teaching, such statements subtly convey the idea of an obsolete tradition

35. S. Mudgal, *Advaita of Śaṅkara: A Reappraisal,* p. 175.

36. S. Dasgupta, *A History of Indian Philosophy,* vol. I, p. 494.

37. C. Eliot, *Hinduism and Buddhism,* vol. 2, New York, 1954, p. 211.

grafting on new tenets, whether original or derived. Hence all the bitter laments over the 'excessive' dependence of Advaita upon sacred texts and Vedantic orthodoxy. Hence all the endeavors to explain and excuse the Advaitin's 'narrow-mindedness', indicating that, after all, he was a son of his time, the limits of which he could not exceed, no matter how he tried. In the above-mentioned work by C. Eliot one finds the following argument about Śaṅkara: "But since his whole object was to revive the traditions of the past and suppress his originality by attempting to prove that his ideas are those of Bādarāyaṇa and the Upaniṣads, the magnitude of his contribution to Indian thought is often underrated."[38]

Of course, it goes without saying that renewing Brahmanism, the roots of which were nourished by Vedanta, was not a mere restoration of conceptual schemes prevalent before the rise of heterodox schools. But Advaita, which lent scope and significance to this process, was by no means just a chaotic mixture of Buddhism and Brahmanism with a handful of other ideas derived from various systems thrown in. If one assumed it to be this sort of mixture, one could only regard the traditional religion as some accidental and obsolete container for a new content.

I try to show in this book how Advaita succeeded in reshaping and assimilating some major notions that originated within the Buddhist frame of thought. But even more important for understanding Śaṅkara's teaching is the problem of Advaita's attitude towards sacred tradition, towards Vedic sayings. The sacred tradition here is not simply a bursting wineskin which cannot contain new wine: after audacious 'heretics'—the Buddhists and the Jainas—dared to doubt the infallibility of the Vedas, Śaṅkara had to rethink the role of sacred scripture, trying to tie it more strongly to the core of his own teaching. Finally, in spite of the obvious similarity between Śaṅkara's and the Mīmāṃsākas' attitude to the Vedas, Advaita's

38. C. Eliot, *Hinduism and Buddhism,* vol. 2, p. 312.

belief in the eternity and absolute importance of scripture was not just an artless repetition of Pūrva-Mīmāṃsā dogmata. When concepts that look identical at first glance, fall within the gravitational fields of different premises, centripetal forces shape them in their own peculiar way.

In order to determine Śaṅkara's place in the history of Indian culture, it was essential to deliberate over the way the sacred texts, and sacred tradition in general, were refracted in his system. That is why I have presented Advaita first in its vehement opposition to 'heretical' schools and to Lokāyata, and subsequently in its comparison with Pūrva-Mīmāṃsā. In order to achieve a more vivid perception it seemed a good idea to trace an outline of the system against a strange background, and then check the accuracy of the contours by seeing it in relation to its closest yet still different orthodox counterpart. However, what was meant to be merely a formal method for organizing the material, produced unexpected results. This method revealed some important inner tenets of Advaita, precisely because attention was brought to the role of sacred scripture in Śaṅkara's teaching. It turned out that Vedic texts play a serious theoretical part in securing an inner intellectual balance to his system, valid for every specific problem arising in course of the polemics.

This method not only clarified the main direction of the work but also the concrete means of its accomplishment. Besides textual analysis and historical and philosophical deliberation, there was occasional need to resort to a more specific analysis of Śaṅkara's theological concepts. Though I tried as far as possible to avoid somewhat strained comparisons between Advaita and Christianity, certain notions of Christian hermeneutics (even in the absence of any direct references to it) helped bring to light Śaṅkara's attitude to revelation and, in a wider context, to his philosophy of language.

One can find many features in common between Advaita and Western religious and philosophical systems: similar points could be determined in the scholastic teachings of Thomas Aquinas and Bernard de Clairvaux, as well as in the mystic Christianity of Meister Eckhart; indeed, they can be traced as far as some notions of German dialectical theology or Christian existentialism. It seems that in the history of philosophy the same problems keep surfacing with surprising regularity. They come up again and again but receive different interpretations—and different solutions—depending on the intellectual life of the time and predominant cultural dispositions. Finally, it is sometimes important to draw comparisons even between distant concepts and systems to clarify what is really dissimilar in them. In his review of a German edition of Mircea Eliade's famous book on Yoga, Paul Hacker underlines the necessity to approach the study of theological distinctions between religious and philosophical systems by way of philological or historico-philological investigation. He further specifies: "Das Unterscheiden ist hier doch wohl wichtiger als die Feststellung von Ähnlichkeiten, die, füz sich allein Betueben, allzu leicht zu einer falschen Gleichsetzung wizd" ("The difference here is much more important than any determination of similarities, since the latter being treated by themselves, lead only too easily towards a false concept of identity.")[39] I have tried to abide by this warning while working on this book.

39. P. Hacker, Review of Mircea Eliade's *Yoga, Unsterblichkeit und Freiheit,* Zürich, 1960. In *Zeitschrift für Missionswissenschaft und Religionswissenschaft,* Münster, no. 46, 1962, p. 318.

CHAPTER II

The Beginning of Vedanta: A Historical Sketch

1. *VEDANTA AND HETERODOX SCHOOLS IN HISTORICAL RETROSPECTIVE*

One of the most popular notions in the history of philosophical and religious thought in India is that of extraordinary mutual tolerance allegedly displayed by different teachings. In the words of S. Radhakrishnan, "That is why the heretic, the sceptic, the unbeliever, the rationalist and the freethinker, the materialist and the hedonist all flourish in the soil of India."[1] This apparently peaceable—and surprising—disposition of opposing views has usually been explained by the 'harmonious' and 'antidogmatic' character of the Indian tradition. In the interesting collection of comments on the posthumously published *Inklusivismus*[2] by P. Hacker, this tradition is discussed primarily from the standpoint of its ability to incorporate alien ideas. Special flexibility and tolerance are ascribed to both Buddhism and Śaṅkara's Advaita; these features are judged to be indications of their maturity as compared with other philosophical systems. The latter are mostly regarded as preparatory stages to a higher order of reflection.

To my mind, though, one can maintain the thesis of special tolerance of these religious and philosophical

1. S. Radhakrishnan, *Indian Philosophy,* vol. I. New York, 1951, p. 27.

2. Vide: *Inklusivismus, Eine indische Denkform,* Wien, 1983.

teachings only with regard to their interpretations at the level of ordinary life, ritual and other 'applied' versions. At the level of metaphysical tenets, however, we encounter in Indian philosophy and religion a diverse and colorful picture of the collision of different currents and concepts.

While one is trying to comprehend the role played in the history of Indian thought by heterodox and 'heretical' schools, as well as by some unconventional currents within the orthodox framework, the very notion of the development of this philosophy inevitably changes. It becomes clear that its rhythm and direction are to a great extent determined by the mutual opposition and struggle of the main philosophical systems.

The shaping of philosophical teachings which consciously opposed themselves to Brahmanist orthodoxy had been preceded by a stage of unrest closely connected with the crisis of the previous forms of Vedic religion. According to the classical work of S. Belvalkar and R. Ranade, "the evidence ... would go quite a long way to confirm, in the first place, what we have said above ... the existence in the Upaniṣadic period of a large mass of 'heretic' or 'heterodox' philosophy outside the pale of Brahmanism, but perceptibly influencing the tone and trend of its speculation in ways more than one."[3]

The early opposition to Brahmanism was formed mostly by the efforts of errant preachers, or *parivrājaka's* (wanderers, in the terms of the Upaniṣads) and *śramaṇa's* (ascetics, those who mortify the flesh). Mendicant teachers, wandering with their disciples, often expressed views deviating from orthodox tenets. The Buddhist Pali canon mentions six of the most popular *śramaṇa* teachers as early as the fifth century BC.[4] One of them—Makkhali

---

3. S. K. Belvalkar, R. D. Ranade, *History of Indian Philosophy,* vol. 2, *The Creative Period,* Poona, 1927, pp. 443-444.

4. The usual list of teachers who were widely known to take part in discussions with the Buddhists includes the names of Pūraṇa Kassapa, Ajita Keśakambalin, Pakudha Kaccāyana, Sanjaya Belatthiputta,

Gosāla—is considered to be the founder of the so-called Ājīvika sect,[5] some ideas of which had a considerable impact on Buddhism itself.

Within the framework of Ājīvika a concept of rigid natural determinism was elaborated. This concept of *niyati,* (lit.: fixed, restrained order of things; hence—necessity, destiny, fate) excluded the intervention of any supernatural or divine powers—and also excluding the very possibility of individual free choice. Along with the denial of the basic tenets of traditional religion, this school of thought stressed a fatalistic notion of the vanity of any human effort that aimed at change. Thus, simultaneously with the criticism of Brahmanic ideas, the Ājīvakas arrived at the conviction of the absurdity of any notions of freedom and moral responsibility, as well as the denial of accepted ethical norms. Finally, the concept of *karma* in their system lost most of its moral implications and became closely identified with the impersonal operation of *niyati.* A famous German scholar, Hermann Jacobi, once voiced the opinion that even the Buddha and the legendary founder of Jainism, Mahāvīra, were much indebted in their concepts to these 'heretics' and that they formed dissimilar notions, consciously distancing themselves from these early critics of Brahmanism.[6]

Nigantha Naṭaputa and Makkhali Gosāla. A more detailed account of their activities can be found in a somewhat biased study of Indian philosophy by Walter Ruben in which the greatest emphasis is placed on 'materialistic' or 'naturalistic' trends (W. Ruben, *Geschichte der indischen Philosophie,* Berlin, 1954, pp. 104-111.

5. *Ājīvika,* from *ājīvaka*, a religious mendicant, somebody who is following special rules with regard to finding his livelihood *(ājīva)* in different parts of the country. The most comprehensive work on the history of the Ājīvika sect was written by A. Basham (A. L. Basham, *History and Doctrines of the Ājīvikas*, A Vanished Indian religion, London, 1951).

6. Vide: H. Jacobi, Introduction to the *Jaina Sūtras*, Part II, *Sacred Books of the East*, London, vol. 45, p. xxvii ff.

Unlike the Ājīvakas, later 'heretics'—the Buddhists and the Jainas—left intact the traditional notions of *karma* and liberation. However, these heterodox teachings also contributed significantly to undermining the former Brahmanic religion based on sacrifice. One might note that 'heretical' schools and Lokāyata (Indian materialism) mainly opposed the minute regulation of human life by Vedic injunctions, rejecting some obsolete and cumbersome Brahmanic rites.

Having introduced the ideal of monastic community *(saṅgha)*, Buddhism indirectly encroached upon the forming social base of Brahmanism—the institution of the four *varṇas* and the four 'stages of life' *(varṇāśramavyavasthā)*. It is well-known that the Buddhists preached the equality of all people regardless of their social status. They believed in honouring as Brahman a person on the way to liberation and not the one who laid claim to it by his birthright. They considered to be most beneficial from the standpoint of moral and religious merit not the consecutive passing of all four stages[7] but the direct transition to the higher plane of resignation from worldly cares. That was the plane symbolized by the monk's role, wholly absorbed by the desire to be liberated from the cycle of reincarnations *(saṃsāra)*. In the words of S. Mudgal, "so tired were the people of Brahmin sacerdotalism, that they responded fully to the call of Buddhism."[8] According to him, "[T]he Buddhist movement, institutionalised, organised, and having imperial patronage and general sympathy, with their monasteries and universities, monks and nuns, coming from all orders of the society, was sympathetically received, and fashionably accepted.[9]

7. That is, the stage of an unmarried student getting Vedic lessons from a teacher *(brahmacārin)*, that of a householder *(gṛhastha)*—a Brahman performing the duties of the father of the family, that of an anchorite living in the forest *(vanaprastha)*, and finally that of a religious mendicant *(sannyāsin)*.

8. S. Mudgal, *Advaita of Śaṅkara: A Reappraisal*, p. 170.

9. Ibid.

One might note that heterodox teachings opposed not only Brahmanism. In the eyes of the Buddhists and the Jainas, it was not only the adherents of other schools but very often even the followers of other currents of thought within their own system who were regarded as heretical, even as their own teachings were heretical for the traditionalists. Brahmanic orthodoxy was quick to realize what constituted the core of contradictions separating it from the heterodox opponents, and usually lumped them together under the name of *"nāstika"*. The best known definition of the term is given in *Manu-smṛti* (II.3): "the follower of *nāstika* is a man who does not recognize the authority of the Veda."[10] Teachings of this kind gradually became rather popular. Their prevalence, judging by the testimony of orthodox opponents, continued till the fourth and third centuries BC.

Up to this time similar new sects were appearing while the existing ones were often splitting up into smaller branches. The Jaina canonical texts enumerate as many as 363 schools *(diṭṭhi);* the Buddhist *Dīgha-ṇikāya* classifies 62 teachings opposing Buddhism. Indeed, the concrete figures are more or less arbitrary, but they are incontestable evidence of disunity and rivalry. The prolification of ideas and sects was a sure sign of imminent decline.

For fairness' sake one should say that religious beliefs and philosophical teachings based on traditional orthodoxy were no less varied. However, in spite of all the multitude of voices inside the Brahmanic universe the common tuning fork for every one of them was the Vedic texts. A somewhat new conception is slowly making its way here: all ritual rules and ethical norms, as well as all

---

10. Cf. a similar interpretation of *nāstika* in the *Mahābhārata* (XII. 162.7; XII. 15.33; XII. 12.4). There is also a well-known etymological reconstruction by Pāṇini (*Aṣṭādhyāyī,* IV.6) who derives *nāstikamata* from *na-asti,* saying that *nāstika* is a person who maintains that there is no 'other world' *(paralokaṃ nāsti),* that is, any existence after death. The later interpretiton of *nāstika* is, strictly speaking, applicable only to the Lokāyatikas.

philosophical notions, are ultimately just an outward projection of a certain common foundation.

Nostalgic longing after lost spiritual unity and the related consolidation of traditional elements coincided with the weakening influence of heterodox teachings. The reasons for the decline of *nāstika* can be found in the changing political and economical situation in India and in the inner development of the 'heretical' doctrines.

During its flourishing, Buddhism enjoyed the patronage of many mighty rulers. It is generally known, for instance, that the Buddhist *saṅgha* received active support from a Maurya, king Aśoka, in the later part of his reign, that is, in the second half of the third century BC. Buddhism also experienced the extensive growth of Mahāyāna with the blessing of a Kushana King Kaniṣka at the end of the first and the beginning of the second century AD.[11] After the Gupta dynasty came to power, royal assistance was also rendered to Brahmanic sects. A renewed and modified version of Brahmanism later acquired the name of Hinduism.[12] Hinduism in its various forms, often rather far removed from the initial orthodoxy,

---

11. Scholars are of the opinion that the policy of religious tolerance practice by Aśoka at the beginning of his reign was later replaced by an obvious inclination towards Buddhism. Judging by the 'Schism decree' concerning Buddhist *saṃgha*, as well as by the materials of third Buddhist council that was convened during Aśoka's time, the king was fully aware of the importance of Buddhism for the strengthening of his empire. As for Kaniṣka, it was at his time that such outstanding philosophers as Aśvaghoṣa and Nāgārjuna were preaching in North India. During Kaniṣka's region the Buddha's images start to appear on royal coins; and Mahāyāna was spreading as far as Central Asia, through Tibet and Bactria. About Buddhist kings of India vide: R. Thapar, *Aśoka and the Decline of the Mauryas*, Oxford, 1961; B. N. Puri, *India under the Kushanas*, Bombay, 1964; A. K. Warder, *Indian Buddhism*, Delhi, 1970, etc.

12. For precision's sake there is a need to explain that the term *Hinduism* referring to orthodox tradition of early Mediaeval India, started to appear in scholarly studies on Indian religion and philosophy as late as the nineteenth century. Usually the implication is that

became more and more popular due in part to the practice of generous donations to the Brahmins and to Hindu temples. Up to the reign of a later Gupta King, Harṣa, (*c*. 606-48) who was personally rather close to Buddhism but tried to encourage equally all religious cults, Buddhism in India was still quite viable. But already, according to the notes of a Chinese Buddhist pilgrim I-Ching, who visited the country between 671 and 695, "the teaching of the Buddha is becoming less prevalent in the world from day to day."[13] The decline of Buddhism was probably to some extent caused by the marked waning of important city centers.

During the reign of the Gupta dynasty, the efforts of the rulers towards more centralization and social stability were on the whole beneficial for the renaissance of orthodox beliefs and traditions.[14] But one should note that in the

---

Hinduism (as compared to early Brahmanism) is characterized by a shifting of emphasis to the whole complex of religious and philosophical problems, as well as by its ability to address wider social strata of the country. Vide: V. Möller, *Die Mythologie der vedischen Religion und das Hinduismus*, Stuttgart, 1966; P. Hacker, "Zur Geschichte und Beurteilung des Hinduismus, Kritik einiger verbreiteter Ansichten," in *Orientalistische Literaturzeitung,* no. 59, 1964, pp. 231-45.

13. I-Ching, *Record of the Buddhist Religion As Practised in India and the Malay Archipelago* (AD 671-95), Oxford, 1896, p. 17. Vide also: C. Eliot, *Hinduism and Buddhism,* vol. 2, pp. 97-106.

14. It is not such a rare occurrence in world history that dispositions of the subjects are determined primarily by the preferences of the monarch. Indeed, Brahmanism never really disappeared in India: it continued to exist in everyday ritual practice, household rites and local beliefs. However, owing to royal support Buddhism succeeded in securing predominance at least for a short period of time. Probably the situation was somewhat akin to that described by Thomas Babbington Macauley when he discussed the destiny of the Reformation in England. In his words, Restoration was so easy here because "the fact is that the great mass of the people was neither Catholic nor Protestant, but was, like its sovereign, midway between the two sects .... The nation, as it was clearly ready to profess either religion, would, beyond all doubt, have been ready to tolerate both." Lord Macauley, *Historical Essays,* London, 1910, pp. 251, 255.

gradual weakening of Buddhism an important role was played by some of its own inner tendencies.

Mahāyāna proved to be extremely susceptible to the doctrinal and ritual peculiarities of Tantrism and Śaktism. It appears that inner rivalries and continuous mutual strife, as well as extremes of Buddhist Tantrism, such as Vajrayāna,[15] were to some extent instrumental in the loss of authority. Various local beliefs now freely penetrated Buddhist teaching, also changing its mode of worship and rites. Often such a fusing together became possible through the mediation of Hinduism. C. Eliot says: "The Hindu reaction against Buddhism became apparent under the Gupta dynasty but Mahayanism in its use of Sanskrit and its worship of Bodhisattvas shows the beginnings of the same movement. The danger for Buddhism was not persecution but tolerance and obliteration of differences."[16]

Unlike Buddhism, Jainism probably never faced a real danger of being swallowed up by the Brahmanic tradition. Perhaps that was the reason why the threat to Jainism

---

15. *Vajrayāna* (from *vajra*, a thunderbolt or a diamond) is the third current (along with Hīnayāna and Mahāyāna) in the religious teaching of Buddhism. This esoteric sect appeared in the North-East of India and later spread to bordering regions, primarily to Tibet. The main core of the teaching is the idea of releasing dormant powers within human nature—first of all sexual energy, which is used for the instantaneous accomplishment of spiritual liberation *(mokṣa, nirvāṇa).* Vajrayāna based itself on local pre-Buddhist cults, genetically ascending to various types of worship of a Mother Goddess. This Goddess played the part of a female counterpart of energy *(śakti)* of the higher Godhead; the female primary source or energy was usually identified with *Māyā* (magic illusion) or Śiva's spouse, Kālī-Durgā. Parallel with Buddhist Vajrayāna, currents of Hindu Tantra were developing. For more detailed account of Buddhist Tantric notions and their interrelations with a Śaivite trend of Hinduism see: S. Dasgupta, *Introduction to Tantric Buddhism,* Calcutta, 1950; A. Wayman, *The Buddhist Tantras. Light on Indo-Tibetan Esotericism,* New York, 1973; H. V. Günther, *The Tantric View of Life.* Berkeley, 1973; W. D. O'Flaherty, *Asceticism and Eroticism in the Mythology of Śiva,* London, 1973.

16. C. Eliot, *Hinduism and Buddhism* vol. 1, Introduction, p. xxxviii.

was, so to speak, more direct. It is believed that a Maurya King, Candragupta, (second half of the fourth century BC was probably himself a Jaina, but later the Jainas (like the Ājīvakas) were persecuted both by the Buddhists and by the Brahmanists. Vivid accounts of persecutions of the Jainas were preserved even in works written by their orthodox opponents.[17] Small but rather stable Jaina communities can now be found mainly in the south of India.

It is quite clear that the most uncompromising break with Vedic religion came in the teaching of the Lokāyatikas, or Indian materialists.[18] In the words of T. Stcherbatsky, "the spirit of negation and indignation against the fetters of traditional moral and connected religious values was perhaps nowhere as vivid and evident as among Indian materialists.[19] And Haribhadra, a Jaina who lived about the ninth century, says in his compendium:

> The Lokāyatikas speak thus: there is no God, no cessation / of *saṃsāra* /,
> there is no duty and no unlawful / act /, no fruit of merit or sin.[20]

---

17. Vide: C. Eliot, *Hinduism and Buddhism*, vol. 1, p. 114 ff.

18. The name of the system (Lokāyata) is usually etymologized as *lokāyata*, that is, worldly, connected with the world. Synonymous names are *Cārvāka*, meaning either sweet talks (from *caru* pleasant, sweet and *vāk*, speech) or the teaching of gluttons (from a verb root *carv*, to chomp, to chew). Sometimes, though, Indian materialism is also called *Barhaspatya-mata*, after the name of the legendary sage Bṛhaspati, the author of the lost *Bṛhaspatisūtras*; some passages from these *sūtras* are cited by the opponents of Lokāyata.

19. T. Stcherbatsky, *"K istorij materializma v Indii,"* 'Vostochniye zapiski', Part I, Leningrad, 1927.

20. Haribhadra, *Ṣaddarśanasamuccaya*, Tenali, *a.o.*, p. 27:

Lokāyatā vadantyevaṃ nāsti devo na nirvṛtiḥ /
dharmādharmau na vidyate na phalaṃ puṇyapāpayoḥ //

The opponents of the Lokāyatikas reproachfully emphasized the unrestrained hedonism of this teaching, but even they had to admit that " [T]hose loving worldly songs ... regarding only wealth and love to be human goals and denying the sense of 'other world', follow the teaching of the Cārvākaṣ".[21] It looks as though the Lokāyatikas' views were tending to coincide with the opinions of ordinary people, quite remote from philosophical discussions.

The ontology of Indian materialists was not very developed; sometimes it is explained by the rather low level of scientific knowledge at the time. (True, the same situation did not prevent Vaiśeṣika from elaborating a developed and completely speculative natural philosophy and metaphysics.) Judging from accounts of the opponents, the Lokāyatikas paid some attention to epistemological and logical problems,[22] but it is difficult to say anything specific about their views in this field, as no work by Indian materialists has survived.

Orthodox religion was strengthened under Gupta patronage. It also submitted to a complex process of renewal and transformation. Discarding obsolete rituals, it became more flexible, easily absorbing regional cults and popular local deities. Numerous objects of worship were more and more often regarded as the emanations of the one Godhead. The sign of the times was mutual coordination, concering not only ritual but also doctrine.

---

21. Mādhava, *Sarva-darśana-saṅgraha,* Poona, 1966 *(Cārvāka-darśana): lokagāthāmanurundhāno ... arthakāmāveva puruṣārthau manyamānāḥ pāralaukikamarthamapahnuvānāścārvākamatamanu-vartamānā(ḥ).*

22. For instance, Kauṭilya in his *Arthaśāstra* mentions Lokāyata as one of the 'reasoning systems' *(ānvīkṣikī): sāṃkhyaṃ yogo lokāyataṃ cetyānvīkṣikī,* that is, the teachings that "examine /things/ through reasons, *(hetubhir anvīkṣamāṇā).* In *Manusmṛti* the Lokāyatikas are indentified with 'reasoning logicians' *(haitukāḥ),* and according to Medhātithi's commentary to this text (IV.30), the Lokāyatikas are logicians, denying the authority of the Vedas *(vedavirodhītarka-vyavahāriṇaḥ).* In the same commentary (VII.43) the author speaks about the 'logical science' *(tarkavidyā)* of the Cārvākas.

What is more, the Hindus were quite ready to extend their notion of *avatāra* to embrace Buddhism and other 'heretical' systems: the Buddha, for instance, was considered to be an embodiment of one of the traditional Gods.[23]

At the same time (by the first century AD), six philosophical schools directly connected with Hindus doctrine were already shaped. These schools, or *darśanas* (lit.: seeing, looking at; hence view) are Sāṃkhya and Yoga, Nyāya and Vaiśeṣika, Pūrva-Mīmāṃsā and Vedanta.[24] Unlike 'heretical' teachings, they are sometimes characterized as *"āstika"* systems (from *āstika*, a person who recognizes the existence of other worlds), or, often enough, as the orthodox systems. The last system to be formed was Vedanta, which was most closely connected with Vedic texts.

By the beginning of Śaṅkara's epoch, heterodox movement in India—and primarily its Buddhist current—had virtually spent its momentum. The appearance of Vedanta more or less predetermined the outcome of this process, while the preaching and philosophical activity of Śaṅkara probably precipitated the ousting of Buddhism. However, Buddhism successfully continued (and is continuing still) outside India; having left its native soil, it

23. For example, in *Matsya-purāṇa* which appeared according to accepted opinion about the sixth century AD, the Buddha is even included in the Hindu pantheon as one of the Viṣṇu *avatāras*. One must say, however, that in similar cases the Buddha is assigned the role of a tempter who is supposed to lure the weak and wavering into the pitfalls of a false doctrine.

24. As previously noted, the orthodox philosophical schools form pairs, the parts of which are rather close to each other and, simultaneously, mutually complementary in their main tenets. So, Vaiśeṣika's philosophy of nature and atomistic postulates need as logical correlative the reasoning foundations and techniques of Nyāya; the dualistic realism of Sāṃkhya is supplemented by the theistic approach and meditative practice of Yoga; while the ritualism and linguistic interests of Pūrva-Mīmāṃsā were preparing the way for the spiritualistic monism of Vedanta. However, all these systems are united by their unconditioned acceptance of the authority of Vedic sayings.

acquired tremendous popularity and underwent extraordinary transformations, which, of course, can not be examined here. What is relevant for this book is the fact that all further development of religious and philosophical thought in India continued, with some insignificant exceptions, to be guided by unswerving devotion to Vedic orthodoxy. And the greatest significance was undeniably acquired by Vedanta.

Nevertheless, during the transitional period, while the stress was so radically shifting back to orthodox schools, Buddhist views were sometimes surfacing in new forms in the works of early Vedantins, who were paving the way for Śaṅkara's Advaita.

2. *PREDECESSORS OF ŚAṄKARA*

In trying to examine the succession of teachers who influenced Śaṅkara and more or less directly contributed to the forming of Vedanta, it would be a vain effort to persist in looking for an absolute chronology of their life and activity. Attempts of this kind have proved useless more than once. Owing to certain peculiarities of Indian culture, time and its precise determination obey rules that are in some respects quite different from those concerned with exact fixation of events and accuracy of dating.[25] A popular Hindu belief that every man comes to this world many times and, therefore, it is not really too important when he said something worthy of attention, did not promote interest in determining the place of phenomena upon the time axis, especially if these phenomena belong to ancient or early mediaeval periods.

---

25. These problems are still widely discussed by the Indologists; without going into details one should note that the image of phenomenal time characteristic of Indian culture is an essentially cyclic one. For the western world a similar cyclicity inherent in paganism became surmounted by Christianity, while time itself was forcibly straightened by the only significant historical event—the incarnation of Christ.

Because of this, there is nothing to do but to rely on a relative chronology. Here one is helped by the extant texts that abound in cross-references, citations, lists of well-known names and schools. Perceptible attempts of Indian orthodox authors to secure a firm foothold for their teachings in Vedic sayings is somewhat akin to the scholastic tradition of the European Middle Ages: both here and there one can easily discern a striving to read all answers in the holy scripture, assiduously demonstrating the correspondence of a developed idea to theological premises. (One might add in parentheses that the demonstrations are in both cases strictly and consistently reasoned.)

This may be the appropriate moment to deviate slightly from the subject of the book in order to specify what could be the sense of the term "holy scripture" in Indian culture. Sacred scripture is, of course, the four Vedas, taken in the broad sense of the word; that is, the four *saṃhitās*—the collections of hymns, chants, sacrificial mantras and magic spells (*Ṛgveda, Sāmaveda, Yajurveda* and *Atharvaveda*), their corresponding *brāhmaṇas* (brahmanical explanations), *āraṇyakas* (forest texts, that is, religious writings composed by hermits living in the forests) and *upaniṣads* (philosophical texts). Orthodox teachings must inevitably and without fail recognize the authority of Vedic writings. The authorship of the Vedas is ascribed to God-inspired poets or sages *(ṛṣi),* and consequently, these texts are regarded as *śruti* (lit.: heard), that is, eternally heard or communicated, actually, a revelation.[26] In contrast to that, epic writings (for instance, the *Mahābhārata* together with its most esteemed part, *Bhagavadgītā,* and

26. We are by now quite used to the definition of Christianity as the religion of the Scripture (*Schriftreligion*, in the term of German theologians); even the Muslims included the Christians in the list of *ahl al-quiṭab* (the people of the Book). With some necessary reservations to be elaborated below, this definition might be extended to Hinduism. At this point I would like only to emphasize that, unlike the *Bible*, the *Torah* or the *Koran*, the *Vedas* exist eternally and do not have a Creator: even the Gods, who are sometimes regarded as the authors, are just as

the *Rāmāyaṇa*), *purāṇas* (lit.: ancient, old), containing theogonic and cosmogonic myths, *sūtras* (fundamental treatises on exegetics, philosophy, poetics, grammar, etc.) are nothing but sacred tradition, or, to put it in Sanskrit terms, *smṛti* (lit.: remembered), writings and codes remembered (and composed) by human teachers.

It is quite clear that sacred tradition is wholly basing itself on sacred scripture—in other words, that *smṛti* texts can by no means contradict *śruti* texts; indeed, any discrepancies between them should be explained away from the standpoint of revelation. According to ancient Brahmanic rules, the reading of the Vedas was allowed only to the 'twice-born' *(dvija*—those who have undergone a 'second birth', through investiture with the sacred thread), or to the representatives of the three highest *varṇas*. Hence, a widespread definition of the epic and puranic writings as 'the fifth Veda', destined for women and *śūdras;* it was supposed that they transmit basically the same Vedic knowledge, only slightly simplified and adapted to the imperfect understanding or ritual impurity of these listeners.

Any independent teaching within the framework of orthodoxy had, on the one hand, to comply with Vedic tradition *(āmnāya),* and, on the other, to follow some influential teacher's tradition. The general practice of the authors of Indian philosophical treatises and compendiums of seizing every opportunity to refer to previous authorities also has an unmistakeable scholastic tinge.

In Śaṅkara's words, a true teacher's tradition is called *"saṃpradāya"* (transmission, granting; that is, a handing over of an established doctrine from teacher to teacher). Śaṅkara values the knowledge of this tradition more highly than any kind of learning or erudition. He writes, "[A] conceited knower might say: I shall reveal the essence of *saṃsāra* /bonds/ and the essence of liberation, /I shall

---

mythologic and conventional in their authorship as the legendary sages; their role is limited to the transmission of sacred knowledge.

reveal/ the essence of the *śāstras* but he is himself confused and is stupefying others since he rejected the teachers' tradition of deliberation on the essence of the *śāstras* and came to the refutation of scripture and to mental constructions opposing scripture.[27]

Of course, not all the teachers and predecessors are equally venerated by Śaṅkara. Depending on the degree of closeness to their systems, as well as on his personal esteem, Śaṅkara addresses his direct or indirect teachers differently and bestows his praise on them differently. The codes of veneration here more or less coincide with the traditional classification of teachers' titles in Brahmanism,[28] though there are certain individual preferences and interpretations.

---

27. Śaṅkara's Commentary on the *Bhagavadgītā (Gītābhāṣya)*, XIII. 2: *evaṃ manvāne yaḥ sa paṇḍitāpasadaḥ saṃsāramokṣayoḥ śāstrasya ca arthavattvaṃ karomītyātmahā, svayaṃ mūḍhaḥ anyāṃśca vyāmohayati śāstrārthasaṃpradāyarahitatvāt śrutahānimaśrutakalpanāṃ kurvan.*

Cf. also his commentary on *Kenopaniṣad*, I. 4: "Indeed, Brahman can be grasped only through the instructions of teachers, transmitted from one to the other, and not owing to reasoning, nor through intelligence or many heard /texts/, ascetic practices, sacrifices, etc." *(brahma caivamācāryopadeśaparaṃparayaivādhigantavyaṃ, na tarkataḥ pravaṇamedhā-bhuśrutatapoyajñādibhiśca.)*

The instructions of the teachers are referred to as *ācāryopadeśa*. One should note here an interesting word combination *paraṃpara*, that is, from one to the other. This will be discussed later, in the course of comparing Advaita and Pūrva-Mīmāṃsā, since for the Mīmāṃsakas it plays quite a particular role in their conception of sacred scripture.

28. Vide, primarily, the works by a well-known Indian historian of religion and culture P. V. Kane, e.g. his *History of Dharmaśāstra*, vol. 2, p. 1. Poona, 1941. Mainly on the basis of *Viṣṇusmṛti* he maintains that a *guru* (lit.: heavy, weighty, important in the broad sense of the word means usually any older, venerable or respected person who is worthy of esteem; in the strict sense the term defines a kind of a spirtiual parent or a first preceptor who gives the youth his initial instruction, *mantras* and prayers, reads to the youth the first *śāstras* and performs the necessary ceremonies before the investiture. Another general term for a teacher is *adhyāpaka* (from the verb root °*adhī*, to turn the mind towards something, to understand, to study), or a teacher of sacred

For example, a *guru* for him is usually a teacher who is instructing his disciple personally, through direct contact, while an *ācārya* is more often not so much a spiritual guide, investing the student with the sacrificial thread, but an influential thinker who is remembered owing to his connection with particular writings. However, in one of Śaṅkara's own works we find a somewhat more vague description: "An *ācārya* is he who can memorize and grasp the affirmations and negations /in a discussion/, who is endowed with calmness, inner control and mercy, who knows the texts of Vedic tradition, who rejects seen and unseen enjoyments, who is withdrawn from all the actions and /their/ means, who knows Brahman, who is abiding in Brahman, who does not break the rules of conduct."[29] One might note that according to Vedanta, an *ācārya* is primarily an authoritative commentator on one of the fundamental texts of this system, *Brahmasūtra*. An *upādhyāya* occupies a much lower position in the hierarchy of preceptors, since he gives instruction only on particular points connected with Vedic knowledge. Sometimes Śaṅkara and other Vedantins define their teachers as *ācārya-deśīya*, or *almost ācārya*, meaning that the statements of a venerable teacher contain only a part of the truth and can raise doubts. From time to time a highly esteemed preceptor who is not fully entitled to the name of an *ācārya* is

---

knowledge. There are two main kinds of these preceptors, an *ācārya* (from *ācāra*, conduct, custom, traditional usage or established rule), a spiritual teacher who comes to instruct the youth in Vedic knowledge after initial training given to him by the *guru*; an *ācārya* invests the pupil with the sacrificial thread, instructs him in the Vedas and sacrificial laws, and gives him some knowledge of religious mysteries. An *upādhyāya* (from *upādhi*, a peculiarity, attribute, qualification), that is, a teacher who subsists by teaching some particular knowledge, sometimes a particualr part of the Vedas or some auxiliary works based on the Vedas *(vedāṅgas)*.

29. Śaṅkara, *Upadeśasāhasrī (Gadyabandha,* I. 6): *ācāryastūhāpohagrahaṇadhāraṇaśamadamadayānugrahādisaṃpanno labdhāgamo dṛṣṭādṛṣṭabhogeṣvanāśaktaḥ tyaktasarvakarmasādhano brahmavit brahmaṇi sthito 'bhinnavṛtto.*

addressed as *bhagavan*, (that is a venerable one, an illustrous one). That is how Śaṅkara often refers to Gauḍapāda, who did not write his own commentary on *Brahmasūtra*.

Thanks to Śaṅkara's constant references to basic texts, as well as Vedanta teachers tradition of Vedanta, one can form a fairly clear notion of the relative chronology that binds together the life and creative activity of Vedanta preceptors.

The line of teachers starts undoubtedly with Bādarāyaṇa, the author of *Brahmasūtra*, who is addressed by Śaṅkara as *bhagavan*, or, more often, as *sūtra-kāra* (that is, the creator of the *sūtra*).

The *Brahmasūtra* of Bādarāyaṇa (or *Vedāntasūtra*, as it is sometimes called)[30] occupies quite a special place among all Vedantic writings. Indeed, the text forms a part of the so-called triple-canon *(prasthānatraya)* of Vedanta. Literally, *prasthāna* means departure, setting out (from the verb root *prasthā*, proceed to, set out); however, in theological and philosophical systems the term acquires a new meaning: that of a method or canonical system. The first and the foremost canonical source of Vedanta is the *śruti-prasthāna*, or the canonical base of revelation, formed by the Upaniṣads. The second, or *smṛti-prasthāna* (canonical base of remembered tradition) is presented by *Bhagavadgītā*, while the *nyāya-prasthāna* (canonical base of reasoning) is *Brahmasūtra*. According to Vedantic tradition, *Brahmasūtra* presents the teaching of the Upaniṣads systematically and consistently; Bādarāyaṇa's text gives an aphoristic and concise rendering of the main notions of revelation.

---

30. Other, less widespread names are *Śārīrakasūtra* (Sūtra on an embodied /soul/), *Bhikṣusūtra*, since the text was destined first of all to religious mendicants *(bhikṣu)*, and *Uttara-Mīmāṃsāsūtra*, or the *sūtras* of the school of Uttara-Mīmāṃsā (as contrasted to those of the Pūrva-Mīmāṃsā). The first of these names is most frequently used by Śaṅkara.

Earlier I touched upon the inevitable difficulties connected with the attempts to fix an exact dating of important religious and philosophical works. Bādarāyaṇa's text is no exception. Indian scholarly tradition of modern times, usually inclined to increase the age of the sources, attributes it to 500-200 BC. However, proceeding from mutual cross-references of Bādarāyaṇa and Jaimini, Paul Deussen maintained that this work was written more or less simultaneously with *Mīmāṃsāsūtra* (not earlier than 200 BC and not later than AD 400-500).[31] S. Dasgupta puts Bādarāyaṇa's work closer to the earlier limit of this time interval.[32] According to A.B. Keith, it could not have been created later than the second century AD.[33] Basing on some references to the Buddhist notion of *śūnya-vāda*, H. Jacobi places *Brahmasūtra* between AD 200-450.[34] On the whole, scholars are rather unanimous, considering the most probable date for *Brahmasūtra* sometime between the second century BC and the second century AD.

Nothing much is known about Bādarāyaṇa himself; probably, he is more a legendary than a historical figure—a kind of generalized image of the very first Vedanta teacher. A later Vedantist, Vācaspatimiśra, identifies him with Vyāsa, a mythological compiler of Vedic hymns; in his *Bhāmatī* Vācaspatimiśra also calls Bādarāyaṇa an embodiment of Viṣṇu's intelligent energy.

The *sūtras* of Bādarāyaṇa are undoubtedly the accepted theoretical source of Vedanta; nevertheless, they are certainly not as significant as the later interpretations made by numerous commentators. Indeed, the work is extremely terse; each *sūtra* consists literally of two or three words

---

31. P. Deussen, *Das System des Vedanta*, p. 22.

32. S. Dasgupta, *A History of Indian Philosophy*, vol. 1, p. 418.

33. A. B. Keith, "The Karma-Mīmāṃsā", *Journal of the Royal Asiatic Society*, 1907, p. 492.

34. H. Jacobi, "The Dates of the Philosophical *Sūtras* of the Brahmans", *Journal of American Oriental Society*, 1911, vol. 31, p. 29.

(mostly, they are the names,[35] bound together by case inflections) which are incomprehensible without some development and clarification of their content, and, consequently, without an interpretation. One might remember in this connection that the very term "*sūtra*" means primarily a thread, a string; that is, a cord running through or holding together the beads of more detailed deliberations. A western scholar once aptly defined the *sūtras* of Bādarāyaṇa as a synopsis of lectures. In fact, *Brahmasūtra* was meant to be memorized by heart; for Vedantic students it obviously served as reference points, introducing an extensive and lengthy preaching of the teacher, while the latter, in his turn, formed a foundation for subsequent interpretations and new polemical arguments.

All the commentators on *Brahmasūtra* abide by the initial compositional structure of the text, which is divided into four chapters, or lessons *(adhyāya)*, each of them containing four parts *(pāda)*. The text or Bādarāyaṇa contains about 550 *sūtras* and more than a hundred *adhikaraṇas* or topics for consideration.[36]

The first chapter of *Brahmasūtra* is called *Samanvaya* (lit.: succession, regular sequence), that is, harmony. Its main goal is to show that all the sayings of the Upaniṣads, dealing with the higher reality, refer to the eternal Brah-

---

35. According to linguistic theories of ancient India, the names *(nāma)* apply to—any definitions of objects, phenomena, notions, as well as to all their possible qualifications, so the term is extended to embrace adjectives, adverbs, etc.

36. It is impossible to be more precise, since the terseness and, consequently, some mysteriousness of the text allow for arbitrary joining together and separation of different fragments. Śaṅkara, for example, singles out as many as 555 *sūtras* and 192 *adhikaraṇas*; the latter are provided by separate titles. For Rāmānuja *Brahmasūtra* has 545 *sūtras* and 140 *adhikaraṇas*; according to Madhva, 534 *sūtras* and 123 *adhikaraṇas*; Niṃbārka counts as many as 549 *sūtras* and 161 *adhikaraṇas*; for Vallabha *Brahmasūtra* numbers 554 sūtras and 171 *adhikaraṇas*. Other versions are possible, since there are other ways of distinguishing separate units of meaning within *Brahmasūtra*.

man as the source and the only foundation of the universe. The second one, *Avirodha*, or absense of contradictions, aims at the refutation of the opponents' views on the nature of the world and embodied souls. Here one can find the polemics with the Sāṃkhya notion of *prakṛti* as the origin of the world, the dispute with the Vaiśeṣika concept of atoms, with heterodox teachings of the Buddhists and the Jainas, as well as some Vedanta arguments against conceptions of certain theistic orthodox schools, for instance, against those of Pāñcarātra. In the third chpater, *Sādhana* (lit.: an effort, or means), the author deliberates on the ways and means of liberation *(mokṣa)* and discusses some characteristics of hermits and religious mendicants. Finally, the fourth chapter, entitled *Phala,* or fruit, is concerned with theological problems connected with ultimate liberation: the difference between *deva-yāna* (the path of gods) and *pitṛ-yāna* (the path of the manes) which open before a human soul after death, etc. From a theoretical point of view the most interesting are the first four *sūtras* of the first *adhyāya,* dealing with the nature of Brahman, as well as the two first *pādas* of the second *adhyāya,* containing the Vedanta notion of causality and its role in the dispute with the Sāṃkhyayikas and the Buddhists.

Though the concise text of *Brahmasūtra* does not allow one to form a definite opinion about the position of its author, still it is possible to assume that Bādarāyaṇa's concept probably boiled down to a version of the theistic Bhedābheda (identity-and-difference). According to this doctrine, Brahman is inherent in the world as its innermost essence, and, simultaneously, it transcends the world as its higher ruler and omnipotent God the Creator *(Īśvara).* The universe is regarded as a real emanation of Brahman, as its own modification or evolution *(pariṇāma)* in time and space. Sometimes, however, while discussing the nature and attributes of individual souls, the author enumerates possible standpoints without indicating which of them is preferable to him.

Vedanta tradition ascribes one of the first attempts to comment upon *Brahmasūtra* to Upavarṣa. Śaṅkara, for instance, mentions his commentary, allegedly called *Śārīrakasūtravṛtti;* however, this work did not survive. It is assumed that it was Upavarṣa who was the first to divide Vedic texts into 'parts of action', or ritualistic sections *(karma-kāṇḍa),* and 'parts of knowledge' *(jñāna-kāṇḍa),* that contributed towards a more precise definition of themes and problems in Vedanta. Upavarṣa was also interested in some epistemological problems connected with the use of the six *pramāṇas*, or means of valid knowledge. Finally, according to Śaṅkara's testimony, Upavarṣa was the first Vedantin to draw attention to the paradoxical essence of *ātman*, which eludes ordinary intellectual understanding. The views of Upavarṣa are referred to by the Vedantins Śaṅkara, Rāmānuja and Yāmuna, as well as by Śabara, the adherent of Mīmāṃsā.

Yāmuna, in his treatise *Siddhi-traya* (Triple grasping), reminding the reader of an earlier tradition, gives the name of one of the first Vedanta preceptors, Taṅka. This thinker is also mentioned in Rāmānuja's *Vedārtha-saṅgraha* (A collection of sayings on the essence of the Vedas). Taṅka is believed to have written a commentary on *Chāndogyopaniṣad*; some sentences from this work are preserved in the writings of Śaṅkara and his followers, as well as in the writings of philosophers of Rāmānuja's school.

A little more is known about another Vedantist of that time, Bhartṛprapañca. Śaṅkara often mentions and cites him in the commentary on *Bṛhadāraṇyakopaniṣad* (though he does not call Bhartṛprapañca by name, references to this Vedantin are reliably established by a later tradition). It was probably Bhartṛprapañca who elaborated a popular simile, equating Brahman and the world to the ocean and its waves. Later this simile was often used by Yādava and Rāmānuja. In the words of Śaṅkara (who is paraphrasing Bhartṛprapañca's statements), "Brahman is simultaneously dual and one. Just as water is real, so its modifications are also real: the waves, the foam, the bubbles. They come and go, but they are a part of the ocean and, because of that, they are real. In the same way this multiform /universe/ is real, like the waves, ... but the higher Brahman itself is the water of the ocean."[37] For Bhartṛprapañca himself the admission of two equally real forms of the existence of Brahman quite consistently led to the belief in the necessary combination of the path of knowledge and the path of action, that is, the combination of the knowledge of Brahman and ritual practice. However, Śaṅkara cites Bhartṛprapañca's words only in order to refute them. According to him, these views are "opposed to *śruti,* to *smṛti* and logical reasoning",[38] because the higher Brahman can be only one, and it is devoid of any qualities or attributes.

Bhartṛprapañca's notion of the two forms or two manifestations of Brahman found its further development in the ideas of the Bhedābheda school, which was represented by Bhāskara (*c.* eighth century), Yādava (eleventh century) and Niṃbārka (second half of the eleventh century), as well as in some conceptions of Rāmānuja's followers. They regarded the idea of complementing true knowledge by good deeds as extremely appropriate.[39] The logic of reasoning here is quite clear: if the world is as real as the higher Brahman, it could not be a matter of indifference for the ultimate liberation of a person whether he is acting well (that is, in conformity with Vedic injunctions) during

---

37. Śaṅkara, Commentary on *Bṛhadāraṇyakopaniṣad,* V. I.1: *evaṃ ca dvaitādvaitātmakamekaṃ brahma /yathā kila samudro jalataraṅgaphenabudbudādyātmaka eva /yathā ca jalaṃ satyaṃ tadudbhavāśca taraṅgaphenabudbudādayaḥ ... evaṃ sarvamidaṃ dvaitaṃ paramārthasatyam eva jalataraṅgādisthānīyaṃ samudrajalasthānīyaṃ tu paraṃ brahma.*

38. Śaṅkara, Commentary on *Bṛhadāraṇyakopaniṣad,* V.I.1: *tasmācchrutismṛtinyāyavirodhād ....*

39. It was Bhāskara, probably a younger contemporary of Śaṅkara, who gave a precise wording to the doctrine of 'combination of knowledge and actions' *(jñāna-karma-samuccaya),* which subsequently became so popular with Vedanta scholars of the Viṣṇuite school.

each successive episode of his *saṃsāric* existence. In other words, the augmentation of merits and securing of an auspicious *karma*, according to these systems, is directly conducive to *mokṣa.* (Within the orthodox tradition only Śaṅkara was bold enough to suggest that no human action—including the rites prescribed by the Vedas—leads directly to liberation.)

One of the early teachers of Vedanta who was clearly inclined to the notion of non-dual *(advaita)* Brahman was *Draviḍa* (or Dramiḍa). He invented a subtle fable which exquisitely illustrates the foundations of Advaita. Once a king sent his young son and heir to be brought up in the family of a poor hunter. The boy grew up without any knowledge of his high rank and status. However, as soon as he came of age he was told about the true state of things. Having heard about his title, the boy at once acquired the dignity and confidence fitting to his rank. That is just the way, says the Vedantin, every person lives in this world: as soon as he hears that his *ātman,* or Self, is identical with the higher Brahman, his inner nature is revealed to him. He acquires liberation, and after that no force in the world can bring him back to his previous condition. Judging by the commentary of Ānandagiri, Śaṅkara considered Draviḍa to be the knower of sacred scripture *(āgama-vid),* as well as the knower of the teachers, tradition *(saṃpradāya-vid).*

In his Commentary on the fourth *sūtra* of the first *pāda* of the first *adhyāya* of *Brahmansūtra* Śaṅkara cites three *kārikās* that were later determined to belong to the Vedantin Sundarapāṇḍya.[40] His contribution was mainly in the sphere of logical and epistemological problems. It is

---

40. These *kārikās* are placed at the very end of the commentary to the above-mentioned *sūtra*; their sense does not go beyond a mere illustration to Śaṅkara's reasoning. The text of the *kārikās* runs as follows (usually their metrical lines are not singled out in Śaṅkara's commentary on *Brahma-sūtra*): *api cāhuḥ—gauṇamithyātmano 'satva putradehādibādhanāt / sadbrahmāhamityevaṃ bodhe kāryaṃ kathaṃ bhavet //anveṣṭavyātmavijñānāt prāk pramātṛtvamātmanaḥ /aniṣṭaḥ*

believed that in his Commentary on the *Bhagavadgītā* Śaṅkara implies the doctrine of Sundarapāṇḍya when he mentions a logical method of prior superimposition and subsequent denial *(adhyāropa-apavāda)* used in Advaita with reference to phenomenal attributes of Brahman. Unfortunately, the whole of Sundarpāṇḍya's *Kārikās* has not survived.

Now we can leave the shifting soil of conjectures and fragmentary data in order to examine in more detail the systems of three Vedanta teachers who had a profound influence on Śaṅkara's Advaita. They were a grammarian and philosopher, Bhartṛhari; an Advaitin, Gauḍapāda; and an older contemporary of Śaṅkara, a philosopher who was also drawn to Mīmāṃsā, but probably finished as a Vedantin, Maṇḍanamiśra. We can form a more considered and justified opinion about the essence of their teachings, since the main works of these philosophers are still extant.

Bhartṛhari lived probably during the fifth and sixth centuries. Some scholars tend to identify him with a celebrated Sanskrit poet of the same name, the author of a

---

syātpramātaiva pāpmadoṣādivarjitaḥ / dehātmapratyayo yadvatpramāṇatvena kalpitaḥ //laukikaṃ tadvadevadaṃ pramāṇaṃ tvātmaniścayāt //.

"But some say:

When false names are rejected like 'a son', 'a body' and so on,
when the false Self and the figurative Self are seen as unreal,
When the consciousness awakens: 'I am really Brahman',
how could any action be /possible/?
Before the knowledge of the longed-for *ātman* appears, this *ātman* can be regarded as a knowing subject,
But the knower, having rejected the blemishes
of sin, becomes himself the desired goal of his own wishes.
Just as the body is arbitrarily ascribed to *ātman* with the help of the means of valid knowledge,
Everything remains unchanged in this world until the realization of *ātman.*"

The authorship of Sundarapāṇḍya was allegedly determined by a later Advaitin Ātmasvarūpa who commented on Padmapāda's *Pañcapādikā*, that is, wrote a sub-commentary on the first four *sūtras* of Śaṅkara's Commentary on *Brahmasūtra.*

three-part cycle of poems called *Śatakatrayam* (Three hundreds): *Nīti-śataka*, or A hundred /poems/ on moral duty; *Śṛṅgāra-śataka,* (A hundred /poems/ on carnal longing) and *Vairāgya-śataka*, (A hundred /poems/ on renunciation). One might say that the general mood of the last *Śataka* is more or less in conformity with popular views on Vedanta; so the image of the poet at least does not contradict the main ideas of Bhartṛhari the philosopher, though *Śatakatrayam* gives a smoother interpretation of Vedanta, without any of the peculiarities and marks of the rather unusual system of Bhartṛhari the grammarian. Anyway, whether we are dealing with namesakes or there was only one Bhartṛhari—a sage and a poet—I will analyze here only the teaching of Bhartṛhari, the author of the famous treatise *Vākyapadīya* (A treatise on the sentence and the word), as well as of some extant fragments of the commentary on Patañjali's *Mahābhāṣya* (that is, of a subcommentary on Pāṇini's *Aṣṭādhyāyī*).[41]

According to Indian tradition, while he was still very young, Bhartṛhari was very enthusiastic about the ideas of Buddhism, but later he became a staunch supporter of orthodox Brahmanism. The Vedantic position of Bhartṛhari—which, however, is not entirely free from some Buddhist influence—can be clearly discerned in *Vākyapadīya* and, even more so, in the partly extant portions of its commentary, *Vṛtti.*[42]

---

41. Lately *Vākyapadīya* is receiving much attention from historians of philosophy. Besides the usual textological and philosophical analysis, repeated attempts are made to examine Bhartṛhari's system in the light of present-day notions of linguistic philosophy. One might note in this connection the following works: K. Kunjunni Raja, *Indian Theories of Meaning,* Madras, 1963; M. Biardeau, *Théorie de la connaissance et philosophie de la parole dans le brahmanisme classique,* Paris, 1964; B.K. Matilal analyzes Bhartṛhari's teaching from the standpoint of logical positivism (B.K. Matilal, *Epistemology, Logic and Grammar in Indian Philosophical Analysis,* Mouton, Den Haag, 1971).

42. There is some dispute among scholars over the authorship of *Vṛtti.* The most prevalent opinion is that it belongs to Bhartṛhari himself; however, Madeleine Biardeau regards it as a later work from

The treatise itself is composed of three parts *(kāṇḍa)*; the first one deals with the nature of Brahman, hence its title *Brahmakāṇḍa,* the second one discusses complete sentences *(vākya),* and the third *kāṇḍa* analyzes words *(pada)* as sense units forming phrases of the language. The essence of the grammarian's teaching is outlined already in the first two *kārikās* of the metrical treatise:

> Endless, eternal Brahman is the nature of the Word,
> which cannot be destroyed;
> From it is manifested the evolving world
> through the nature of things.
> Though it is known by sacred tradition as one,
> it shelters different potencies.
> And even if the potencies are not separated /from it/,
> they are manifested as if apart.[43]

The metrical form of *Vākyapadīya* helps the philosopher to find aphoristically elaborated wordings for his notions, it also contributes to creating a tinge of solemn mythological pathos characteristic of the treatise. The word mentioned here is not just something pronounced, uttered—no, it is Speech, Language itself, existing before the creation of the world; Speech that creates both the universe and ordinary human language.

Unlike the Naiyāyikas and the Vaiśeṣikas, who regarded words as just external, unnecessary shells, envel-

---

one of Bhartṛhari's disciples, Harivṛṣabha. In her opinion, the views of the author of *Vṛtti* represent a further stage of development of the notions characteristic of *Vākyapadīya,* a further progress towards classical Advaita (vide: Bhartṛhari, *Vākyapadīya Brahmakāṇḍa, avec la Vṛtti de Harivṛṣabha;* traduction, introduction et notes par Madeleine Biardeau, Paris, 1964, pp. 5-11).

43. Bhartṛhari, *Vākyapadīya (Brahma-kāṇḍa),* I.1:
anādinighanaṃ brahma śabdatattvaṃ yad akṣaram /
vivartate 'rthabhāvena prakriyā jagato yataḥ //1//
ekameva yadāmnātaṃ bhinnaṃ śaktitavyaprāśrayāt /
apṛthaktva 'pi śaktibhyaḥ pṛthaktvena ca vartate // 2//
(*Vākyapadīya* of Bhartṛhari, edited by Prof. K.V. Abhyankar and Acarya V.P. Limaye, Poona, 1965.

oping the inner content of perceptions, Bhartṛhari places the word inside the very core of consciousness. The Naiyāyikas usually referred to the example presented by newborn infants and dumb persons who are devoid of speech but are obviously conscious and capable of forming ideas. However, according to Bhartṛhari, the foundation of every idea is a non-manifested, latent word—a kind of seed *(bīja)* of thinking and consciousness in general. This word, which is entirely silent in the beginning but slowly manifests itself is presented in three forms: as a 'seeing' *(paśyantī)*, a 'middle' *(mādhyama)* and a 'pronounced' *(vaikharī)* speech;[44] that is, as a mental image of desired object, as an inner urge to act, which finds its expression in a command or in a silent reasoning to oneself and, finally, in an ordinary spoken utterance.

However, Bhartṛhari probably would not be so interesting for us as Śaṅkara's predecessor and one of the founders of Advaita, if his teaching boiled down simply to the admittance of an indissoluble relation between language and consciousness. His former sympathies for Buddhism might have induced him to take yet another step and connect language with being. Almost on the same lines as the Buddhist Vijñānavāda, the grammarian identifies a perceived object, a perceiving subject and the very state of perception, merging them together in the fourth, the higher form of speech *(parā vāk)*. The notion of *parā vāk* appears in the commentary to the 142nd *kārikā* of

---

44. Bhatṛhari, *Vākyapadīya (Brahmakāṇḍa)*, I. 142:
vaikharyā madhyamāyāśca paśyanty āścaitad adbhutam /
anekatīrthabhedāyās trayyā vācaḥ paraṃ padam //142 //
The pronounced one, the middle one and the seeing one
form the many divisions
of the triple speech, /which finds for itself/
a marvelous and higher abode.

According to Harivṛṣabha, the 'seeing' form of speech is still full of inner potencies, but "the highest seeing form does not contain false modifications, it is unsoiled and beyond ordinary world practice". *(Paraṃ tu paśyantīrūpam anapabhraṃsam asaṅkīrṇaṃ lokavyavahārārītam /.)*

Vākyapadīya; scholars may still discuss the probabilities of Bhartṛhari's authorship of *Vṛtti.* But the idea of higher speech seems quite appropriate in the general context of Bhartṛhari's writing.

It is true that for Bhartṛhari himself—as distinct from the Buddhists—the highest, the only reality is nothing but the sacred, initial Word of the Vedas, which forms a foundation for each new cycle of the world creation. In the text of the *Vākyapadīya* one can read:

> From the Word alone comes this evolving /of the world/,
> so teach the knowers of the sacred tradition,
> From Vedic verse all this starts to rotate for the first time.[45]

This sacred word, placed in the beginning of the world as a sort of homogeneous unity, as an unchangeable matrix, giving birth to everything existing in the universe, is, simultaneously, the higher Brahman. The symbol of this Brahman as taught by the Upaniṣads is the mystical syllable *Oṃ*.

It may be out of place, here to deliberate on quite a different tradition, which posits the Word, λο'γos, at the very source of being itself; still, it may be worthy of attention that creative activity of the Word in Christianity is expressed by its role as a verb. But going back to Bhartṛhari, one becomes aware that Brahman for him is fully defined by the term *sphoṭa-śabda,* or, an utterance that is bursting, swelling up. If one remembers the traditional Indian etymology, which derives the very word Brahman from the verb root *bṛh* meaning to swell up, to grow, to expand, Bhartṛhari's definition seems quite pertinent. But the verb root *sphuṭ,* as well as its derivations *sphuṭa* and *sphoṭa* have yet another shade of meaning: the

45. Bhartṛhari , *Vākyapadīya (Brahmakāṇḍa),* I. 120:
śabdasya pariṇāmo 'yamityāmāyavido viduḥ /
chandobhya eva prathamametadviśvaṃ vyavartate //120 //

verb also means to appear, to become manifested, while *sphoṭa* is not just an appearance or manifestation, but a certain state of mind when, after the word has been pronounced, the consciousness is suddenly lit up by the image of the object. The evolving of a mental image, brought about by the correctly pronounced utterance, is likened here to the creation of the universe, based upon its correct name.[46] So from Bhartṛhari's standpoint, the knowledge of Brahman can be achieved primarily through the science of grammar, that is, the teaching about words, their appropriate use and distribution:

> Since the one is split up many times by the dividing /during the time/ of creation,
> The higher Brahman is grasped through the knowledge of grammar.[47]

---

46. One is reminded here how in a well-known story by Arthur Clarke the accomplishment of the existence of the universe and, ultimately, the end of the world is connected with the finding of the true name of the God. The science fiction writer is somewhat superficially using Buddhist realities (the scene is in Tibet) but does not seem to realize that, according to the Buddhist or Brahmanic tradition, the revelation of the true name would have led only to the ending of one world cycle—and the beginning of the following one. The holding of the world in its 'folded' state is possible only on the stage of a latent, not-yet-pronounced Word.

47. Bhartṛhari *Vākyapadīya (Brahmakāṇḍa)*, I. 22:
yadekaṃ prakriyābhedairbahudhā pravibhajyate /
tad vyākaranamāgamya paraṃ brahmādhigamyate //22 //

However, M. Biardeau has certain reservations with regard to the liberation promised for those learned in the science of grammar:

"si Bhartṛhari promet le selut aux connaisseurs et aux usagers du language correct, ce salut reste indéfini; appelé tantôt mokṣa, tantôt apavarga ... il est aussi à l'occasion appelé abhyudaya, qui est l terme couramment employé dans la Mīmāṃsā et la Grammaize de l'école de Pāṇini, pour désigner à la fois la prosperité terrestre et la bonheur céleste après la mort comme fruit du dharma" ("[I]f Bhartṛhari promises salvation to the knowers and the users of the right language, this salvation remains undefined; sometimes called *mokṣa*, and sometimes *apavarga* ... it is also on some occasions called *abhyudaya*, the term currently employed in Mīmāṃsā and in Pāṇini's Grammar school in order to define simultaneously earthly prosperity and heavenly happi-

It is clear that grammar *(vyākaraṇa)* is understood here in a very broad sense and the second and third parts of *Vākyapadīya*, dealing with linguistic matters, are actually just auxiliary interpretations of the notions presented in *Brahmakāṇḍa.*

Śaṅkara, for whom Bhartṛhari was a highly venerated teacher, never engages in open polemics with him. Nevertheless, one can get some idea of Śaṅkara's divergence from the teaching of the grammarian from the critique of Bhartṛhari's system that can be found in the works of a later Advaitist, Vimuktātman (*c.* thirteenth century). In his treatise *Iṣṭasiddhi* (realization of the desired) Vimuktātman notes that a word or a saying *(śabda)* could be regarded as an object, and therefore it could never be an inner Self, or *ātman* of living beings. And since the Upaniṣads insist on the identity of *ātman* and Brahman, Bhartṛhari's teaching is evidently deviating from orthodox tradition. It looks as if Śaṅkara himself would not go as far as that in his differences with this famous predecessor, but still, even for him, Bhartṛhari is in many respects too 'mythological' and one-sided.

In the eyes of later Vedanta, Bhartṛhari lacked primarily a concept of *ātman*, an ability to relate the mental and psychic life of an individual to higher reality. One might note that another teacher and predecessor of Śaṅkara—Gauḍapāda—devoted himself mainly to this subject. One should not, of course, examine his teaching in the light of a present-day 'psychologism'—his aim and his task were somewhat different from that—but he did elaborate a singular analysis of mind and consciousness, which was directly projected upon the cosmological picture of the world. Gauḍapāda's sphere of interests was greatly influenced by the Buddhist Vijñānavāda. Just like Bhartṛhari, he tried in his own way to develop and restructure some Buddhist ideas, adjusting them as far as possible to the

---

ness acquired after death as a result of the corresponding *dharma*.") M. Biardeau, *Théorie de la connaissance et philosophie de la parole dans le brahmanisme classique*, p. 268.

accepted orthodox tradition. Some scholars, for instance, V. Bhattacharya, who published Gauḍapāda's main work—his *Kārikā* on *Māṇḍūkyopaniṣad*—are of the opinion that practically all his notions were simply borrowed from Buddhist teaching.[48] In contrast to this attitude, another well-known Indian scholar, T.M.P. Mahadevan, insists that Gauḍapāda was a direct follower of Upaniṣadic tradition and so it is quite out of the question that Buddhist doctrines could have any impact on his thought.[49] However, the correctness of similar statements can be judged only after at least a preliminary acquaintance with the work of one of the first Vedantins.

Max von Walleser, German Indologist, thought that Gauḍapāda lived at the beginning of the eighth,[50] though lately scholars are inclined to the opinion that he lived much earlier (*ca.* fifth and sixth centuries). According to Vedantic tradition, Gauḍapāda was not Śaṅkara's immediate contemporary and is separated from him by at least one generation. Towards the end of his commentary on Gauḍapāda's *Māṇḍūkya-kārikā* Śaṅkara hails him as a *paramaguru,* that is either as a great teacher or the teacher of the teacher. (In the living chain of Vedantists who transmitted their teaching orally between Gauḍapāda and Śaṅkara there is another teacher, Govindapāda).

As mentioned above, Gauḍapāda was the author of the philosophical treatise *Māṇḍūkya-kārikā* (its other names are *Gauḍapāda-kārikā, Gauḍapādīya-kārikā* and *Āgama-śāstra* (a *sāstra* on Vedic tradition). Sometimes Gauḍapāda

---

48. Vide: V. Bhattacharya, *The Āgamaśāstra of Gauḍapāda,* Calcutta, 1943 (Introduction).

49. T.M.P. Mahadevan, *Gauḍapāda: A Study in Early Advaita.* Similar views were expressed by S. Mudgal: "The Crypto-Buddhism of Gauḍapāda and Śaṅkara, therefore, was mere 'play acting', and 'transcendentalism' was a bait to catch the Buddhist in the Vedanta net." S.G. Mudgal, *Advaita of Śaṅkara: A Reappraisal,* p. 187.

50. Max von Walleser, *Der ältere Vedanta,* pp. 16-17.

is regarded as the author of other writings (usually of a Tantric kind) but this attribution is rather doubtful.

The first chapter *(prakaraṇa)* of *Māṇḍūkya-kārikā,* titled *Āgama,* is a commentary on *Māṇḍūkyopaniṣad.* It is interesting to note that the text of this Upaniṣad, divided into twelve prosaic fragments, is fully included in *Māṇḍūkya-kārikā* and is not known to exist independently. It led some scholars (among them such serious Indologists as Paul Deussen) to presume that Gauḍapāda himself was the author of this late Upaniṣad. That hypothesis—bordering on sacrilege in the eyes of an orthodox thinker—does not find any historical or textological corroboration. In Viṣṇuite Vedanta tradition, especially for Rāmānuja and Madhva, the whole of the first chapter of *Māṇḍūkya-kārikā,* including the metrical commentary, is considered to be *Māṇḍūkyopaniṣad.*

Āgama-prakaraṇa starts with the analysis of the four states *(avasthā)* of consciousness, or, as Gauḍapāda hastens to add, of the four steps *(pāda)* to liberation *(mokṣa).* The first one is the state, characteristic of every person *(vaiśvānara),* or consciousness during wakefulness *(jāgarita).* It is determined by the orientation towards external objects and enjoys simple sensations (smell, taste, color, etc.). The second one—*taijasa,* or brilliant, luminous—begins during a dreaming state *(svapna)* when consciousness is absorbed by its own inner content. The third step of consciousness is made during profound sleep without dreams *(suṣupta);* there it becomes wise *(prājña),* becomes a united, indivisible entity *(ekībhūta)* and because of that is also called *prajñānaghana,* or, literally, a lump of consciousness. (In Śaṅkara's words from his commentary on *Māṇḍūkya-kārikā,* the details are indiscernible here under the veil of night.) In Gauḍapāda's metrical *Kārikā,* where he tries to summarize the deliberation on the first three states of consciousness, one reads:

> External knowledge/is grasped/ everywhere by
> the consciousness belonging/ to every person,
> internal knowledge—by the luminous one,

The lump of consciousness is the wise one;
so one is remembered as triple.[51]

One might think that a wise consciousness is the supreme goal taught by the Upaniṣads—and presented by Gauḍapāda, the Vedantin. Actually, it is more complicated than that. According to *Māṇḍūkyopaniṣad*, there is yet another, utmost state, where there is absolutely no opposition between external and internal, between sleep and waking, darkness and light, anxiety and bliss. This peculiar state cannot be expressed in words, it is called the fourth one *(turīya)* and is defined primarily in an apophatic way: as something unseen, beyond empirical practice, impossible to grasp, without any signs, unthinkable, indescribable (*'adṛṣṭam avyavahāryam agrāhyam alakṣaṇam acintyam avyapadeśyam', Māṇḍūkyopaniṣad,* 7). In Gauḍapāda's commenting *Kārikā* this passage is clarified as follows:

These two /states/, the one /belonging/ to every person
and the luminous one, are regarded
as bound by cause and effect,
Even the wise one is bound by cause, but both of them
do not exist for the fourth one.
The wise one does not discern anything—
neither itself nor the others,
neither truth nor lie,
But only this fourth one is eternal
witness of everything.[52]

---

51. Gauḍapāda, *Māṇḍūkya-kārikā,* I (this *kārikā* is attached to the sixth saying of *Māṇḍūkyopaniṣadi:*
bahiṣprajño vibhurviśvo hyantaḥprajñastu taijasaḥ /
ghanaprajñastathā prājña eka tridhā smṛtaḥ //1//
(Eight Upaniṣads, with the Commentary of Śaṅkarācārya, vol. 2, Calcutta, 1978).

52. Gauḍapāda, *Māṇḍūkya-kārikā,* I.11-12:
Kāryakāraṇabaddhau tāviṣyete viśvataijasau /
prājñaḥ kāraṇabaddhastu dvau turye na sidhyataḥ //11//

In other words, only the mysterious fourth state is really beyond any duality, beyond any restless world activity. The notion of non-duality *(advaita)* of the higher reality ultimately lent its name not only to Gauḍapāda's teaching but also to the system of Śaṅkara. The trend within orthodox philosophy which was founded by them later became known as Advaita-Vedanta. When he opposed the restless activity of usual knowledge and experience to this ineffable and unintelligible entity, Gauḍapāda was basing his thoughts mainly on Buddhist concepts. And it was in Buddhism that Gauḍapāda borrowed the notion of the *illusiveness* of manifold world activities and perceptions that are being cut short and exhausted in the moment of true seeing. The term, used to define the falseness of any duality, was that of the Buddhist *māyā.*[53] As one can read in the first chapter of *Māṇḍūkya-kārikā.*

---

nātmānaṃ na parāṃścaiva na satyaṃ nāpi cānṛtam /
prājñaḥ kiñcana saṃveti turyaṃ tat sarvadṛk sadā //12//

The notion of a seer, a witness is borrowed by Gauḍapāda from the Upaniṣads, in particular, from a famous fable about two birds, one of which (symbolizing the empirical Self) is tasting of a sweet fruit, while the other (the higher spirit, or *ātman*) is only watching (vide: *Muṇḍakopaniṣad,* III. 1.1).

53. The word *māyā* can be found in *Śvetāśvataropaniṣad,* IV.10, where it signifies a divine creative power and is more or less identified with *prakṛti,* or nature, as the origin of the universe. Indeed, it was only in Buddhist Śūnyavāda that the notion of *māyā* was developed into a consistent doctrine of the illusiveness of the phenomenal world. One sees, for example, in Nāgārjuna's *Mādhyamika-kārikā,* VII, 34, the following definition:

Just like /illusive/ *māyā,* just like a dream,
just like the city of the /heavenly musicians,/
the Gandharvas,
Just like a beginning is this state, it is called
the momentary, /changing flux/.
Yathā māyā yathā svapno gandharvanagaraṃ yathā /
yathotpādas tathā sthānaṃ tathā bhaṅga udīritaḥ //34//.

However, Gauḍapāda and Śaṅkara relate *māyā* to the Vedic metaphor of a 'hidden' *(gūḍha)* Brahman (cf., for instance, *Kaṭhopaniṣad,* I.3.12).

When a soul wakens from sleep, /evoked/
by endless *māyā,*
It reveals something undual, devoid of sleep or dreams,
something unborn.[54]

However, unlike the Buddhists, who left open the question of an ontologial status of the higher reality, Gauḍapāda maintains that this fourth state, which cannot be grasped by the usual means of rational knowledge, is nevertheless undoubtedly real and is nothing but the higher Self—that is, *ātman*, essentially identical with Brahman. One of the means to get closer to this unique entity is, according to Gauḍapāda, meditation on the sacred syllable *Oṃ*, where each of the first three states is in its turn associated with one of the sounds composing this syllable by the rules of Sanskrit phonetics. (That is, *Oṃ* is divided into: *a-u-ṃ*). One might say that *turīya* does not find a direct correspondence in the sound structure of the syllable; the symbol of the fourth state is a dot *(bindu)* as a part of the graphical image of *anusvāra,* or the nasal aftersound, belonging to the preceding vowel.

In the last chapters of Gauḍapāda's work, called "The Chapter on Falseness" *(Vaitathya-prakaraṇa)* and "The Chapter on non-duality" *(Advaita-prakaraṇa),* he examines the nature of the empirical world and the problem of its creation. The Advaitist notes that the causality doctrine of Sāṃkhya, according to which the effect is presented as an evolution *(pariṇāma)* of the real primal entity (for the Sāṃkhyayikas it is *prakṛti* which is naturally evolving and transforming itself into the real universe), leads to the infinite regress *(anavasthā)* of the chain of

---

54. Gauḍapāda, *Māṇḍūkya-kārikā,* I.16:
anādimāyayā supto yadā jīvaḥ prabudhyate /
ajaṃanidramasvapnamadvaitaṃ budhyate tadā //16//
One might note that in the next *kārikā* Gauḍapāda is further specifying: "[T] his duality is nothing else but *māyā*"—*māyāmātram idaṃ dvaitam* (I. 17).

cause and effect. At the same time, the Naiyāyikas' and the Vaiśeṣikas' conviction that the effect is qualitatively different from the cause amounts to admission of the possibility of emergence of real from unreal—and as such cannot provide a satisfactory explanation of the creation of the world. The only doctrine free from these contradictions is, to his mind, that of Mahāyāna with its concept of *ajāti* (absence of birth). According to this concept, both creation and the existence of the world are essentially illusory. What is more, Gauḍapāda practically equates states of sleep and waking, asserting that all our perceptions are similar to dreams and serve just as empty signs of absent and essentially unreal things:

> Wise people say that the states of dreaming and waking are the same,
> Because different things are identical, and there is a reason for this, which is known.
> And what does not exist in the beginning and in the end, does not occur even now.
> These /perceived objects/ are similar to false /illusions/ but still they are defined as true.[55]

According to *Māṇḍūkya-kārikā*, the world of individual souls and external objects is just a projection of one indivisible consciousness *(citta)*. However, it is important not to overlook the fact that—in contrast to momentary *vijñāna* taught by the Buddhist schools—this consciousness, forming the background and foundation of the perceived universe, is identical with the eternal and immutable *ātman* of the Upaniṣads. In the words of Gauḍapāda,

---

55. Gauḍapāda, *Māṇḍūkya-kārikā,* II. 5-6:
svapnajāgaritasthāna hyekamāhurmanīṣiṇaḥ /
bhedānāṃ hi samtvena prasiddhenaiva hetunā //5//
ādāvante ca yannāsti vartamāne 'pi tattathā /
vitathaiḥ sadṛśāḥ santo 'vitathā iva lakṣatāḥ //6//

God, /who is/ *ātman*, thinks himself through his own Self, owing to his *māyā*;
And then he realizes different /objects/—this is the thesis of Vedanta.[56]

The assumption of the absolute reality of the higher consciousness allows Gauḍapāda to construct a peculiar hierarchy of different levels of being and their respective levels of perception. Though the first three states of consciousness, as well as the phenomenal world in general, are real only relatively and illusively, they are still radically different from simple mistakes and errors. Of course, it would not be difficult to trace Gauḍapāda's concept back to the Buddhist doctrine of two truths, but one should always bear in mind that in *Māṇḍūkya-kārikā* the interest is concentrated not on the problem of profane (*saṃvṛta*, lit.: covered, concealed) and higher methods of knowledge, but on that of the inter-relations of the planes of reality of everything that exists. Gauḍapāda's notion of the grades of reality and consciousness found a further development in Śaṅkara's Advaita. Finally, just as it was later in Śaṅkara's system, the ultimate liberation from *saṃsāra* is regarded in *Māṇḍūkya-kārikā* as the achievement of the already achieved *(praptasya prāpti)*, that is, as a return to some originally existing entity. It can be revealed not through ritual worship of Īśvara, or personi-

56. Gauḍapāda, *Māṇḍūkya-kārikā*, II. 12:
Kalpayatyātmanā 'tmānamātmā devaḥ svamāyayā /
sa eva budhyate bhedāniti vedāntaniścayaḥ //12//
Somewhat later (*Māṇḍūkya-kārikā*, II.16) Gauḍapāda explains how and in what order 'thinking' or imagining proceeds from *ātman*: in the beginning *ātman* forms an illusory notion of individual soul; only later, through an effort of creative imaginaiton, does *ātman* project outward images of the objects desired by the soul, as well as the images of actions and reaped fruit of *saṃsāra*. In his commentary on Gauḍapāda's *Kārikā* Śaṅkara emphasizes that the fantastic picture of this universal dreaming is still essentially different from the Buddhists' concept, since for Gauḍapāda even this world illusion has its inner support in real *ātman*.

fied God, but only owing to a particular kind of knowledge *(jñāna):*

> It is said that unthinkable, unborn knowledge
> is not different from the known /Brahman/.
> The known Brahman is unborn and eternal: /just so/
> the unborn /Brahman/ is revealed through
> the unborn /knowledge/.[57]

The fourth chapter of *Māṇḍūkya-kārikā* is entitled "The Chapter on the Extinguishing of the Burning Coals" *(Alātaśānti-prakaraṇa).* In its ideas, its style and terminology it is so close to some Mahāyāna works that it looks like a direct imitation of the treatises by Nāgārjuna and Asaṅga. The illusory creation of the world is explained here by a vibration of consciousness *(citta-spanda),* which has close parallels in the philosophical constructions of Vijñānavāda. In the words of Gauḍapāda,

> This pair of the perceiver and the perceived
> /is produced/ just by the vibration of consciousness,
> And consciousness is devoid of objects—that is why
> it is declared to be eternally unbound.[58]

Knowledge or consciousness is divided into a worldly *(laukika)* one, which starts during ordinary waking state, a pure worldly *(śuddha-laukika),* or perceptions in dreams, and above-worldly *(lokottara)* one (vide: *Māṇḍūkya-kārikā,* IV. 87-88). These terms almost literally reiterate the terminology of the Buddhist *Laṅkāvatāra-sūtra* (III. 65).

Since all worldly activity is for Gauḍapāda practically equated with dreaming, it seems quite appropriate that

57. Gauḍapāda, *Māṇḍūkya-kārikā,* III. 33:
akalpakamajaṃ jñānaṃ jñeyābhinnaṃ pracakṣate /
brahmajñeyamajaṃ nityamajenājaṃ vibudhyate //33//

58. Gauḍapāda, *Māṇḍūkya-kārikā,* IV. 72:
cittaspanditamevedaṃ grāhyagrāhakavaddvayam /
cittaṃ nirviṣayaṃ nityam asaṅga tena kīrtitam //72//.

the crossing of its limits is defined as waking *(prabodha)*. Certainly, it is not accidental that he calls the liberated sages the awakened ones *(prabuddhāḥ, buddhāḥ);* here one can recognize another sign of the Advaitist's sympathies towards Buddhism. Some scholars (among them V. Bhattacharya) tend to identify the intangible yoga *(asparśa-yoga),* or, yoga, free of touches and bounds, which is mentioned by Gauḍapāda in the fourth chapter of his *Kārikā* (IV.2) as a path to the higher bliss, with the ninth *dhyāna* of the Buddhists.

To my mind, however, it is hardly correct to insist on the identity of the main notions of Gauḍapāda's Advaita and Buddhist doctrines. Though in some passages of his commentary on the *Kārikā* of his teacher Śaṅkara has to admit that sometimes Gauḍapāda does share some opinions of the Vijñānavādins, he hastens to add that it is done only to refute the views of the materialists who believe in the real existence of external objects (vide: Śaṅkara's commentary on Gauḍapāda's (*Kārikā*, IV.27). One might remember in this connection T. M. P. Mahadevan's words to the effect that Gauḍapāda used the ideas and terminology of the Buddhists only as a sort of sophisticated bait in order to lure them into the net of orthodox philosophy. At the end of *Māṇḍūkya-kārikā* Gauḍapāda has to dissociate himself from the Buddhist concepts: the danger of confusion was decidedly too great:

> Since the knowledge of awakened and omnipresent one does not touch /objects and other/ souls,
> All souls, just like that,/are not connected with objects/ —but it was not said by the Buddha.[59]

However, the interpretation (and eventually, the translation) of this rather vague *kārikā* is based primarily on Śaṅkara's commentary; and Śaṅkara directly identifies this awakened *ātman* with Brahman and the higher

---

59. Gauḍapāda, *Māṇḍūkya-kārikā*, IV. 99:
kramate na hi buddhasya jñānaṃ dharmeṣu tāyinaḥ /
sarve dharmāstathā jñānaṃ naitadbuddhena bhāṣitam //99//.

knowledge. And Brahman, reminds the Advaitist, is known only from the Upaniṣadic sayings.

The problem of the similarity of certain of Gauḍapāda's notions with Buddhist ideas borders a more general problem of the historical influence of Buddhist concepts on Śaṅkara. F. Whaling finds it historically probable that "the Advaita Vedanta set forth by Gauḍapāda was different from the Vedanta that had gone before, and much of that difference can be explained by reference to his conscious or unconscious debt to Mahāyāna Buddhism."[60] Of course, it was not just a chance coincidence that a later Advaitin Śrīharṣa (*c.* twelfth century) in his work *Khaṇḍanakhaṇḍakhādya* (Assimilation of chapters on refutation) could declare that he really has no essential divergences of opinion from the Mādhyamikas, since, to his mind, Buddhist Śūnyavāda is very close to Advaita.[61]

Indeed, it is difficult not to notice how much Śaṅkara is indebted to his predecessor. They are quite in agreement in defining the higher reality as non-dual *(advaita),* that is, devoid of any attributes; they are quite close in their views on *māyā*; and, finally, both of them identify the higher *ātman* with knowledge, or supreme consciousness. It was directly from Gauḍapāda's *Kārikā* that Śaṅkara derived more particular details of his teaching: such as his concept of the levels of being and knowledge, his simile of an individual soul and space *(ākāśa)*, his favorite example of a rope that looks like a snake from a distance, an example that was extremely useful in illustrating perceptual errors. In the *Kārikā* of Gauḍapāda one finds the division of sacred texts into sayings that have absolute value (the so-called sayings 'on the absence of difference,—*abheda*) and those that have relative value and depend on context, though in Śaṅkara's system a similar tenet played an essentially different part. T.M.P. Mahadevan, who was

---

60. F. Whaling, *Śaṅkara and Buddhism*, p. 23.

61. Vide: Phyllis Granoff, *Philosophy and Argument in Late Vedanta: Śrī Harṣa's Khaṇḍanakhaṇḍakhādya,* Dordrecht, 1978.

certainly far from identifying the ideas of Advaita and Buddhism, was still of the opinion that "doctrinally, there is no difference whatsoever between what is taught by Gauḍapāda in the *Kārikā* and what is expounded by Śaṅkara in his extensive works."[62]

Feeling that similar statements were perceptibly straining a point of discussion, and trying to take into account the undeniable fact that Gauḍapāda was standing in dangerous proximity to Mahāyāna concepts, some scholars try to separate the views of the two Advaitists by indicating that Śaṅkara's ideas underwent an important evolution. In the words of S. Dasgupta, Śaṅkara's development from his Commentary on *Māṇḍūkya-kārikā* to the Commentary on *Brahmasūtra* was marked by the growth of 'realism'.[63] A minute analysis of the evolution of Śaṅkara's conceptions was carried out on the same general lines by Paul Hacker. To his mind, an early stage of Śaṅkara's writing is represented by his Commentary on *Māṇḍūkya-kārikā*, commentary on *Māṇḍūkyopaniṣad,* Commentary on *Taittirīyopaniṣad* and, partly, his treatise *Upadeśa-sāhasrī* (A thousand teachings). It was the time when Śaṅkara allegedly shared Gauḍapāda's interest in Yoga, as well as in the Vijñānavāda version of Buddhism, widely using in his works the ideas and even the terminology of Buddhism. The most profound influence on Gauḍapāda and Śaṅkara was, according to Hacker, exerted by the concepts of *Laṅkāvatāra-sūtra* and by the writings of Nāgārjuna and Vasubandhu.[64] Hence the inevitable conclusion that in his works of the later period Śaṅkara was, so to speak, atoning for the sins of his early enthusiasm of Mahāyāna. And in the words of F. Whaling, Śaṅkara's

---

62. T.M.P. Mahadevan, *Gauḍapāda: A Study in Early Advaita*, pp. 231-232.

63. S. Dasgupta, *A History of Indian Philosophy*, vol. 2, p. 29.

64. Vide: P. Hacker, *Beiträge zur Geistesgeschichte Indiens*, Leiden, 1968.

own development was in some ways a development away from Gauḍapāda and Buddhism.[65]

However, instead of dividing into stages the essentially integrated creative activity of Śaṅkara to my mind there are far more fundamental grounds, for trying to single out the subsequent stages in the development of Advaita. Gauḍapāda, who got carried away by some of the ideas of Vijñānavāda, voluntarily assumed the task of supplying a bridge between Buddhist doctrines and orthodox tradition. As for Śaṅkara, he actually left behind both Mahāyāna and the somewhat 'heretically' colored teaching of Gauḍapāda, and one should note that he forged ahead of them in the very beginning, in the work where he was so lavish in his praise of a *paramaguru*. When one is analyzing a relatively short Commentary on *Māṇḍūkya-kārikā*, it virtually leaps to the eye that Śaṅkara's sincere respect for his teacher does not prevent him from taking certain liberties with the basic text. I would not say that he consciously distorts the tenets of the *Kārikā*; he rather proposes essential additions which sometimes entirely change the perspective of Gauḍapāda's work.

When *Māṇḍūkya-kārikā* deals with pure consciousness, which is devoid of any attributes, uncreated, but by its own efforts creating the world of phenomena, Śaṅkara does not omit to specify that the entity that is implied here is nothing else but the higher Brahman of the Upaniṣads. Even for the obviously Mahāyānic passage about the vibration of consciousness he selects a *śruti* saying, that the higher reality is not bound by any relations.[66] And the guarantee against a psychological interpretation of *Māṇḍūkya-kārikā*—an interpretation that would directly pave the way to the Buddhist 'heresy'—is secured by

65. F. Whaling, *Śaṅkara and Buddhism*, p. 24.

66. *Sa yattatra kiṃcitpaśyatyananvāgatastena bhavati asaṅgo hyayaṃ puruṣa iti* /"He is not touched by anything that he sees in this state, because this Puruṣa is devoid of bounds" (*Bṛhadāraṇyakopaniṣad*, IV. 3.15). Here the passge deals with dreaming *(svapna)*, but in the very

Śaṅkara owing to his reference to the authority of sacred tradition. That is why he supplements the last (the hundredth) *kārikā* of the fourth chapter of Gauḍapāda's work with an extensive conclusion which completely changes the context of the basic saying. Gauḍapāda's *Kārikā* runs as follows:

> This hard-to-define, deeply hidden, unborn,
> equal and wise
> State having awakened, this /state,/devoid of
> differences, we worship with all our force.[67]

And how does Śaṅkara respond to that? The move is quite simple: instead of Gauḍapāda's term *padam* (state, step, part) he inserts *Brahmanam*, which glibly enters the structure of the stanza, coinciding with the replaced word even in its grammatical form—the accusative of the neuter gender. In my opinion, twists of that kind were meant to be not only an outward method for securing 'heretical' ideas a safe harbor inside the orthodox tradition. This is not the place for more details; we will encounter a similar manipulation when we analyze Śaṅkara's polemics with the Buddhists. However, one cannot overlook the fact that the same mechanism is used again in his later writings. The core of this method is by no means exhausted by introducing the notion of divine entity into the exposition,

---

next saying of the Upaniṣad (IV.3.16) the same words are literally reiterated with reference to Puruṣa who has returned to his awakened state. And when Śaṅkara cites this text in his commentary on *Māṇḍūkya-kārikā* (IV.72), he is clearly implying both meanings and both passages.

67. Gauḍapāda, *Māṇḍūkya-kārikā,* IV.100:
durdarśamatigambhīramajaṃ sāmyaṃ viśāradam /
buddhvā adamanānātvaṃ namaskurmo yathābalam //100//
It is quite interesting to note that immediately after this *kārikā* is placed the well-known conclusion of Śaṅkara, in which he praises the higher Brahman and deferentially addresses his *paramaguru,* Gauḍapāda.

which could well do without it for the inner logic of the development of ideas,—but is mainly clarified from the Advaitist's foothold in Vedic texts.

Unlike the above-mentioned early Vedantins, Maṇḍanamiśra lived approximately at the same time as Śaṅkara. He had already become a recognized teacher by the time when Śaṅkara was only starting his work; according to some extant evidences, he survived his younger contemporary. Indian scholars are generally of the opinion that Maṇḍanamiśra lived in the seventh century,[68] while Western Indologists put it later. According to the orthodox tradition, Śaṅkara personally met Maṇḍanamiśra during his wanderings and even defeated him in philosophical disputes.

Maṇḍanamiśra left many different works; it is interesting to note that they are written in the traditions of various orthodox schools. Among his other works three treatises composed in the spirit of Pūrva-Mīmāṃsā became widely known and commented upon: *Mīmāṃsānukramaṇikā* (The enumeration of Mīmāṃsā categories), *Bhavanā-viveka* (The distinction of becoming) and *Vidhi-viveka* (The distinction of injunctions). Fairly popular was also his epistemological work *Vibhrama-viveka* (The distinction of errors), as well as some philosophical writings, composed from the standpoint of grammar theories. The only Vedantic work of Maṇḍanamiśra is his treatise *Brahma-siddhi* (Realization of Brahman), which had a profound impact on the development of post-Śaṅkara Advaita.

Brahma-siddhi comprises four parts that subsequently treat such matters as the nature of Brahman, the foundations of philosophical discourse, the essence of Vedic injunctions and the ways of achieving ultimate liberation. Even this treatise betrays a considerable Mīmāṃsā influence (especially the impact of Kumārila's ideas), but what

---

68. Among these scholars one might name S. Kuppuswamy Sastri, who published a reliable edition of *Brahma-siddhi* (Vide: *Brahma-siddhi* by Ācārya Maṇḍanamiśra, with commentary by Śaṅkhapāṇi, edited by S. Kuppuswamy Sastri, Madras, 1937, Introduction, p. lviii).

is particularly noticeable here is the imprint of Bhartṛhari's teaching about the Word. It is Speech itself that rules the world, forming the basis of all worldly things: "And the world follows the form of the speech—that is why it is known either as the evolution of the speech, or as its revelation."[69] Consciousness itself, the very ability to think, is identified by him with an inner form of speech that accompanies every possible object.[70] Following Bhartṛhari—and even directly referring to him—Maṇḍanamiśra considers meditation on the sacred syllable *Oṃ* to be one of the means of knowing the higher reality, and hence one of the means of liberation from *saṃsāra*. In his words, "he who knows the essence of *ātman* of all /beings/ is instructed to meditate on this /syllable/.[71]

Though Maṇḍanamiśra himself did not call his system by the name which it later acquired from Advaita followers, this name—Bhāvādvaita (*bhāvādvaita*, lit.: *Advaita* of being)—reflects one of the essential concepts of the Vedantin. According to Maṇḍanamiśra, the higher Brahman *exists* and is revealed along with the cessation of all world manifoldness and diversity *(prapañcābhāva)* and the folding of nescience, or *avidyā (avidyānivṛtti)*. Indeed, the ending of *avidyā* and the emergence of true knowledge is in itself equal to the confirming of the existence of the higher Brahman, and, thereby, to its realization. The opponents, in the words of the Vedanta, usually imply that "allegedly it is impossible to admit a

---

69. Maṇḍanamiśra, *Brahma-siddhi*, I.2: *vāgrūpānvitaṃ ca jagat ato vāco vipariṇāmo vivarto vāvasīyate* /.

70. One reads in *Brahma-siddhi* (I.2): "the thought is the very potency of the speech, and so, when it is drawn inside, there is left only the subtle speech potency; and everywhere the understanding of objects follows the form of the speech." "*vākśaktireva vā citiḥ tatpratisaṃhāre 'pi sūkṣma vākśaktirityeke sarvathā vāgrūpādhīno jñeyabodha iti* /."

71. Maṇḍanamiśra, *Brahma-siddhi*, I.2: *sārvātmyavida eva tena dhyānopadeśaḥ* /.

simultaneous /existence of the two states/ in one and the same reality, but /we/ object to this, /saying that it is possible,/ since here one reality is defined through the forms of being and non-being."[72] In other words, the higher Brahman in Advaita can be defined both cataphatically—as a *positive* liberation *(mokṣa)*—and apophatically—through a *negation* of the false, illusory world of *avidyā*. This dual approach to the realization of Brahman reflects the inner duality of the realization itself, which is achieved through this knowledge.

Maṇḍanamiśra often emphasizes that Brahman is grasped neither by perception, nor by logical inference or other means of valid knowledge. These means, or *pramāṇas* (of which there are six, according to Maṇḍanamiśra's Advaita, as well as Pūrva-Mīmāṃsā) cannot lead an adept to the higher reality. The only exception is partly made for the 'evidence of authority' *(śabda)*, however, the Advaitist specifies that the authority should not be interpreted here simply as the opinion of the wise or as something generally accepted. To Maṇḍanamiśra's mind, only the Vedas can really lead to Brahman: "The seers say that it is known from sacred tradition; and this /Brahman/ is defined through the destruction of any division and diversity."[73]

Up to this point the views of Maṇḍanamiśra examined here do not apparently differ much from the later Advaita of Śaṅkara. Nevertheless, one should not forget that some notions of his system raised serious objections from the younger contemporary, as well as a severe critique on the part of many of Śaṅkara's followers. The problem concerns mainly Maṇḍanamiśra's attitude to Vedic ritual and traditional religious injunctions. Trying as far as possible to reconcile and bring together the concepts of Pūrva-

72. Maṇḍanamiśra, *Brahma-siddhi,* III.106: *nanvekatve tulyakālatāpyanupapannā na ekasyāpi vastuno bhāvābhāvarūpeṇa vyapadeśāt* /.

73. Maṇḍanamiśra, *Brahma-siddhi,* I.2: *āmnāyataḥ prasiddhiṃ ca kavayo 'sya pracakṣate /bhedaprapañcavilayadvāreṇa ca nirūpaṇam* /

Mīmāṃsā with those of Vedanta, Maṇḍanamiśra stresses the absolute, immutable significance of Vedic precepts. And here, one should say, he could hardly count on Śaṅkara's agreement, since the latter assigned to traditional religion only the role of a subsidiary step on the way to liberation. The author of *Brahma-siddhi* appeared to be far closer in this respect to Bhāskara, one of the founders of Viṣṇuite trend within Vedanta.[74] Probably some inclination towards Viṣṇuism to some extent explains also his insistence upon a special condition, indispensable for the unity of a soul with the higher Brahman; this condition is represented by love, passionate affection, which in the first place induces an adept to seek the higher entity. In Maṇḍanamiśra's words, "it is established that Brahman is essentially bliss, the higher self-luminosity of *ātman*; the *ātman* is essentially bliss, since it is attained through the higher passion."[75] Passionate love *(prema),* preached by Maṇḍanamiśra, bears a strong resemblance not only to *bhakti* (lit.: being a part of, hence—attachment, devotion), propounded by Rāmānuja and Vallabha, but also to the 'gentle tenderness' *(sneha),* which is so important for the religious mysticism of Madhva and other Kṛṣṇaites.

If Śaṅkara essentially restrained himself from holding open disputes with the older Vedantin, many of his followers later engaged in polemics with Maṇḍanamiśra in their theoretical works. It was Sureśvara (*c.* eighth century) who was probably the mostly successful in this polemics. Incidentally, according to Vedanta tradition, it was Maṇḍa-

---

74. As previously mentioned, Bhāskara (*ca.* eighth century), who was a propounder of the concept of 'the combination of knowledge and actions' *(jñāna-karma-samuccaya),* in some respects bitterly opposed Śaṅkara's Advaita. This Vedantin, who could certainly be regarded as a forerunner of Rāmānuja, maintained that an adept, aspiring for unity with Brahman, should resort also to accumulating religious merits *(puṇya).*

75. Maṇḍanamiśra, *Brahma-siddhi,* I.1: *tasmādātmaprakāśaprakṛṣṭānandasvabhāvameva brahmeti yuktam /ānandasvabhāva ātma paramapremāspadatvāt /.*

namiśra himself, who, having succumbed to Śaṅkara's arguments, in the later period of his life changed his name and, calling himself Sureśvara, decided to write only Advaita works. In his treatise *Naiṣkārmya-siddhi* (The realization of non-activity), as well as in his sub-commentary to Śaṅkara's commentary on *Bṛhadāraṇyakopaniṣad* (called *Bṛhadāraṇyakabhāṣya-vārttika*), Sureśvara approached Maṇḍanamiśra's teaching in the true spirit of Śaṅkara. At the same time, one of the elements of Sureśvara's polemics proved to be extremely significant for post-Śaṅkara Advaita. Unlike Maṇḍanamiśra, Sureśvara maintained that the origin of universal nescience *(avidyā)* is the higher Brahman itself and not an individual soul; this issue later became a point of divergence of two influential schools within Advaita-Vedanta. After Sureśvara, Maṇḍanamiśra's teaching was opposed by the philosophers Sarvajñātman (*ca.* the beginning of the tenth century), Vimuktātman (the beginning of the thirteenth century). The latter became one of the founders of an Advaita school called Vivaraṇa.[76]

However, Maṇḍanamiśra's teaching, in its turn, found many adherents even among the followers of Śaṅkara. The most prominent of them was, undoubtedly, Vācaspatimiśra (the beginning of the tenth century). Just like Maṇḍanamiśra, he considered *avidyā* to be rooted not in the higher Brahman, which is eternally pure and therefore unsoiled by nescience, but in the limited and darkened soul *(jīva)* of a living being. The concept of *jīva* as the support and locus (*āśraya*, lit., refuge) of *avidyā* became a specific trait of the Advaita school Bhāmatī, called after the title of the main work by Vācaspatimiśra—his sub-commentary *Bhāmatī* (The brilliant one), written on Śaṅkara's commentary on *Brahmasūtra*. It was with

---

76. The school is given this name after the main work by Prakāśātman—*Pañca-pādikā-vivaraṇa*, or The clarification of *Pañca-pādikā*. *Pañca-pādikā* was written by Padmapāda, Śaṅkara's closest disciple.

Vācaspatimiśra—and so, indirectly, with Maṇḍanamiśra—that Prakāśātman disputed the locus of *avidyā*. Maṇḍanamiśra was an accepted authority also for the Advaitins Ānandabodha (*ca.* twelfth century), the author of the treatise *Nyāya-makaranda* (The honey of reasoning); Citsukha (*ca.* thirteenth century); and Madhusūdanasarasvatī (*ca.* the beginning of the seventeenth century).

So, on the whole, the system of Maṇḍanamiśra proved to be more important for later Advaita than for the teaching of Śaṅkara. Besides strictly theoretical problems raised in his works, one should probably mention the fact that it was thanks to him that the literature of Advaita became enriched with a new genre—the prosaic treatise of the '*siddhi*' type. In works of this kind, a doctrinal tenet is proposed or specified by the author only after a thorough consideration of the opponent's arguments. It is believed that the pattern for *Sphoṭa-siddhi* and *Brahma-siddhi* of Maṇḍanamiśra was provided by *Vijñaptimātratā-siddhi* of the Buddhist philosopher Vasubandhu. And the *siddhi* treatises of Maṇḍanamiśra were followed by Sureśvara's *Naiṣkāmya-siddhi,* by *Iṣṭa-siddhi* (The realization of the desired) of Vimuktātman, by *Advaita-siddhi* (The realization on the non-dual) of Madhusūdanasarasvatī, as well as by similar works by later Vedantins.

Now, when Śaṅkara is placed inside the Vedanta tradition, which started to develop even before his time, one can outline both the problems that were of interest to him—and the totality of opposing teachings from which he tried to distinguish his own system. It seems clear that the content of Śaṅkara's doctrine should be searched for at the point of intersection of three main philosophical trends: the grammarians' philosophy of language, the Vedic orientation of Pūrva-Mīmāṃsā and the Buddhist teachings of the Mahāyāna fold. Actually, these three vectors (in their various combinations) had already defined the theoretical constructions of the three principal predecessors of Śaṅkara: Bhartṛhari, Gauḍapāda and Maṇḍanamiśra. For these essentially transitional thinkers the result of their theoretical efforts was shaped mainly by the mechanical law of simple 'addition of forces' and a rather incoherent mixture of manifold ideas. However, in the case of Śaṅkara's system we are dealing with a consistent concept of being and knowledge. After a brief historical digression devoted to the Advaitist's life and work, we shall return to the analysis of his teaching, examining it from this point of view. Then it will be possible to show how the crucible of Advaita successfully melted down the fragments and vestiges of alien (or just unacceptable) concepts that served as raw material for the new teaching.

CHAPTER III

Biography of Śaṅkara and His Main Works

1. *ŚAṄKARA'S LIFE*

We know both too much and too little about Śaṅkara's life. The hagiographical tradition of Vedanta overflows with descriptions of wonderful signs and prophecies, fantastic occurrences and brilliant aphorisms that accompanied literally every day and hour of the Advaitist's earthly existence. Meanwhile, the reliable data are quite scanty and difficult to single out from the colorful mass of contradictory evidence.

There are several accepted biographies of Śaṅkara, but some of them are still unpublished. The only source of this genre available to me was a present-day compilation by V.S. Radhakrishna Sastri, entitled *Srī-Śaṅkara-vijaya-makaranda,*[1] and therefore I also made extensive use of the previously mentioned book by Mario Piantelli, where tales from various hagiographies are brought together. In the last chapter of his work Piantelli gives a short synopsis of the extant biographies of the Advaitist, making use not only of Sanskrit sources, but also of manuscripts in other Indian languages.

Probably the earliest of all Śaṅkara's biographies is the one traditionally ascribed to Citsukha. Like other works of this kind, it includes in its title the word *vijaya,* that is, victory, conquest, and is called *Bṛhat-śaṅkara-vijaya* (The

1. Vaidya V.S. Radhakrishna Sastri, *Srī-śaṅkara-vijaya-makaranda,* Tiruchy, 1978.

conquest of great Śaṅkara), or, sometimes, *Guru-śaṅkara-vijaya* (The conquest of teacher Śaṅkara). The author declares himself to be a native of Kerala; he says that he comes from the same part of the country as Śaṅkara and so was able to preserve the evidence even about the early childhood of the great teacher.

The most authoritative and the most widely-cited hagiography of Śaṅkara belongs to Ānandagiri. While Citsukha's work is sometimes regarded as doubtful (some scholars cannot exclude the possibility of a later forging), *Prācīna-śaṅkara-vijaya* (The collection of tales about Śaṅkara's conquest) by Ānandagiri is quite an accepted and reliable source, which is well-attributed and dates back to the 14th century. However, as some scholars have noticed, the biography of Śaṅkara in this text is supplemented by evidence of the events, that had taken place in the monastery of Kāñcī under the priors, or *jagadgurus*, bearing the same name of Śrī Śaṅkarācārya.

Another popular biography was composed by the Vedantin Vyāsācali; it is entitled *Vyāsācalī-śaṅkara-vijaya.* Though the tradition relates it to the Śaṅkara who is of interest for us now, one must note that its hero is often called either Vidyāśaṅkara, or Śaṅkarānanda; therefore, there is a definite possibility of confusion between the founder of Advaita and a certain Śaṅkarānanda who flourished in Kashmir about the 11th century. Incidentally, the same nickname was used also with reference to Śaṅkaramiśra—a renowned commentator of the Vaiśeṣika school.

Finally, among the most well-known hagiographies of Śaṅkara, one usually mentions *Saṅkṣepa-śaṅkara-vijaya* (A short rendering of Śaṅkara's conquest), which is ascribed to the Advaitist Mādhavācārya, sometimes considered to be a brother of the celebrated Sāyaṇa Mādhava, the author of the compendium *Sarva-darśana-saṅgraha.* The composer of the biography is often identified with the sage Vidyāraṇya, who wrote one of the simplest and most intelligible manuals of Advaita metaphysics—the treatise *Pañcadaśī* (Fifteen chapters). Based on this evidence, the biography should be probably dated back to the fourteenth century. Nevertheless, quite recently compelling arguments were offered that *Saṅkṣepa-śaṅkara-vijaya* was composed in the second part of the 17th century, perhaps even later, and was primarily the fruit of protracted disputes between Vedantic monasteries. In the opinion of the Indian scholar W.R. Antarkar,[2] this hagiography is nothing more than a moderately skillful forgery, made in Śṛṅgerī monastery and destined to substantiate its claims on certain rites connected with Śaṅkara's life. Indeed, this hagiography, which is attributed to Mādhavācārya-Vidyāraṇya, contains almost no new material, mostly following the earlier sources. Its original value is not great, but it still remains a much-cited and convenient synopsis of many legends related to the Advaitist's life.

Mario Piantelli mentions another interesting biography—*Śaṅkara-vijaya-vilāsa* (An exquisite/rendering/of Śaṅkara's conquest). Its authorship is ascribed to one of Śaṅkara's minor disciples; his name is supposed to be Cidvilāsayati. However, this text probably owes its existence to the dispute between two South Indian monasteries. The hagiography is composed in the form of a dialogue between one of a Śaṅkara's pupils and a certain Vijñākāṇḍa, but the greater part of its material is borrowed from *Bṛhat-śaṅkara-vijaya.*

Some of the less-known biographies probably also deserve at least a brief mention. Among them one should note Govindanatha's text, published at the end of the last century and entitled *Keralīya-śaṅkara-vijaya* (Śaṅkara's victories in Kerala); it mainly relates to the local Kerala tradition of Śaṅkara's biographies. There is an unpublished manuscript, containing the poem "Śaṅkarābhyudaya" (The rise of Śaṅkara), and written in the 17th century by a religious poet Rājacūḍāmaṇi Dīkṣita. A

2. Vide : W.R. Antarkar, "Saṅkṣepa Śaṅkara Jaya of Mādhavācārya or Śaṅkara Digvijaya of Śrī Vidyāraṇyamuni," *Journal of the University of Bombay,* vol. 41, no. 77, November, 1972.

celebrated Vedantist Sadānanda, the author of a popular treatise *Vedāntasāra* (the essence of Vedanta), composed at the end of the fifteenth century, is supposed to be the author of the hagiography *Śaṅkara-digvijaya-sāra* (The essence of Śaṅkara's conquest of the world). In the monography by M. Piantelli are also enumerated some of the later biographies of Śaṅkara, manuscripts of which are kept in the libraries of Madras, Kañcī and other places.[3]

In what way do the celebrated hagiographers depict the life of the great Vedantin? First of all, descriptions of his destiny start with events that took place well before his birth. As previously mentioned, Śaṅkara is most often regarded as an earthly incarnation of Śiva, and so, as befits an *avatāra* of God, his birth is preceded by miraculous signs. Śiva, who is sitting atop the Kailāsa mountain together with his heavenly consort, gives the other gods a solemn promise to descend to the earth in order to reinstate the shattered foundations of true knowledge—that is, of Vedanta. It is interesting that many of the well-known Vedantists were also regarded as incarnations of various gods: Maṇḍanamiśra was considered an embodiment of Brahma; Sadānanda, of Viṣṇu; Citsukha, of Varuṇa; and Ānandagiri, of Agni.

According to an old legend, in a small village in Kerala, at the extreme south of India, there once lived a Brahman, whose name was Vidyādhirāja; he came of the family of Nambūṭiri, which was famous for its wealth and learning. The only son of Vidyādhirāja, Śivaguru, or in other versions Cūrṇin, from his early youth was distinguished by his inclination towards asceticism and a secluded way of life. All of his father's eloquence was needed to persuade the youth to postpone sacred vows and marry a suitable girl. Śivatārakā (some hagiographers call her Āryāmbā), daughter of a learned Brahman from a neighboring village, became his wife. As one can judge from the highly

3. Vide : M. Piantelli, *Śaṅkara e la rinascita del brāhmanesimo,* pp. 217-24, especially pp. 223-224.

significant names, the young couple enjoyed the special protection of Śiva himself (Śivaguru means, of course, the teacher Śiva, while Śivatārakā means either Śiva's eye, or Śiva's falling star).

In spite of a virtuous life and unswerving performance of all rites, the couple remained childless for a long time. After many years they finally decided to go to Trichūr, where there was an important Śaivite sanctuary, Vṛṣādrināth, known as a popular place of pilgrimage. They wanted to ask the gods' blessing for a child. It was there that Śivaguru saw in a dream an old man who offered him a choice between a hundred quite happy and successful sons—and just one son, destined to become a great sage but condemned also to a short and severe life. According to *Vyāsācalīśaṅkara-vijaya,* Śivatārakā also saw Śiva in a dream; the god was not disguised but was revealed to her in all the brilliance of his glory, riding the bull Nandi. He openly declared to the woman that her son was destined to become a great Vedanta teacher. After husband and wife had awakened and told each other their dreams, they suddenly heard the voice of Śiva, who exclaimed: "I will myself be born as your son!"

The birth of the wonderful child was accompanied by heavenly music and singing, the sweet fragrance of flowers and unusual meekness of savage beasts. The body of the newborn child was dazzling in its brilliance; on top of his head one could clearly discern a crescent, the sign of Śiva; on his palm there was a mark left by the god's trident; while on his breast, by the heart, there was an image of a coiled cobra; finally, on his forehead one could see a trace of the third eye.[4] The hagiographies also give astrological data, that make it possible to know something about the time of his birth, though they relate mainly to month, day

---

4. All these signs directly correspond to the accepted iconography of Śiva. For instance, the crescent that adorns his headdress on almost all pictures symbolizes the cup with the drink of immortality *(amṛta).* The trident is supposed to emphasize that Śiva rules over three worlds *(triloka)*—the nether world, the earthly world and the heavenly world;

and time of day, rather than to a specific (even if legendary) year. The very name Śaṅkara means auspicious, merciful; it is one of the most sacred and revered of Śiva's names.

Just as wonderful, according to the biographies, was the early childhood of the future teacher. According to one of the legends, Śaṅkara's mother once returned home to find a large cobra, coiled around his neck; while she was still looking at it, stunned by the horrible sight, the cobra turned into a necklace of sacred flowers and fruits. It is said that while he was only one year old, the child could already speak and read Sanskrit. According to the hagiographies, once some children were arguing with each other about the number of seeds inside a large melon. Young Śaṅkara said that the number of the seeds would correspond to the number of gods who had created the universe. And how great was the wonder of everybody present, when, having cut the melon, they found inside only one seed! The most detailed account of Śaṅkara's childhood, including some less-known tales, can be found in *Śaṅkṣepa-śaṅkara-vijaya.*

Soon before Śaṅkara was to celebrate his fifth year, his father Śivaguru was dead (this is probably why the adherents of Dvaita-Vedanta often refer to Śaṅkara as the son of the widow). Soon the boy was invested with a sacred thread and so could start the study of the Vedas, as well as the arts and sciences based on the Vedas. (They are usually called *Vedāṅga,* that is, the limbs of Veda, or the parts of Veda.) Śaṅkara soon surpassed by his learning all

---

or that he is the lord of the three times—past, present and future; and that he appears in the three states of consciousness—the waking state, the dreams and the deep sleep state. The cobra is the sign of eternal renewing and, simultaneously, the sign which bars the way to anyone who would be bold enough to approach Śiva without first renouncing his own personality. The third eye of Śiva, which burns by its blaze all the objects of the ordinary world, signifies absolute seeing, the vision that surpasses the difference between subject and object (which are in their turn represented, respectively, by the left and the right eyes of the god).

the local Brahmanic teachers; he was often asked for advice and spiritual guidance not only by his neighbors but also by the nearby villagers. As befits the true hero of a hagiography, Śaṅkara from early childhood felt an irresistible inclination towards the life of a hermit *(sannyāsin)*, but the entreaties of his mother held him back from taking sacred vows.

When he was almost eight, an unusual occurrence took place which is unanimously related by all of his biographers. The problem was that it was time for his earthly life to end. It was then that, according to the hagiographies, under Śivatārakā's very eyes her son was suddenly caught by an enormous crocodile that dragged its prey to the river. Śaṅkara managed to cry out to his mother, telling her that a promise to become a *sannyāsin* would be the same as a new birth and would, therefore, save him from this violent evil or bad death *(durmaraṇa)*, which was considered in India to be one of the greatest misfortunes and even sins. So Śivatārakā finally agreed that her son would become a hermit, the crocodile released its victim, and Śaṅkara's life span was doubled (by some accounts, multiplied four fold). On the same day Śaṅkara left his native home, having promised, though, to return before his mother's death, in order to console her and then to perform her funeral rites.

The young hermit went to the north. He walked until he finally reached the banks of the Narmadā River, where at that time were many Śaivite sanctuaries. Having looked into one of the caves situated under the shade of the sacred trees, Śaṅkara saw a group of *sannyāsins* surrounding an imposing old man, who was deeply engrossed in meditation. He folded his hands respectfully, approached the old man, and, having stretched before him on the ground, exclaimed: "I bow down before revered Govinda, my teacher!" Govinda asked the boy to introduce himself and then greeted him fervently as a long-promised disciple, a future great sage and an earthly incarnation of Śiva. In later hagiographies, however, such as the compilation of V.S. Radhakrishna Sastri, the emphasis is different:

Śaṅkara hastens to introduce himself to Govinda as the great Śiva, who only temporarily assumed a human form.[5] In any case, Govinda was not bewildered by these speeches of the child; it seems he had been waiting for Śaṅkara for quite a long time, having been forewarned by Gauḍapāda. Thus began the discipleship of the young *sannyāsin* under the guidance of Govinda.

Different hagiographies describe Śaṅkara's stay on the banks of the river in slightly different ways. According to *Bṛhat-śaṅkara-vijaya,* the period of discipleship under Govinda continued for two years, but there are other estimates. Regardless of lengths this time was extremely productive, since it was at the feet of Govinda that Śaṅkara became acquainted with the foundations of Advaita. It was probably at this time that he composed many of his Śaivite hymns, some philosophical treatises and the Commentary on *Bṛhadāraṇyakopaniṣad.* It goes without saying that it was during this period that Govinda first showed Śaṅkara the *Māṇḍūkya-kārikā* of Gauḍapāda, which served as a basis for a deferential commentary by the pupil.

As to Śaṅkara's main work, his Commentary on the *Brahmasūtra,* its creation has inspired a special legend. According to *Saṅkṣepa-śaṅkara-vijaya,* while Śaṅkara was staying with Govinda for his second year, suddenly a great flood came. After severe rains the waters of the Narmadā inundated the villages in the area and finally

---

5. Moreover, in the same *Śrī-śaṅkara-vijaya-makaranda* Śaṅkara boldly engages in self-praise during the whole of the chapter, telling Govinda :

I am the pure Śiva, defined as the beginning,
as truth and bliss;
If someone were to say that my essence is not that of the
beginning and bliss, it is not so,
for I am immutable, imperishable.

Ahamānandasatyādilakṣaṇaḥ kevalaḥ śivaḥ /
ānandādirūpaṃ yattannāhamacalo 'vyayaḥ //14//.

V.C. Radhakrishna Sastri, *Śrī-śaṅkara-vijaya-makaranda,* X.14.

rose up to the very entrance of the cave, where the teacher and his disciples were engrossed in meditation. Having seen what had happened, Śaṅkara pronounced a special incantation (a *mantra* 'on the drawing of the waters') and put his begging bowl on the threshold. The torrents of water immediately rushed into the small bowl and soon disappeared there, while the river again resumed its natural course. It was then that Govinda remembered Bādarāyaṇa's famous prophecy, according to which the best commentary on his text would be written by somebody who would succeed in taming the wild river.

Having received the blessing of Govinda, Śaṅkara, according to Vedantic tradition, managed to compose in four years commentaries on all the works of the 'triple canon', that is, on the *Brahmasūtra,* on *Bhagavadgītā,* as well as on the principle Upaniṣads.

Hagiographical legends tell us about the young Śaṅkara's journey to the sacred mountain Kailāsa, where for the first time he personally encountered Śiva in the form of Dakṣiṇāmūrti, or as the giver of true knowledge. It was at that time that Śaṅkara performed a pilgrimage to Benares. On the banks of the Gaṅgā river—in Benares, as well as in the ancient sanctuary of Badarīnātha—he stayed until he received tidings of his mother's grave illness.

Returning home, Śaṅkara found his mother on her deathbed. According to *Bṛhat-śaṅkara-vijaya* and *Saṅkṣepa-śaṅkara-vijaya,* Śivatārakā entreated her son to console her and dispel her fears. It is said that Śaṅkara tried at first to acquaint her with the essence of Advaita, but the image of an illusive world, based on an impersonal *ātman*, only frightened the poor woman still more. And so, the young ascetic, having forgotten for the time being his higher philosophy, chanted hymns devoted to Śiva and Viṣṇu; this chanting helped his mother to meet her death with greater calm and courage. Finally, though his *sannyāsin* vows did not in principle allow for following the usual ritual practice, which ordinarily befitted the only son (a *sannyāsin* was considered to be beyond any worldly and family ties), Śaṅkara performed all the necessary funeral rites.

Soon after his mother's death, Śaṅkara had to endure another blow: his teacher Govinda was also dying. According to most of the hagiographies, Śaṅkara came to say farewell to his teacher, accompanied by his own first disciple, Padmapāda.[6] Much later, on one of the Narmadā islands, where Śaṅkara had paid his last respects to Govinda, a temple was erected which became an important center of Hindu pilgrimage. From the Narmadā, according to Vedantic tradition, Śaṅkara started for the famous city of Prayāga, accompanied by Padmapāda and several other disciples, including Citsukha.

It was in Prayāga, in the words of the hagiographers, that Śaṅkara's meeting with the most noted Mīmāṃsakas—Kumārila and Prabhākara took place. One might mention here that the biography of Kumārila has survived to these days only owing to some episodes inserted in the traditional biographies of Śaṅkara. According to these sources, Kumārila was born in a Brahmanic family of South India and from his early youth decided to dedicate

---

6. In *Bṛhat-śaṅkara-vijaya* and *Prācīna-śaṅkara-vijaya* we meet the first and the most beloved of Śaṅkara's pupils under a different name; these texts tell of the Brahman Sanandana, the native of Ahobala. As for his other, more famous name, its appearance is explained by a popular legend. The story goes as follows : some years after the first meeting of Śaṅkara and Sanandana, when the Advaitist was in Benares together with his pupils, he asked them to go and fetch his clothes that were drying on the other bank of the Gaṅgā. While other pupils deliberated on the most suitable way to cross the river, Sanandana, without thinking twice about it, rushed across the Gaṅgā, hurrying to fulfil the wish of his teacher. Like Saint Peter, he literally walked over the water. However, he was far more resolute and certainly more modest than the Apostle—he did not even notice the miracle. Nevertheless, the miracle did not pass unnoticed by the eyewitnesses, and Sanandana got his nickname—Padmapāda, that is, having lotus feet. Padmapāda received his initiation directly from Śaṅkara, and it is believed that it was for him that the teacher composed his treatise *Ātma-bodha,* The awakening of *ātman.*

all his efforts to the struggle against the 'heretical' doctrines of the Jainas and the Buddhists.[7] By the time of their meeting with Śaṅkara, Kumārila and his pupil Prabhākara (so he is presented in most of the Advaitist's hagiographies) could boast of many victories during public philosophical disputes. Their opponents during these popular contests were mainly the 'heretics', the enemies of Brahmanic orthodoxy,[8] but generally any philosopher and any errant preacher could take part in the dispute. The opponents might belong to different schools or to one and the same school—what really counted was good memory, cleverness and skill in verbal wrangling. Actually the image of oral disputes presented by the biographies does not differ greatly from the descriptions of philosophical contests held at the courts of the kings, descriptions amply provided by *Bṛhadāraṇyakopaniṣad* and *Kauṣītakopaniṣad.*

It goes without saying that in the hagiographies where Śaṅkara is the main hero he invariably defeats all his opponents. It is believed that after one such dispute Śaṅkara acquired a new pupil—none other than Prabhākara's son, Pṛthivīdhara (and according to some hagiographies even Prabhākara himself, and—not long before his death, having repented his former views—Kumārila).

More plausible, though, was an Advaita conversion of another well-known Mīmāṃsāka—Maṇḍanamiśra. The episode of Maṇḍanamiśra's dispute with Śaṅkara

---

7. It is said that, having disguised himself as a Buddhist monk, Kumārila even got his instruction from celebrated Buddhist teachers, so that the could get a clear notion of the ideas of his opponents. This kind of ruse proved to be somewhat risky : according to the hagiographies, Kumārila lost one eye, in a Buddhist monastery and only divine intercession helped save his life.

8. It is said in *Bṛhaṭ-śaṅkara-vijaya* and *Śaṅkara-vijaya-vilāsa* that Kumārila's victories over the 'heretics' indirectly contributed to the death of his former teacher, the Buddhist Sugata; after that, Kumārila had no option but to commit a ritual suicide.

(Saṅkara-maṇḍana-saṃvāda) was described extensively in *Bṛhat-śaṅkara-vijaya* and *Saṅkṣepa-śaṅkara-vijaya.* Unlike Śaṅkara, according to the hagiographies, Maṇḍanamiśra was not a *sannyāsin,* but a learned and pious householder *(gṛhastha)*, who had reached the heights of wisdom due to his unswerving obedience to ritual injunctions. Śaṅkara came to his house just at the time when Maṇḍanamiśra was occupied with preparations for the yearly ceremony of memorial sacrifice. With his impertinent remarks and direct ridicule, the young ascetic forced Maṇḍanamiśra to engage in a dispute with him, having set the condition that in case of defeat, the adversary would leave his household and become an errant mendicant. According to legend, the contest between Śaṅkara and Maṇḍanamiśra continued for fifteen days without any intermission. It is related that after it was over, the Advaitist had acquired a new disciple.[9] As mentioned above, Vedantic tradition identifies Maṇḍanamiśra (who, of course, had to assume a new name at his initiation) with one of Śaṅkara's followers—Sureśvara.

The hagiographers differ in their efforts to give a precise determination of the time spent by Śaṅkara in Benares, though his visit to the sacred city is not disputed. Vārāṇasī, or Kāśī, as it is most often called in Śaṅkara's biographies, the city of a thousand temples, had for a long time drawn many pilgrims—or simply travellers—from all over India. It was there that the preaching of the Advaitist expanded greatly; among his listeners and opponents were not only orthodox-minded Hinduists, but also Buddhists and Jainas.

---

9. According to popular legend, after the defeat of Maṇḍanamiśra, his wife (as the incarnation of Sarasvatī, the spouse of Brahma) decided to dispute with Śaṅkara. Her questions concerned mainly the sphere of human love, and Śaṅkara could answer them only after a month of delay during which he gained the necessary experience by temporarily entering the dead body of the king Amarūka. One might note that the legend provides an indirect explanation for the origin ot Tantric and Śakta works by Śaṅkara, as well as his erotic poems.

In Benares, Śaṅkara resided with his disciples in one of the most famous *ghaṭṭas,* that is, the sanctuaries used for performing funeral rites on the banks of the Gaṅgā River. This *ghaṭṭa* is known by the name Maṇikarṇikā, or, the earring/of Śiva/. According to legend, it was the very first piece of earth fished out of the primeval waters by the trident of the God. Sitting in this *ghaṭṭa,* Śaṅkara received alms, taught pious Hindus and converted 'heretics'. The Advaitin's image still occupies the most honorable place in the neighboring temple of Viśvanātha.

However, the story of Śaṅkara's stay in Benares would not be complete if one were to omit a popular tale about a *cāṇḍāla,* which was probably composed with Buddhist influence. It is said that once a *cāṇḍāla,* that is, a person of mixed *varṇa*—a son of a *śūdra* and a *brahman* woman (in orthodox belief, the most miserable and despised being)—was encountered by Śaṅkara and his disciples on one of the narrow streets of the city. The Advaitist, afraid of the ritually impure touch of the wretched man, ordered him to clear the way and let them pass. He got quite an unexpected rebuke. Directly referring to Advaita tenets about the unity of *ātman,* the *cāṇḍāla* boldly defended the idea of the original equality of all living beings. According to the same legend, Śaṅkara bowed down to the *cāṇḍāla* and, having acknowledged his blunder, composed on the spot a poem about the higher *ātman* that shines forth equally both in a *dvija* Brahman and in an untouchable *cāṇḍāla.*

After Benares, Śaṅkara continued his travels. The hagiographies relate that he not only indefatigably preached Advaita, but also founded Vedantic monasteries *(maṭha)* in various parts of India, organized after the Buddhist pattern. Most of the biographers are of the opinion that the main monasteries, which were founded by Śaṅkara when he was about thirty, were established in the following order: Dvārakā, Badarīnātha, Purī, Śṛṅgerī and Kāñcī. Sometimes, though, this sequence varies; and usually the list of monasteries is supplemented by other *maṭhas* in various combinations.

It is generally believed that Śaṅkara assigned the *sannyāsins,* who shared Advaita notions, to ten monastic orders—according to the number of main monasteries—and instructed each order to stay in the place prepared for it.[10] At present, only four associations of Śaṅkara's followers remain truly monastic in character; they are the monastic orders of Bhāratī, Sarasvatī, Tīrtha and Āśramin. All the rest have become more or less secular organizations.

According to the hagiographies, Śaṅkara died in his thirty-third year, surrounded by his numerous followers and disciples. Even today several Hindu monasteries contest the honor of being regarded as the place of the teacher's last repose. According to *Prācīna-śaṅkara-vijaya,* Śaṅkara died in Kāñcī, while the compilers of some of the biographies give preference to the sanctuary of Kedāranātha. *Saṅkṣepa-śaṅkara-vijaya* relates that Śaṅkara actually did not die at all, but, having climbed the mountain Kailāsa, assumed his original divine form. The Advaitist's demise is dealt with in the same spirit in *Śaṅkara-vijaya-vilāsa,* the text that seems most prone to relating absolutely fantastic events.

Of course, it is no simple task to gain an understanding of the peculiar intertwining of fantasies and reality that characterizes the accounts of Śaṅkara's life. Let us make at least a preliminary effort, singling out some reasonably reliable facts from the whole conglomerate of colorful legends.

---

10. The monastery in Dvārakā corresponds to the monastic order of Āśramin; that of Badarīnātha, to the order of Giri; the Purī monastery, to the order of Araṇya; the Śṛngerī monastery, to the order of Bhāratī; and the Kāñcī monastery, to the order of Sarasvatī. To five other monasteries were assigned the monastic orders of Tīrtha, Purī, Vaṇa, Parvata and Sāgara. As one can judge by the very names, the order of Āśramin was supposed to abide to monastic shelters, or *āśramas*; the orders of Araṇya and Vaṇa were to stay in the forests; the monks belonging to the orders of Giri and Parvata, in the mountains; those of the Sāgara order, on the seashore; those of the Purī order, in the cities; and the monks of the Tīrtha order had to remain in the centers of pilgrimage.

First of all, the question that naturally arises concerns the exact dating of his life. It is fairly understandable that hagiographies provide us mostly with astrological data. If one were to rely on the material of *Bṛhat-śaṅkara-vijaya,* Śaṅkara was born in the year Nandana, or the twenty sixth year of the sixty-year cycle, in the lunar month Vaiśākha (corresponding to May-June), under the Zodiac sign of the Archer. *Saṅkṣepa-śaṅkara-vijaya* confirms these data, specifying that this notable event took place on a Monday, and determining the phases of the moon. According to M. Piantelli,[11] these astrological characteristics correspond to only two possible dates: AD 568 and 805. Relative dating of the year and day of Śaṅkara's birth are accepted by all the biographies composed within the sphere of influence of the monastery of Kāñcī, though some extant South Indian versions of Śaṅkara's biography offer a different date.

According to the same *Bṛhat-śaṅkara-vijaya,* the Advaitist's death falls on the month Vṛṣabha (April-May), or, possibly, Pauṣa (December-January) of the year Raktākṣin, or the 58th year of the sixty-year cycle. So if one believes the hagiographies, Śaṅkara died, probably, in his thirty-third year : either in 600 or in 837 year AD.[12]

As for the Western tradition, for quite a long time scholars adhered to a definite dating. In 1877 a German scholar, Prof. K.P. Tiele, in his essays on ancient religions suggested as a probable date of Śaṅkara's life an interval between788 and 820. He based his estimate on the evidence of a later Vedantin, Yajneśvara Śāstri, who cites in his treatise *Aryavidyā-sudhākār* (The moon of noble knowledge) an earlier work by Bhaṭṭa Nīlakaṇṭha, entitled *Śaṅkara-mandāra-saurabha* (The fragrance of Śaṅkara's

11. Vide: M. Piantelli, *Śaṅkara e la rinascita del brāhmanesimo,* pp. 12-13.

12. M. Piantelli, *Śaṅkara e la rinascita del brāhmanesimo,* pp. 103-4.

paradise tree).[13] Somewhat later, an Indian scholar, K. Pathak, found corroboration for these data in a treatise by an anonymous mediaeval author.[14] On must note that in principle the reliability of these source is not much higher than that of the hagiographical materials. Still, the date 788-820 was accepted as a serious working hypothesis by such prominent Indologists as F. Max Müller, A. Macdonell, A.B. Keith, M. Winternitz.[15] Later this dating became generally accepted by their followers.

Nevertheless, after some time many serious scholars agreed that the dating of Śaṅkara's life needed closer definition, and that its limits should be set farther back in the post. Similar views were advocated by Indian scholars K. Telang,[16] T. Chintamani[17] and S. Kuppuswami Sastri.[18] Also inclined to an earlier dating is a well-known Japanese Indologist, Hajime Nakamura.[19] An Italian scholar, G.

---

13. Vide : T.R. Chintamani, "The Date of Śaṃkara", *Journal of Oriental Research,* Madras, vol. 3, pp. 39 ff.

14. K.B. Pathak, "The Date of Śaṃkarācārya", *Indian Antiquary,* vol. 2, Bombay, p. 175.

15. Vide, for instance : F. Max Müller, *Three Lectures on the Vedanta Philosophy,* London, 1894; A.B. Keith, *The Karma-Mīmāṃsā,* London, 1921; M. Winternitz, *Geschichte der indischen Literatur,* vol. II, Leipzig, 1913; and also, with some reservations, S. Dasgupta, *A History of Indian Philosophy,* vols. 1-2.

16. K.T. Telang, "The Date of Śaṃkarācārya", *New Indian Antiquary,* vol. 13, p. 95 ff.

17. T.R. Chintamani, *The Date of Śaṃkara,* pp. 39-56.

18. S. Kuppuswami Sastri, Introduction to *Brahmasiddhi,* Madras, 1937, p. lviii.

19. A synopsis of the initial Japanese version of the work by Hajime Nakamura *A History of Early Vedanta Philosophy* (Hajime Nakamura. *Shoki no Vedanta Tetsugaku,* Tokyo, 1950) was made by G. Morichini. Vide : G. Morichini, "History of Early Vedanta", *East and West,* IsMEO, Rome, 1960, pp. 33-39. Lately, however, a revised edition of Nakamura's book was published in English: H. Nakamura, *A History of Early Vedanta Philosophy,* Delhi, 1983.

Tucci, reminds us of a similar opinion from French historian, P. Demiéville[20] ; to his mind, the former date should be reconsidered and set back at least 45-50 years. D. Ingalls also prefers to place Śaṅkara in the first half of the eighth century.[21]

Quite recently much attention has been paid to Śaṅkara's mention of or indirect reference to his opponents—both predecessors and contemporaries. It is regarded as definite that in Śaṅkara's works one can find traces of his polemics with the Buddhists Diṅnāga (*ca.* the end of the fifth century) and Dharmakīrti (the beginning of the seventh century),[22] a Mīmāṃsāka Kumārila,[23] There are also references to Bhartṛhari and Gauḍapāda. That means that the earliest limit of Śaṅkara's activity cannot be set earlier than AD 650. On the other hand, the latest limit is usually determined by the commentary of Vācaspatimiśra on Śaṅkara's work. One of Vācaspatimiśra's writings is definitely dated *ca.* AD 840; and it is generally accepted that he is at least one generation younger than Śaṅkara—that is, the date should be placed about AD 800.

In trying to pin down the dates of the Advaitist's life, it proved useful to take into account indirect evidence, provided by Jaina and Buddhist sources. However, as noted by the Indian scholar K. Kunjunni Raja, judging by the material of *Tattva-saṅgraha* (a collection of the essence of various teachings) by Śāntarakṣita (AD 705-62) and the commentary by Kamalaśīla (713-63), Śaṅkara's teaching had not yet become important and well-known at the time

20. Vide : G. Tucci, *Minor Buddhist Texts,* part 2, IsMEO, Rome, 1958, p. 8.

21. D.H.H. Ingalls, "Śaṃkara's Arguments against the Buddhists", *Philosophy East and West,* vol. 3, January 1954, no. 4, p. 292, note 2.

22. Vide : K.B. Pathak, "Bhartṛhari and Kumārila", *Journal of the Bombay Branch of the Royal Asiatic Society,* vol. 18, p. 213.

23. Vide : V. Bhattacharya, "Śaṃkara and Diṅnāga", *Indian Historical Quarterly,* vol. 6, p. 169.

of these Buddhist authors.[24] It looks as if early pre-Śaṅkara Vedanta was not yet regarded by the 'heretical' teachers as a serious system of opposing thought. As for Śaṅkara's own name, it was not even mentioned in contemporary Jaina and Buddhist works.

So the hopes of giving more precise dates for Śaṅkara's life and activity through the use of his adversaries' works proved to be mostly premature. One has to agree with Hajime Nakamura, who wrote that "the scholarly tradition of Śaṅkara became influential only in the context of later social development.[25] Still, starting from AD 900, Vedanta becomes an object of severe criticism, for instance, in Jaina sources (one is reminded of *Yaśastilaka* of Somadeva, who was a Digambara), while the only system worthy of attention from the standpoint of the Jainas was Śaṅkara's school.[26]

Summing up the efforts of the scholars to clarify the chronology of Śaṅkara's life, one must admit that—in spite of all their skill and even subtlety—they did not attain any noticeable progress. And when, for example, a prominent Japanese scholar, Sengaku Mayeda, who specializes in Śaṅkara's work and has published many critical editions of his writings, regards as most likely the interval between 700 and 750 AD, he still has reservations, specifying that other points of view on this matter are also justified to some extent.[27] Indeed, a Dutch scholar, Til-

---

24. K. Kunjunni Raja, "On the Date of Śaṃkarācārya and Allied Problems", *Adyar Library Bulletin*, vol. 24, parts 3-4, 1960, p. 139.

25. Hajime Nakamura, "Bhāskara, the Vedāntin, in Buddhist Literature", *Annals of the Bhandarkar Oriental Research Institute*, Golden Jubilee Volume, vols. 48-49, Poona, p. 122.

26. Hajime Nakamura, "Vedanta as Noticed in Mediaeval Jain Literature", *Indological Studies in Honor of W. Norman Brown.* New Haven, 1962, p. 192.

27. Vide : Sengaku Mayeda, *Śaṃkara's Upadeśasāhasrī,* critically edited with introduction and indices, Tokyo, 1973.

mann Vetter, who painstakingly summed up not only the data from Sanskrit sources, but also the existing critical literature, had no option but to return to a fairly long period from AD 650 to 800.[28] At this rather vague interval we must stop for the time being.

As for the famous *digvijaya* of Śaṅkara, or, the conquest of the parts of the world, there is really no grounds for any doubt as to the victorious journey of the Advaitist throughout the country. Śaṅkara was undoubtedly not only a philosopher and an astute theoretician, he was also one of the most prominent religious figures and a gifted preacher, spreading his own teaching. One glimpses this both in the hagiographies, where the teacher invariably defeats his adversaries, and in the echoes of lively disputes and contests that are recorded in his own works. Śaṅkara's main opponents were the Buddhists. Though the decline of Buddhism started long before Śaṅkara, his active preaching, directed against this heterodox teaching, certainly contributed to the gradual forcing out of the 'heretics'. But, as observed by F. Whaling, "Śaṅkara not merely refuted the Buddhists negatively, he also played his part in the Hindu renaissance which was loosening the popular hold of Buddhists over the people."[29]

Another moment is quite worthy of attention. If one maintains the thesis of the direct impact of Buddhism on Śaṅkara, this impact would be doubtless perceptible primarily in the sphere of practical religion. Śaṅkara succeeded in reforming or, to be more precise, in constructing all over again, the monastic organization of Hinduism, in many respects taking as a model the Buddhists *saṅgha,* or

28. Vide : Tilmann Vetter, *Studien zur Lehre und Entwicklung Śaṅkaras,* Wien, 1979, pp. 11-12. From critical studies Vetter uses mainly the above mentioned works by K. Kunjunni Raja, T. Chintamani and Hajime Nakamura, though he also pays attention to the articles by E. Frauwallner and the book on Dharmakīrti, written by E. Steinkellner, that do not directly deal with Śaṅkara.

29. F. Whaling, *Śaṅkara and Buddhism,* p. 35.

religious community. The hagiographies enumerate ten Hindu monasteries founded by Śaṅkara, as well as ten monastic orders of *sannyāsins*. Four of these monasteries—Śṛṅgerī, Kāñcī, Dvārakā and Purī—still retain their full significance. Even now the organizational structure of Southern Hinduism, which had been the main object of Śaṅkara's care, is regarded as more firm and solid than its Northern counterpart. The ascetics who are supposed to follow Śaṅkara's creed are called *daśanāmin*, that is, having ten names—in memory of the ten former monastic orders. Meanwhile, all other *sannyāsins* are usually defined as *daṇḍin* or *ekadaṇḍin* (from *daṇḍa*, or the sacred staff of an ascetic). On the whole, in the words of F. Whaling, "Śaṅkara introduced Buddhist principles of organisation and lifelong asceticism into Hindu monastic life, and provided for the first time some sort of guiding authority to lay down and preach right principles of philosophy and religion.[30]

Hinduism is also much indebted to the influence of Buddhist religious practice, assimilated through Śaṅkara's mediation, for its rejection of bloody sacrifices, as well as of some extreme Śaktist practices. According to the living Hindu tradition, it was Śaṅkara, for instance, who brought to an end the practice of worship of the dog-headed Śiva in one of the most popular centers of pilgrimage, the city of Ujjayinī. (This strange form of worship was based upon one of the lesser known myths of the victory of Śiva, who had assumed the form of the dog Khaṇḍobā, over a mighty Asura Maṇimalla; this form of worship presumed and allowed for the corresponding 'doggish' behavior of the adept). Travelling over Kāmarūpa (present Assam), Śaṅkara introduced into more sensible limits the Tantric ritual practice of the 'left hand', the practice that was mainly based on magic and erotic excesses.

What is not, however, reflected adequately in critical literature, is the problem of the relationship between

30. F. Whaling, *Śaṅkara and Buddhism*, p. 30.

Śaṅkara's Vedanta and Kashmir Śaivism. Meanwhile, the correspondence between some notions of the Śaivite Pratyabhijñā-darśana (from *pratyabhijñā,* lit.: recognition, which is understood here as a method of sudden realization of God) and Advaita ideas deserves some deliberation—or at least a preliminary analysis.[31] In some respects this similarity can be explained by their respective theoretical and philosophical roots: the history of preparation and development presupposed a slight shading of the Buddhist concepts of Vijñānavāda and Śūnyavāda, superimposed over the traditional Śaivite background. In the teaching of Somānanda (end of the ninth century) emphasis is placed on the knower or knowing subject *(pramātṛ),* who is identified with Śiva and, simultaneously, with the inner Self, or *ātman* of the adept; the inner luminosity *(prakāśa)* or vibration *(spanda, vimarśa)* of *ātman* creates the visible universe. Somānanda's pupils, Utpaladeva and Abhinavagupta (beginning of the eleventh century, maintained, in contrast to Śaṅkara, that the differentiation of energies or potencies, responsible for the creation of the world, is really contained within *ātman* and so cannot be held as illusory. Still, the correspondence of images and terminological preferences seems too striking for mere coincidence. Since Kashmir (in particular, one of the temples, dedicated to the Goddess Sarasvatī, the temple Sarvajñapīṭha) is repeatedly mentioned among the places visited by Śaṅkara during his travels over the country, one might at least presume the possibility of his influence upon the development of local philosophical and religious schools, a process that drew attention after the ninth century.

---

31. Two other schools of Kashmir Śaivism—*krama-darśana* and *kula-darśana*—reveal less common traits with Advaita, though the Kula school incorporates the idea of *Jīvanmukti* (liberation in life), which is characteristic also of Śaṅkara's school. About this vide: Lilian Silburn, *La Mahārthamañjarī de Maheśvarānanda,* avec des extraits du Parimala, Paris, 1968, pp. 14, 22; Lilian Silburn, *Le Vijñāna Bhaïrava,* Paris, 1961.

To make the picture complete, however, one cannot overlook the opinion of Paul Hacker, according to which Śaṅkara was really a Viṣṇuite, and the later legends concerning his alleged Śaivite inclinations can be traced back to one of his biographers, Mādhava (or Vidyāraṇya). Hacker tried to substantiate this—completely original—point of view in one of his articles.[32] To my mind, though, his arguments are far from conclusive; they cannot explain satisfactorily Śaṅkara's critique of the Viṣṇuite doctrine of Pāñcarātra in his Commentary on *Brahmasūtra;* or the emergence of the notion of *māyā*, which is so important for the whole concept of Advaita; or, finally, the authorship of Śaivite hymns, which is ascribed to him by orthodox tradition. Probably Hacker was somewhat misled in this respect by his subconscious strivings to bring Śaṅkara's teaching a bit closer to his own Christian convictions, which, of course, are more easily comparable with the image of the benevolent and merciful Viṣṇu.

As mentioned above, Śaṅkara's death gave rise to two Hindu traditions. The hagiographies, gravitating towards the still flourishing monastery of Kāñcī, and going back to *Prācīna-śaṅkara-vijaya* of Ānandagiri, maintain that the Advaitist died in Kāñcī. In memory of his death a statue was erected, which is now situated in the temple of Kāmākṣī. Another great monastery connected with Śaṅkara's name—the monastery of Śṛṅgeri[33]—supports

32. P. Hacker, "Relations of Early Advaitins to Vaiṣṇavism", *Wiener Zeitschrift für die Kunde Süd-und Ostasiens,* no. 9, 1965, pp. 147-54.

33. Incidentally, a present-day Indian pandit, interested in the life and activity of Śaṅkara—H. Krishna Sastri—maintains that the monastery of Śṛṅgeri was formerly a Śaivite place of worship, which only later, owing to Śaṅkara's efforts, acquired an Advaita bias. In his words, "this explains perhaps why in the Advaita Math of Śringeri there is still a greater bias towards Shaivism and Shaiva worship than towards Vaishnavism and Krishna worship, though the founder, the great Shankaracharya was no respect of creeds nor of any distinction between Śiva and Vishnu." *The Traditional Age of Śrī Śaṅkaracharya and the Maths,* A. Nataraja Aiyer and S. Lakshminarasimha Sastri, Madras, 1962, p. 83.

quite a different version of the legend. It is based on the evidence of the hagiographies, the common source of which is *Saṅkṣepa-śaṅkara-vijaya* by Mādhava. According to these sources, Śaṅkara died near the sanctuary of Kedāranātha (quite close to the temple complex of Badarīnātha in the Himālayas). Even today one can see in Kedāranātha the ruins of the monument which is supposed to have been constructed where Śaṅkara died.

The rivalry between the monasteries of Kāñcī and Śṛṅgeri continues to play an important part in present-day religious and cultural life of the Hindu community. Some Indologists, interested in Śaṅkara and educated within the framework of traditional Hindu learning, were, sometimes quite involuntarily, drawn into the history of petty jealousies and mutual grievances. For instance, a well-known Vedanta scholar, Prof. T.M.P. Mahadevan, agreed to supervise the publishing of a rather colorful and also rather muddled volume dedicated to the sixty-eighth prior of the monastery of Kāñcī—Candrasekharendra Sarasvatī, who included in this collection an autobiographical essay.[34] It is interesting to note that, according to established tradition, the heads of Kāñcī and Śṛṅgeri *maṭhs* always bear the honorary title of *Śaṅkarācārya*, or, the teacher Śaṅkara.

2. *WORKS OF ŚAṄKARA: RELIABILITY OF ATTRIBUTION AND COMPOSITIONAL PECULIARITIES*

During his rather short life Śaṅkara managed to write an enormous number of varied works. Even if one were to exclude the writings whose attribution to Śaṅkara is somewhat doubtful, the scale of his creative activity is still amazing. Indian tradition ascribes to him the authorship of more than 400 extant Vedantic works.

---

34. Vide : T.M.P. Mahadevan, "The Sage of Kāñcī", *Preceptors of Advaita,* edited by T.M.P. Mahadevan, Madras, 1968, pp. 469-548.

Following the proposal of S.K. Belvalkar,[35] for the sake of convenient examination Śaṅkara's works are usually divided into three parts, according to genre characteristics. The first category embraces the commentaries; among them are the *bhāṣya,* or the most authoritative, 'primary' interpretation of basic texts, as well as the *vivaraṇa* and the *ṭīkā,* representing, as a rule, sub-commentaries on commentaries. These sub-commentaries are supposed to interpret both basic texts and their primary explanations. The second group of texts includes mostly hymns, poems, metric incantations and praises of the gods (*stotra, stava* and *stuti*); while the third group consists of independent compositions, treatises and compendia.

Let us now touch upon one of the most controversial problems of present-day Śaṅkara studies—the problem of which works can be attributed to the Advaitist. This question was seriously raised for the first time by Paul Hacker. In one of his earlier articles he writes about the corpus of works which has survived under Śaṅkara's name: [T]he variety of contents makes it highly improbable that all these works should have been composed by one and the same person. So it was inevitable that the majority of historians should have taken the position that all those writings were provisionally to be regarded as spurious, with the only exception of Śaṅkara's main work, the *Brahmasūtrabhāṣya,* and that in the case of all the other commentaries and independent treatises the question of the authorship required investigation.[36] Having

---

35. Vide: S.K. Belvalkar, *Śrī Gopal Basu Mallik Lectures on Vedanta Philosophy,* Part 1, Poona, 1929, pp. 222 ff.

36. These are the lines from P. Hacker's article "Śaṅkarācārya and Śaṅkarabhagavatpāda: Preliminary Remarks Concerning the Authorship Problem", published in *New Indian Antiquary,* (vol. 9, nos. 4-6, 1947, pp. 1-12). However, the text had so many printing errors that the author had to revise it completely for the collection of his works. Vide: P. Hacker, *Kleine Schriften.* Hrsg. von L. Schmithausen. Wiesbaden, 1978, pp. 41-58 (here the reference is to S. 42).

clearly formulated the problem, Hacker also laid down three main principles or methods of investigation for determining the attribution of certain works of Śaṅkara. These principles laid a sound foundation for the later analysis of specific works by the Advaitist; such analysis was made by the German scholar himself, as well as by many of his followers.

First of all, Hacker suggested that one should pay more attention to the colophons of the manuscripts, where the author (allegedly, Śaṅkara) appears under different names and is bestowed with different titles. In the opinon of the scholar, the name (or rather, the title) *Śaṅkarācārya* does not provide confirmation of such authorship—if only because, as mentioned above, "the teacher Śaṅkara" was the title conferred on every head preceptor of the monasteries of Śṛṅgeri and Kāñcī. A more reliable attribution is secured by another popular title—*Bhagavat*, or Lord, which turns up in reference to Śaṅkara in the versions *Bhagavatpāda* and *Bhagavatpūjyapāda*, usually superseding the proper name.

The second investigative method makes use of evidence from the immediate disciples of Śaṅkara—primarily Padmapāda, Sureśvara and Toṭaka. With slightly more caution one might also use the references to Śaṅkara found in the works by Ānandajñāna and Vācaspatimiśra. This method should also take into account the distinguishing between the texts belonging to *Śaṅkarācārya* (and so attributed less reliably), and those allegedly written by Śaṅkara—*Bhagavatpāda* or *Bhagavatpūjyapāda*. But the evidence stemming from the nearest environment to the Advaitist is rather reliable in itself; in most cases, argues Hacker, one can safely depend upon it, while judging the authoritativeness of one or the other work.

And finally, the third principle consists in analysis of the content, as well as of the special terminology of the work in question. In other words, if a text had been written by Śaṅkara, its notions should not contradict the general conception represented in his Commentary on *Brahmasūtra*. Accordingly, the terms used in the text should correspond to the early stage of Advaita development, and not to its later interpretations. In his own articles Hacker sets an example of minute philological analysis of some of Śaṅkara's works, paying meticulous attention to the terms *avidyā, māyā* and *nāmarūpa.*[37]

How do these principles actually function in relation to the three groups of texts representing the creative activity of Śaṅkara?

In the first group, as already noted, the authorship of the Commentary on *Brahmasūtra* is absolutely beyond doubt. This confidence is explained not only by the fact that the authenticity of the work is guaranteed by the evidence of Padmapāda; one must also take into account that *Brahma-sūtra-bhāṣya* provides, so to speak, the point of reference for all other works, as well as for the very image of the Advaitist, who remained in the memory of subsequent generations primarily as *bhāṣyakāra* or, the author of the commentary. Hacker himself regards as completely proved Śaṅkara's authorship of the commentaries on the ten principle Upaniṣads: *Īśā, Aitareya, Kaṭha, Kena, Chāndogya, Taittirīya, Praśna, Bṛhadāraṇyaka, Māṇḍūkya* (which is traditionally united with Gauḍapāda's *Kārikā*) and *Muṇḍaka*. Somewhat less reliable is Śaṅkara's authorship for the *bhāṣya* on *Śvetāśvataropaniṣad.* Making use of Hacker's method, Sengaku Mayeda demonstrated the authenticity of the Commentary on the *Bhagavadgītā,* traditionally ascribed to Śaṅkara.[38] So the most modern philological methods confirm the correctness of the usual belief that Śaṅkara actually composed

---

37. Vide, for instance : P. Hacker, "Eigentümlichkeiten der Lehre und Terminologie Śaṅkaras: Avidyā, Nāmarūpa, Māyā, Īśvara", *Zeitschrift der Deutschen Morgenländischen Gesellschaft,* no. 100, 1950, pp. 246-286.

38. On this vide: Sengaku Mayeda, "The Authenticity of the Bhagavadgītābhāṣya Ascribed to Śaṅkara", *Wiener Zeitschrift für die Kunde Süd-und Ostasiens,* part IX, 1965, pp. 155-94. See also: P. Hacker, "Śaṅkarācārya and Śaṅkarabhagavatpāda", *Kleine Schriften,* p. 49.

the commentaries to all parts of the *prasthāna-traya,* or the triple canon of Vedanta.

Hacker also regards as belonging to Śaṅkara a sub-commentary on *Yoga-sūtra-bhāṣya* by Vedavyāsa, that is the work *Yoga-sūtra-bhāṣya-vivaraṇa,* as well as a short commentary on one of the parts of *Dharmasūtra* by Āpastamba, called *Adhyātma-paṭala-vivaraṇa* (Sub-commentary on the chapter about inner *ātman*).[39] Without going into detail about the argument, I can only say that these two texts are beyond the scope of the present book. Their acceptance as authentic texts by Śaṅkara would have led to the postulation of a separate, pre-Advaitic period of his creative activity.

It is not difficult to realize that the question of Śaṅkara's authorship of the second group of texts cannot be solved by the analysis of their content and table of categories. Of course, the Advaitist's metric works—from erotic, tantric poems to Śaivite hymns—do not contain strict philosophical terminology or logical argumentation. That is why the most reliable method of sorting out Śaṅkara's poems from the enormous mass of religious and mystic poetry of the mediaeval period is the evidence from his disciples and followers. And the Vedantins are of the opinion that Śaṅkara was the author of the poetical cycles *Dakṣiṇāmūrti-stotra* (Praise of the benevolent Śiva), *Gurvaṣṭakam* (Eight poems to the teacher), *Bhaja-govinda-stotra* (Praise of Kṛṣṇa-Govinda[40] and *Śivānandalaharī* (Wave of the

---

39. Vide : P. Hacker, "Śaṅkara der Yogin und Śaṅkara der Advaitin. Einige Beobachtungen." —*Beiträge zur Geistesgeschichte Indiens. Festschrift für Erich Frauwallner. Hrsg. von Oberhammer. Wiener Zeitschrift für die Kunde Süd-und Ostasiens.* parts XII-XIII, 1968-1969, pp. 119-148.

40. A popular name for the *Bhaja-govinda* cycle of poems is *Carpaṭa-mañjarikā-stotra* (The praise of the palm, where the garland of verses lies); sometimes the hymns of *Bhaja-govinda* are called *Dvādaśa-mañjarikā-stotra,* since this cycle, like another of the same time, has twelve *(dvadaśa)* stanzas.

bliss of Śiva).[41] Less dependable is Śaṅkara's authorship of other cycles and single poems. However, he is usually considered the author of the cycle *Bhavānyaṣṭakam* (Eight verses to Bhavānī, or divine Mother), of the hymn *Annapūrṇā-stotra* (Praise to the giver of food), of the cycle *Viṣṇu-ṣaṭ-padī* (Six verses for Viṣṇu), the poem *Gaṅgā-stotra* (Praise to Gaṅgā river), *Devyaparādha-kṣamāpaṇa-stotra* (Praise of the Goddess-Mother for the forgiveness of sins), *Vedasāra-Śiva-stotra* (Praise of Śiva as the essence of Veda), the cycle *Śivanāmālyaṣṭakam* (Eight lines in the name of Śiva), *Śivāparādha-kṣamāpaṇa-stotra* Praise of Śiva for the forgiveness of sins), *Kaupīna-pañcakam* (Five verses about the loin-cloth of an ascetic), *Dvādaśa-mañjarikā-stotra* (Praise in twelve garlands or stanzas), as well as the author of an often-cited but probably spurious cycle *Nirvāṇa-ṣaṭkam* (Six verses on liberation).[42]

One must say that, in spite of the absence of reliable methods to prove the authenticity of all these works, in spite of some vagueness of criteria applied to poetical works by Śaṅkara, still his inclination towards versification, and his skill in attiring religious thoughts with artistic images never raised any doubts. True, at first sight it might appear that poetry transforms only one of the layers of Śaṅkara's thought—and certainly not its summit, but rather the steps leading to it. It might seem that only the lower tier of Advaita, its theistic foundation, is adorned and decorated by Śaivite, sometimes even Śakta (and if one is to believe the tradition, also Viṣṇuite) images, and is strengthened by the passionate striving of mystics and the adept's aspiration to be united with God which bypasses ritual injunctions and logical argumentation.

---

41. Vide, for instance: T.M.P. Mahadevan, *The Hymns of Śaṅkara*, Delhi, 1980; and also S.K. Belvalkar, *Śrī Gopal Basu Mallik Lectures on Vedanta Philosophy*, pp. 222 f.

42. Vide the Supplement to the book : *Ātmabodhaḥ: Self-knowledge of Srī Śaṅkarācārya*, Madras, 1978, pp. 233-310.

To my mind, though—and it was already observed by Rudolf Otto—the theistic background does loom through all of Śaṅkara's creative activity, that is, also through the texture of the most subtle and abstract of his works.[43] This observation by Otto was later wholeheartedly supported by Paul Hacker[44] ; the latter's interest in theistic substructures of Vedanta is in many respects explained by his own proselytic aspirations as well as his clear understanding that for Christian missionaries in India it was much easier to deal with purely religious beliefs of the native people than with a consistent but entirely alien religious and philosophical system. Nevertheless, the observation itself is not devoid of wit and precision. From a formal standpoint it is important for us now that it lends weight to the conviction that the religious and poetical works of Śaṅkara are really authentic (of course, only in the cases when this poetic creativity does not contradict—at least, directly—the philosophical concepts of the Advaitist). One should not overlook the aspect of content: actually, poetry and theology were not dislodged to the periphery of important philosophical essence, but rather continued their own indirect, latent relations with this essence. More evidence in favor of this approach is the history of Advaita develop-

---

43. Vide: Rudolf Otto, *Westöstliche Mystik. Vergleich und Unterscheidung zur Wesensdeutung,* München, 1971, S. 119-160.

44. About that vide: P. Hacker, "Eigentümlichkeiten der Lehre und Terminologie Śaṅkaras", p. 247; P. Hacker, "Śaṅkara der Yogin und Śaṅkara der Advaitin", p. 121; as well as the special review by P. Hacker of the 3rd edition of R. Otto's book *Westöstliche Mystik*: P. Hacker, "Westöstliche Mystik" (review), *Zeitschrift für Missionswissenschaft und Religionswissenschaft,* no. 58, 1974, S. 40-43. A similar point of view is supported by R. De Smet (a doctoral thesis "Theological method of Śaṅkara", published in English, Rome, 1953) and Madeleine Biardeau (M. Biardeau, "Quelques reflexions sur l'apophatisme de Śaṅkara", *Indo-Iranian Journal,* 1959, pp. 81-101). Among more recent publications, conceived more or less on the same lines one might mention Wilhelm Halbfass, *Studies in Kumārila and Śaṅkara, Studien zur Indologie und Iranistik,* Monographie 9, Reinbek, 1983.

ment, which naturally included creative activity of poets and grammarians.

Only the third group of Śaṅkara's work is now left for investigation. It consists of independent writings that are not connected with any 'basic' texts. Śaṅkara's authorship for the philosophical treatise *Upadeśasāhasrī* (Thousand teachings) is firmly established. The authenticity of attribution was reliably demonstrated both for its metrical *(Padya-bandha)* part and for the prosaic *(Gadya-bandha)* one, represented in the critical edition of Sengaku Mayeda (Tokyo, 1973). Far less probable is Śaṅkara's authorship of other short treatises: *Viveka-cūḍāmaṇi* (Pearl of distinction), *Ātma-bodha* (The awakening of *ātman*), *Aparokṣānubhūti* (Not invisible realization) and *Śatā-ślokī* (A hundred *ślokas*). Hacker expressed some doubts concerning the attribution of the compendium *Sarva-darśana-siddhānta-saṅgraha* (A collection of the essence of all schools), which is traditionally ascribed to Śaṅkara.[45] Keeping in mind the different levels of authenticity of these works, one can still use them during the course of investigation, since most often their notions do not contradict the whole of Śaṅkara's system.

A complete list of all works belonging or ascribed to Śaṅkara, quite convenient and specially marked according to the probability of his authorship, can be found in the previously mentioned monograph by M. Piantelli.[46]

Having examined the main works by Śaṅkara from the standpoint of their formal attribution, we will return now to their contents. One should immediately note that the threefold division of the whole corpus of his works has a solid foundation; and the most extensive group of texts, which comes first (the commentaries), is at the same time the most important one.

---

45. Vide: P. Hacker, "Śaṅkarācārya and Śaṅkarabhagavatpāda", *Kleine Schriften,* pp. 55-58.

46. Vide : M. Piantelli, *Śaṅkara e la rinascita del brāhmanesimo,* Appendice al capitolo terzo, pp. i-xiii.

A specific trait of philosophizing characteristic of traditional Indian system—a trait which reminds one of European scholastics—is a discourse that unfolds in the form of interpretation of an original basic text. Just as in the mediaeval religious and philosophical tradition of the West, an indispensable base of philosophical investigation was provided by sacred scripture (in India it is the revelation of the *śruti*) and sacred tradition (in India, the *smṛti*), and the latter includes the systematic and 'orientating' *sūtras* of the founders of the main *darśanas*. All other knowledge was considered to be directly derived from these initial postulates. It is only natural that the most adequate form of inference, that is, of some development of this 'root' *(mūla)* philosophical content was represented by a commentary. That is why philosophical commentary became the most important and principal genre of theoretical activity, and the evolution of any philosophical school presupposed not only the creation of new interpretations of basic texts, but also the writing of sub-commentaries on popular works by authoritative commentators.

The poetical works of Śaṅkara cannot be examined directly within the context of a philosophical investigation, but still they open up some new vistas; they provide some foreshortening or shifting sense, which contributes to the widening of perspective. As for independent works of the Advaitist, they are actually far less original or free than his commentaries. Essentially, the part played by the treatises and compendia belonging or ascribed to Śaṅkara is limited by their auxiliary or propaedeutical functions: they form an introduction to complex religious and philosophical problems, the subtleties of which are traced in the multi-layered interpretations of the basic aphorisms belonging to the initial core of Vedanta. In the words of Sengaku Mayeda, "The study of Śaṅkara has mostly centered around his chief work, the *Brahmasūtrabhāṣya,* and his commentaries on the Upaniṣads. In comparison with these great works the *Upadeśasāhasrī* is a minor one .../However,/in my opinion, there is no better introduction to Śaṅkara's philosophy than the *Upadeśasāhasrī*, especially its Prose Part.[47]

And what is this Commentary on *Brahmasūtra* that is to be chiefly taken into account while investigating Śaṅkara's views? On the one hand, Śaṅkara's Commentary is undoubtedly the most prominent work based on Bādarāyaṇa's text; and on the other, it occupies a central place in all of the Advaitist's work.

Compositionally, the Commentary is conceived as continuous dialogue, where the objections of an imaginary opponent (they are usually defined as *pūrva-pakṣa,* or prima facie statements, literally, something conceived at first sight) alternate with the answers of the Advaitist himself, who uses as arguments the sayings of the Upaniṣads, as well as the *Sūtras* of Bādarāyaṇa. One must say that Śaṅkara sometimes takes liberties with Bādarāyaṇa's aphorisms, allowing himself certain strained interpretations; from time to time he even gives two equally possible interpretations of one and the same *sūtra.* Granted the great respect that the Advaitist had for Bādarāyaṇa, it is quite obvious that the text of *Brahmasūtra* is used only as a sort of canvas to be embroidered with the patterns of his own concepts. Special methods here are evidently subordinated to the general task, and the overall impression is one of the profound inner integrity of the system, the core of which is represented by *śruti* sayings. Śaṅkara's Advaita did not simply appeal to the authority of sacred scripture, as was usually done in other orthodox schools of Indian philosophy. It tried to include the texts of the Upaniṣads into the very fabric of its philosophical constructions, while simultaneously demonstrating the inner unity and absence of contradictions in the whole corpus of these texts.

Defending his views, Śaṅkara tries to anticipate all possible questions and objections of his opponents. (This pattern was quite characteristic of Indian philosophical

---

47. Sengaku Mayeda, Introduction to *Śaṅkara's Upadeśasāhasrī*, p. xi.

literature in general.) Sometimes the Advaitist offers supplementary arguments on behalf of his imaginary opponents, independently drawing logically unavoidable conclusions. Sometimes the pressing of an argument is nothing but a compositional device, designed to create an opportunity to stop for a while and clarify an obscure point—or just to change the course of the reasoning. Of course, the main goal here is not any conflict with real adversaries. It is quite clear that we are dealing rather with a special 'polemic genre' of religious and philosophical investigation where the alleged standpoint of a 'heretic', an 'alien' or even of someone 'sincerely confused' (as in the Sūtras of Bādarāyaṇa) is just a pretext for the development of Śaṅkara's own thought.

Formally, the complementary arguments of the second turn, often simply carrying on the tenets of the opponent in quite an unexpected direction, are called *uttara-pakṣa,* or later view, subsequent examination. As a rule, they should be followed by the final conclusion of the author, that is, by *siddhānta* (final end of an argument, settled opinion).

Tradition distinguishes three methods of philosophical dispute, which presuppose the analysis of the opponent's arguments and subsequent logical conclusion. They are *vāda, jalpa* and *vitaṇḍa.* It is assumed that within the framework of the first method a disputant is really interested in finding the truth. The second method is applied to every case of sophistic polemics, where the essential point is to defeat the adversary by any possible means. The situation is more intricate when one is dealing with a discussion defined by the term *vitaṇḍa;* however, it was this device that appears to have been particularly prevalent in Advaita polemics.

Already the Naiyāyikas, who were disputing with the Buddhists, reproached their opponents for their polemic methods, when the opponent's views had been reduced to absurdity, and the Buddhists were idly picking at the arguments or assertions of the others without attempting to prove their own side of the question.[48] Since, from the Mādhyamikas' point of view, the essence of their main notion—that of *Śūnya,* or, emptiness—could not be grasped in words, this method of polemics was considered to be wholly appropriate. This discrepancy between critical argumentation and inner substantiation of one's own teaching can be regarded as the specific trait of the *vitaṇḍa* dispute. Echoes of such an approach are easily traced in Advaita—if only because the higher reality, according to Śaṅkara, was essentially non-verbal and ineffable, but also self-evident, self-luminous *(svayaṃ-prakāśa)*; its realization presupposed some important turn in the course of the discussion. And even a later Vedantin, the follower of Rāmānuja, Veṅkaṭanātha (thirteenth and early fourteenth century) said that the method of *vitaṇḍa* was quite acceptable both for those desiring only victory *(vijigitsu),* and for those devoid of passions *(vītarāga),* that is, for conscientious, sober polemists.[49]

The objections of Śaṅkara's adversaries—especially numerous in the second, polemical, *adhyāya* of his Commentary on *Brahmasūtra*—are not uniform in their character. As long as Śaṅkara argues with the adherents of the orthodox systems, it is often quite enough for him to demonstrate that his opponents' view differ from *śruti* revelation. Moreover, sometimes he even succeeds in presenting the main notions of other orthodox schools as more or less apt approaches to the ideas of Advaita. Śaṅkara maintains, for instance, that a correct understanding and development of Sāṃkhya concepts is bound to reveal its inner affinity with Vedanta (*Brahma-sūtra-bhāṣya,* II.2.10).

---

48. See, for example, critical observations of a Naiyāyika Vātsyāyana: *Nyāya-sūtra,* I.2.44.

49. Vide: Veṅkaṭanātha, *Nyāya-pariśuddhi,* Chowkambha Sanskrit Series, Benares, 1931, p. 166. About *vitaṇḍa* see also Bimal Krishna Matilal, Foreword, to P. Granoff, *Philosophy and Argument,* pp. x-xii.

However, the most irreconcilable adversaries of Śaṅkara are, without doubt, the followers of the materialist Lokāyata system, as well as the adherents of two 'heretical' schools—the Buddhists and the Jainas—who did not accept the Vedic foundation. It is known that Lokāyata flatly denied the validity of the evidence of authority, while the Buddhists and the Jainas, who had their own sacred texts, still maintained that a reference to authority occupied a subordinate place among other sources of valid knowledge and should be substantiated by arguments based on inference and perception. Such an attitude naturally called for an alteration in the ways and means of the polemics. Using the arguments that were especially popular with his rivals, Śaṅkara pursues the discussion mainly with the help of logic and ordinary common sense. In accordance with the rules of traditional Indian philosophical dispute, Śaṅkara tries to beat them at their own game. His 'rational' critique concentrates primarily on ontological problems; it should probably regarded as a corroboration of the view that for him the 'heretical' teachings and Lokāyata were undoubtedly consistent and internally coherent systems, where gnoseological and ethical aspects are wholly dependent on their ontological foundation.

Still, the discussion, and even the exposition, presented after the pattern of the *vitaṇḍa* method, presupposes a more complex play with an imaginary or real opponent. In my opinion, all of Śaṅkara's polemics, representing an integral part of his commentaries as well as the whole of Śaṅkara's approach to his own system, can be logically divided into two levels.

It has to be borne in mind that in spite of his impeccable skill in reasoning, Śaṅkara attributed to this method only relative value. The limits of logical inference, together with those of ritual practice and ordinary experience, are set within the frame of *aparavidyā,* or profane, phenomenal knowledge. This aspect of Śaṅkara's dispute is intended for the layman—unlearned but also unprejudiced—a kind of a hypothetical newcomer. It is to this class of polemical arguments that Śaṅkara resorts in those parts of his commentaries, the compendia and treatises, specially devoted to the refutation of the views of the Lokāyatikas, the Jainas and the Buddhists.

However, this kind of a critique represents only the lower layer of a real polemics. The actual sense of the Advaitist's arguments would remain hidden, and the reader would be misled, if one did not look simultaneously for the answer that can be figured out during the course of the polemics. After all, an argument offered on the level of *aparavidyā* (or, as it is often called in Advaita, an argument from the standpoint of wordly practice, *vyāvahārika*) may contain insignificant cavils and quibbles; many similar objections, on closer examination, prove to be valid against Śaṅkara's own Advaita. And that is only natural, since the main goal of these arguments is to disarm an opponent, to defeat him in a dispute. They are to be taken for what they are worth: while judging their value, one should keep in mind the context of the polemics.

In contrast to that, the higher level of knowledge (arguments from the higher truth, or, *pāramārthika*) reflects essential divergencies of rival systems. For Śaṅkara it also presupposes a constant appeal to *śruti,* as well as the construction of a coherent picture of reality. To some extent, continuous dicussion with other philosophical and religious schools is characteristic of all theoretical works of the Advaitist; it is implied in various passages of his works, even when the opponents are not directly named and defined.

As will be shown below, such a two-level structure of philosophical polemics correlates with Śaṅkara's notion of the two groups of *śruti* sayings, that is, the *vyāvahārika* (from the point of view of phenomenal practice) and the pāramārthika (from the point of view of ultimate truth). Both groups, each in its own peculiar way, mediate between a specific, personal consciousness and the ultimate spiritual reality (Ātman-Brahman), and contribute to the gradual approach to this new level of existence.

CHAPTER IV

Pure Brahman as Consciousness: Apophatic Theology and the Problem of Contradiction

1. *ŚAṄKARA'S ADVAITA AND LOKĀYATA*

It is probably impossible to find more distant opponents than these two systems. Their comparison is somewhat hindered not only by the remoteness of ideas and philosophical interests, but also by the fact that no work by the adherents of Indian materialism has survived.[1] True, many Indologists now think that Lokāyata might be adequately reconstructed in its main tenets from the material that can be found in the works of its philosophical opponents.[2] So the bringing together of Śaṅkara's teaching and Lokāyata under one heading seems appropriate at least because the Advaitist himself indirectly contributed towards preservation of the ideas of the materialist system.

One of the most valuable sources of Lokāyata are compendia, that is, compositions that give us a short synopsis of major philosophical schools. Their texts some-

1. Some hopes in this respect were formerly placed on the treatise by Jayarāśi Bhaṭṭa, *Tattvopaplavasiṃha,* published in 1940 (*Tattvopaplavasiṃha of Jayarāśibhaṭṭa,* edited by Sukhlalji Sanghavi and R.C. Parikh, Gaekwad Oriental Series, no. 87, Baroda, 1940). However, this work reveals a skeptical inclination, which is quite alien to the fundamental notions of Lokāyata.

2. Vide, for instance : G. Tucci, "A Sketch of Indian Materialism", *Proceedings of the First Indian Philosophical Congress,* Delhi, 1925, pp. 36 f.

times include passages from the lost *Bṛhaspati-sūtra,* ascribed to the legendary founder of Lokāyata. One of these compendia is *Sarva-darśana-siddhānta-saṅgraha,* whose authorship is ascribed to Śaṅkara. Just like the famous *Sarva-darśana-saṅgraha* of Mādhava—a later Advaita follower—it starts with the exposition of the materialists' views. The philosophical systems examined by these Vedantins are organized, so to speak, according to the level of truth inherent in them. Compositionally they are linked by a problem, which suddenly emerges in a preceding system and cannot be solved there; this problem is supposed to be solved in the system that follows. It is difficult to get rid of the impression that Lokāyata is used as a sort of a whetstone for polishing the polemical skills of its opponents. Taking up each of the standpoints characteristic of different systems, the author of a compendium (who personally belongs to the Vedanta creed) moves farther and farther on from Lokāyata, as if climbing ascending steps. Basing himself on Buddhist texts, T. Rhys-Davids even suggested that Lokāyata had been invented by the adversaries of materialism for purely logical purposes—as the extreme case of vulgar, anti-philosophical reasoning, which also should be investigated for the sake of completeness.[3] However, this attitude of the celebrated translator and interpreter of Buddhist works seems a bit excessive. T. Stcherbatsky, for example, never doubted that "Indian materialism was a property of a particular school, which preserved its traditions, developed and practised its teaching."[4]

As mentioned above, many essential aspects of the Indian materialist school did not find full reflection in the dispassionate exposition of compendia. To my mind,

---

3. One can find this observation in the commentary to the translation of *Dialogues of the Buddha.* Vide : T.W. Rhys-Davids, *Dialogues of the Buddha,* vol. 1, Oxford, 1899, pp. 166 ff.

4. T. Stcherbatsky, "K istorii materializma v Indii," *Vostochniye zapiski,* 1. Leningrad, 1927, p. 54.

Lokāyata is more clearly outlined in the polemical statements of its opponents, if only because the opponents were interested in drawing all the conclusions from its fundamental tenets. One should not, of course, overlook a certain partiality of the opponents, who were mostly orthodox in their beliefs: after all, Lokāyata encroached upon the most important Brahmanic values. If one were to believe Saṅkara's exposition, the Lokāyatikas maintained that

The three Vedas are ...
/Only/ the means of livelihood for those,
who are devoid of reason and virility.[5]

Still, the tense opposition of different systems, quite palpable in the critical works of Śaṅkara on the whole provides one with a better and a keener awareness of the general rhythm and vector of philosophical thought than does a sober synopsis of ideas by one of its adherents.

In the first *sūtra* of Śaṅkara's Commentary on Bādarāyaṇa, the views of the materialist philosophers are directly likened to those of ordinary people *(prakṛtā janāḥ)*, quite foreign to philosophical discussions. The Advaitist observes that the Lokāyatikas, just like uneducated laymen, consider only the body to be the conscious *ātman*. Hence the name, under which Lokāyata was known to Śaṅkara: *dehatmavada*, or, the teaching that the Self is identical with the body. Incidentally, in Śaṅkara's compendium one finds the statement from the Lokāyatika standpoint, dealing with this subject:

I am strong, weak, old, young,—
these characteristics /are ascribed/

---

5. Śaṅkara, *Sarva-darśana-siddhānta-saṅgraha*, II. 14-15:
trayo vedās . . .
buddhipauruṣahīnānāṃ jiviketi //15// .
(*Sarva-siddhānta-saṅgraha*, edited with an English translation by M. Raṅgācārya, Madras, 1909).

To the specific, particular body, /which is/ *ātman*,
and there is nothing else besides this.[6]

According to Advaita, the attributes of the body are only temporarily superimposed on the immutable *ātman*, obscuring its eternal nature. And under this category fall not only external, physical characteristics, but also the psychical peculiarities belonging to a person: all emotional features, habits, temperament—in a word, all activity of the senses and reasoning activity. Somewhat later we will examine a minute analysis of consciousness, offered by Advaita; now it is enough to say that all concrete manifestations of psychic life are considered in Advaita to be natural *(prākṛta)* compositions or functions. They are distinguished from *ātman* just for the reason that they can be somehow defined, objectified. In Śaṅkara's preamble to his Commentary on *Brahmasūtra* he deals with the usual confusion between *ātman* and 'object'[7] : "Just having

---

6. Śaṅkara, *Sarva-darśana-siddhānta-saṅgraha,* II.6.
sthūlo 'haṃ taruṇo vṛddho yuvetyādiviśeṣanaiḥ /
viśiṣṭo deha evātmā na tato 'nyo vilakṣaṇaḥ //6// .

7. *Viṣaya,* or object, field, as a horizon or a sphere of activity or perception. In Śaṅkara's Commentary on *Brahmasūtra* it is usually opposed to *viṣayin,* that is, to somebody who is acting or perceiving within this field, to the 'subject', to 'Self'. The semantic pair *viṣayin-viṣaya* is often used in Śaṅkara's Advaita for the purpose of opposing, at least in a preliminary way, *ātman* and all the accidental, 'objective' attributes that are superimposed upon it. However, in the strict sense of the word, there is no complete correlation with our usual, Western notions of subject and object. Later, we shall examine other correspondences, close to the ones mentioned above. (I mean pairs that have their own shades of meaning, for instance: *kartṛ-karma*—doer, maker, agent—action, object; *jñātṛ—jñāna*—knower, subject of perception,—knowledge. The only pair that completely coincides in meaning with *viṣayin-viṣaya* is *kṣetrajña* (the one who knows the field) and *kṣetra* (field); the latter pair can be found in Śaṅkara's Commentary on the *Bhagavadgītā* (XIII. 26). The passage runs as follows : "It is said that the combining of *kṣetra* and *kṣetrajña,* which is, the object and the subject, whose nature is different, is characterized by the superimposition of the attributes of

mutually superimposed on one another their essence and attributes, without distinguishing them, having mixed together the lie and the truth, /having brought together/ eternally different attributes and /eternally different/ bearers of these attributes, one gets, as is usual in worldly practice, false /assertions/ : 'this am I', 'this is mine'.[8]

For those who, owing to ignorance, unconsciously adhere to these views—Śaṅkara continues his reasoning—*śruti* suggests the way of gradual ascension from *ātman,* presented as *annamaya* (lit., consisting of food, that is, the body), through the subsequent steps up to the inner *ātman* (vide: Commentary on *Brahmasutra,* I.1.13). And only for these ordinary people, who identify *ātman* with the body, are Upaniṣadic statements that *ātman* "is not yet found, it should be sought" really meaningful. Actually it is the inner 'witness' *(sākṣin)* of all acts of perception, which makes possible consciousness itself (vide: Commentary on *Brahmasūtra,* I.1.14). This way is in principle open for everyone, except, of course, the people belonging to the *varṇa* of *śūdras,* who are not allowed to read the Vedas (Commentary on *Brahmasūtra,* I.3.34-38).[9]

---

the one/on the attributes/of the other. The confusion/emerges/owing to the non-distinguishing of the own nature of *kṣetra* and *kṣetrajña,* which is similar to the superimposition/of the image/of the snake on the rope, or of silver on the conch shell, when they are not distinguished from each other." *(ucyate kṣetrakṣetrajñayoḥ viṣayaviṣayiṇoḥ vibhinnasvabhāvayoḥ itaretarataddharmādhyāsalakṣaṇaḥ saṃyogaḥ kṣetrakṣetrajñasvarūpavivekābhāvanibandhanaḥ /rajjuśuktikādīnāṃ tadvivekajñānābhāvād adhyāropitasarparajatādisaṃyogavat.)*

8. *tathāpyanyonyasminnanyonyātmakātamanyonyadharmāṃścādhyasyetaretarāvivekena atyaṃtaviviktayor dharmadharmiṇor mithyājñānanimittaḥ... ahamidaṃ mamedam iti naisargike 'yaṃ lokavyavahāraḥ.*

9. In this connection one remembers how P. Deussen, who still professed a touching belief in the power of human reason, suggested that the Vedantins' refusal to allow *śūdras* the study of Vedanta, whose necessary preliminary was the reading of sacred texts, was explained chiefly by the same adjustment to national prejudices which forced

As one can easily see, in Śaṅkara's opinion even ignoramuses are situated in a far better position than the materialist philosophers who persevere in their delusions. The Lokāyatikas' views, essentially opposed to Advaita, are examined by Śaṅkara in the third *adhyāya* of his Commentary on *Brahmasūtra,* but even in the passages of the text, where there is no direct polemics, the main notions of Advaita are used directly against the materialist system.

The Lokāyatikas maintain that consciousness emerges through specific combinations of inanimate primary (or gross) elements *(jaḍa-bhūta)*. According to Lokāyata, there are four of them: earth, water, heat (or fire) and wind (or air).[10] Unlike the orthodox systems of Indian philosophy, the materialists denied the existence of limitless ether, or space *(ākāśa)*.[11] The emergence of consciousness is likened by the Lokāyatikas to the appearance of an intoxicating power during the fermentation of golden syrup, which before the beginning of the process has nothing like that.[12]

---

orthodox thinkers to derive all their knowledge from the Vedas. (Vide : P. Deussen, *The System of the Vedanta,* London, 1972, p. 61).

10. Śaṅkara, *Sarva-darśana-siddhānta-saṅgraha,* II.1/
In the opinion of the Lokāyatikas, the foundation
/of the world/is represented by four elements—
Such as earth, water, heat, wind—and that is all;
/they do not recognize/anything else.
lokāyatikapakṣe tu tattvaṃ bhūtacatuṣṭayam /
pṛthivyāpas tathā tejo vāyur ityeva nāparam //1//.

11. The Lokāyatikas equated the existence of *ākāśa,* which could not be perceived by the sense, to the traditional notion of *karma,* where happiness and unhappiness depend on previous merits *(puṇya)* or sins *(pāpa)* in preceding births. So this 'mythological' *ākāśa* is certainly devoid of any reasonable sense (Vide: Haribhadra, *Ṣad-darśana-samuccaya,* Tenali, 1958, pp. 130-31. Concerning the 'fifth element' in Advaita see : *Sarva-darśana-siddhānta-saṅgraha,* XII. 90-92, as well as Śaṅkara's Commentary on *Brahmasūtra,* I.1.21-22; II.3.1-8.

12. Vide : Commentary on *Brahmasūtra,* III.3.53.

The same example, characterizing the views of the Lokāyatikas, is presented in the compendia of Mādhava and Haribhadra, as well as in the treatise *Tattva-saṅgraha* of the Buddhist philosopher Śāntarakṣita. In Śaṅkara's own compendium a similar case is cited: when red color appears during the combining of differently colored betel leaves, areca nuts and lime (*Sarva-darśana-siddhānta-saṅgraha,* II.7). Thus, consciousness in Lokāyata is represented as a kind of a power or attribute that is inherent in the body and disappears after death with the destruction of the body. Lokāyata was the only school of Indian philosophy which refused to accept the traditional doctrine of *karma* and *saṃsāra.* As a sort of a compensation for the gloomy perspective of inevitable and ultimate death, the Lokāyatikas—one should give them their due—tried to persuade their listeners of the importance and validity of everyday occupations which can make a person happy in this life.[13]

The Lokāyatikas developed their concept of the nature of consciousness based on the data of immediate perception. Indeed, according to ordinary experience, the psychic activity of a person is continued up to the irrevocable destruction of the body. In Lokāyata, direct perception by the senses, or *pratyakṣa,* serves as the only valid source of knowledge and the criterion of actual existence. The materialists deny the validity of logical inference *(anumāna)* and that of authority *(śabda)*, which are accepted, if with some reservations, by all other Indian

---

13. One might note incidentally that Śaṅkara's compendium proves to be especially interesting in this respect, since it is the only extant source that testifies to the Lokāyatikas' attention to the problems of ordinary life, even to the problems of economics:

With the help of/the means/accessible to perception,
that is, agriculture, cattle breeding, trade, politics,
administration and similar occupations,
Let the wise one enjoy bliss on earth.
kṛṣigorakṣavāṇijyadaṇḍanītyādibhir budhaḥ /
dṛṣṭair eva sadopāyair bhogān anubhaved bhuvi //5//.
Sarva-darśana-siddhānta-saṅgraha, II.15-15 1/2.

philosophical schools. The negative attitude of the Lokāyatikas towards inference is to some extent explained by the fact that in the orthodox systems logical argumentation was often used to demonstrate the existence of supersensuous entities. The data of the compendium by Mādhava allow one to suppose that the Lokāyatikas realized also the gnoseological difficulties connected with including deductive reasoning within the framework of a purely empirical system. Actually, the Lokāyatikas regarded inference as a useful instrument, which one could rely upon to some extent, making reservations for its serious inner defects and, so to speak, relative unlawfulness.[14] The necessary corrections must be provided by immediate perception.[15]

The means of valid knowledge *(pramāṇa)*[16] in Advaita are enumerated in the 12th chapter of Śaṅkara's compen-

---

14. In *Milindapañha* (the questions of king Milinda) Lokāyata is even identified with the science of logic, which is treated there as sophistical and deceptive reasoning (the term for it is, incidentally, *vitaṇḍa*), aimed at engaging the opponent in a futile discussion (About this vide: G. Tucci, "Linee di una storia del materialismo indiano", *Opera minora,* Part I, Roma, 1971, pp. 64-65; 94.

15. Though the Lokāyatikas accepted *pratyakṣa* as the only source of valid knowledge, it did not mean that the world, open for their cognition, was regarded as a purely phenomenal one, or woven of subjective sensations. Indeed, carried farther, the Lokāyata position, which does not allow for any criteria of truth and actual existence, other than perception, inevitably leads to agnosticism. Nevertheless, the Lokāyatikas did not take this step. And one might find corroboration for this observation in the fact that they were never interested in searching for the criterion of intersubjectivity. While denying the special role of *śabda* as the evidence of authority, they still did not raise any doubts about the animate and conscious nature of other people—and of course its acceptance depends totally upon the statements of others concerning their perceptions. Probably, the Lokāyatikas proceeded from a supposition of inner similarity or identity of the perceptions of all people, as well as from the assumption that these perceptions somehow correspond to external objects.

16. The basic meaning of *pramāṇa* is measure; hence other derived meanings: the means of valid knowledge (used to 'measure' the objects),

dium; they mostly correspond to the six *pramāṇas* of Pūrva-Mīmāṃsā. These are sensuous perception *(pratyakṣa);* logical inference *(anumāna);* comparison *(upamāna);* evidence of the sacred scripture (*āgama,* which takes the place of the traditional *śabda,* or word of the authority); inference from transmitting some quality of one object to another *(arthāpatti);* as well as *anupalabdhi,* or the conclusion about the absence of some object, based on its imperceptibility. However, the interpretations of the latter *pramāṇa* in Advaita and Pūrva-Mīmāṃsā differ a great deal.

In contrast to the materialists, recognizing so many various and valid means of knowledge, Śaṅkara quickly specifies that the sphere of their use has certain limitations. In the words of the Advaitist.

> [T]here are six *pramāṇas;*
> they relate to something that is called /the domain/ of phenomenal practice, and cannot be applied to *ātman.*[17]

To my mind, the keyword here is *vyāvahārika,* that is, related to practice, connected with the empirical, phenomenal sphere.

In other words, the *pramāṇas* in Advaita can actually connect, bind together (or even permeate) the relations between the entities of the 'natural', ordinary world. Let us go farther, trying to trace the very texture of this world. From Śaṅkara's standpoint, the universe is composed of the magic color play of *māyā,* a veil or magic illusion, which hides some other immutable entity. Just as a rope in the

---

method, proportionality. And the semantic pair of related words *pramātṛ-prameya* means, respectively, the subject and the object of cognition.

17. Vide : Śaṅkara, *Sarva-darśana-siddhānta-saṅgraha,* XII.85-86:
pratyakṣanumānākhyam upamānaṃtathāgamaḥ /
arthāpattirabhāvaśca pramāṇāni ṣaḍ eva hi //85//
vyāvahārikanāmāni bhavantyetāni nātmani /.

hands of a juggler seems to be a snake, and a shell can look from a distance like a piece of silver, the manifold attributes of the world are only temporarily superimposed on its true foundation—the higher Brahman. This superimposition *(adhyāsa),* or *māyā,* is actually the reverse side of the creative power of Brahman, and it is this power or potency *(śakti)* that undergoes changes and transformations, or evolution *(pariṇāma).* The higher Brahman is devoid of any qualities or attributes (it is the so-called *Nirguṇa-Brahman,* or Brahman without definitions); it always remains self-identical and the only one.

Taken in its concealing aspect, *māyā* is nothing but *avidyā*—nescience; not just ignorance or false knowledge, but the only means of perception accessible to us, and simultaneously the only mode of existence of the profane world. The limits of the sphere of action of the *pramāṇas* would become more comprehensible if one were to take into account that *māyā-avidyā* also creates individual peculiarities, as well as, in general, all psychic, 'natural' abilities of each soul. And inside every one of these innumerable souls lies, as its luminous core, pure consciousness, the attributeless *ātman,* originally identical with Brahman. The realization of this identity and the disappearance of the illusory evolution of the phenomenal universe is possible only through the mystical act of dissolution inside Brahman, where the former distinction among subject, object and the very process of cognition, disappears.

But how is an ordinary person to learn about this inner nature? First of all, argues Śaṅkara, everyone, so to speak, feels the *ātman* inside himself; it is a primary reality for everybody, something similar to a Cartesian *cogito.* In the words of the Advaitist, "it is imossible to deny *ātman*, since he, who is denying it, is this very *ātman.*"[18] And besides,

---

18. Śaṅkara, Commentary on *Brahmasūtra,* I.1.4: *ātmanaśca pratyākhyātum aśakyatvāt ya eva nirākartā tasyaivātmatvāt* /, and its almost literal repetition in the second *adhyāya* (II.3.7): "and it is impossible to deny this essence . . . since he who tries to deny is the

the merging of *ātman* and Braman is promised by the evidence of revelation as the only possibility of liberation from the circle of *sāṃsāric* transmigrations. It is only after the reading of sacred texts that a person acquires a relentless desire to know Brahman *(brahma-jijñāsā)*, that is, a desire to come to it, since Brahman, according to Śaṅkara, is this very knowledge (lit.: *vidyā* opposed to *avidyā*).

However, it is not that simple. One the one hand, one cannot be led to the realization of Brahman through moral and religious merits, through performing rites or worship of a personified God, or Īśvara. Finally, as we have seen, one cannot hope to attain the goal through intellectual effort, that is, through accumulation of various intellectual data through well-established *pramāṇas*. In Śaṅkara's words, "with the realization of non-dual *ātman*... having been devoid of the objects, as well as of the subject who could use them, the means of valid knowledge cannot exist either."[19]

It is impossible, according to Śaṅkara, to teach directly the realization of *ātman* (and, therefore, the higher Brahman itself), since every word becomes false and dead, as soon as one tries to use it in order to define the nature of this higher reality. *Ātman* in Advaita is pure consciousness, being one and only one it has nothing by way of parts or attributes. This consciousness is real and unavoidably present in every human experience, but it depends neither upon changeable objects, nor upon methods of inference or perception. Any time one tries to form some kind of notion about it, one is compelled to make use of this entity itself. According to Advaita, *ātman* is the inner foundation of every experience and judgement—and for this reason it

---

nature of this." *(na ceddasasyo nirākaraṇaṃ saṃbhavati /. . ya eva hi nirākartā tad eva tasya svarūpam /.)*

19. Commentary on *Brahmasūtra*, I.1.4: *nahyaheyānupādeyādvaitātmāvagatau satyāṃ nirviṣayāṇyapramātṛkāni ca pramāṇāni bhavitum arhantīti /.*

cannot become its own object. Nothing can be said about it except the undeniable fact that it exists. In the words of Yājñavalkya from *Bṛhadāraṇyakopaniṣad* (II.3.6), there is no other and no better definition of Brahman than *neti, neti*—not this, not this. Śaṅkara's commentary on this passage runs as follows: "Through the removal of all distinctions ... it was said about something that is devoid of any characteristics, that is, devoid of name, form, action, kind or quality.[20] It is pure consciousness, which cannot turn around to grasp its own essence; it is ineffable, indefinable. And that explains, incidentally, why *ātman* cannot be taught directly, and why any attribute ascribed to it is valid only at the level of profane knowledge.

Hence, any content in knowledge (or, for that matter, any attribute of individual consciousness) is just something accidental and interchangeable; it can be 'removed'[21] precisely because it can be objectified. In Śaṅkara's words, this external content is only—up to a certain moment—superimposed *(adhyasyate)* on this inner entity. And it certainly is not accidental that through all the works of the Advaitist there runs the central idea of a profound *incommensurability (apramātṛtva)* of Brahman and the world.

For the sake of completeness I will now make a slight digression, stepping back to the domain of Western religious and philosophical tradition. Already in the teaching of Christian neo-Platonism one can clearly discern two possible approaches to the notion of the dissolution of a human soul in the divine essence. Both of them are based on the idea of the removal of bodily and psychic limita-

---

20. Śaṅkara, Commentary on *Bṛhadāraṇyakopaniṣad,* II.3.6: *sarvopādhi-viśeṣāpohena / yasminna kaścidviśeṣo 'sti nāma vā rūpaṃ vā karma vā bhedo vā jātirvā guṇo vā taddvāreṇa hi śabdapravṛttir bhavati /. Saṅkaropaniṣadbhāṣya,* Vārāṇasī, 1972.

21. This procedure has much in common with the eidetical and phenomenological 'reduction' ('Eποχη') by E. Husserl; the main difference, however, lies in the fact that in Vedānta the recommendations for its realization were not of speculative but rather of a quite practical nature.

tions, but a prominent scholar of Neo-Platonism, E. von Ivanka distinguishes between an 'enstatic' way (characteristic of Evagrius Pontius) and an 'extatic' one (according to Pseudo-Dionisios Areopagites).[22] The former is understood on the lines of the restoration or recovery of the true—that is, divine in its essence—nature of a person; while the latter presupposes the rejection of his own self by an adept, and so, the growing out of his own consciousness, and ultimately the coming out of its limitations.

Probably the closest analogy with Śaṅkara's teaching in the West can be found in the mystic system of Meister Eckhart, where both approaches are united. The key notion of Eckhart's teaching, that of separation *(abegescheidenheit)*, means that a man sinks down into his own essence with the aim of coming in this way to God, having thrown off all finite qualities and attributes. It was Rodolf Otto who discussed the affinity between Eckhart and Śaṅkara, and being too enthusiastic about his concept, the scholar practically identified their systems, overlooking some serious discrepancies of the doctrines. For instance, Eckhart places the stress on the notion of a *gift*, or God's mercy, through which it becomes possible for an adept to go down into his own self; otherwise, this sinking down might bring him only ultimate destruction.[23]

In the previously mentioned review of the 3rd edition of Otto's book, Paul Hacker drew attention to another essential point of divergence between Śaṅkara and Eckhart, namely, their different interpretations of pure being.[24] True, one should note that it was not Hacker but H. Ebeling who was the first to show that Eckhart's doctrine essentially differs from the Thomist one. While for Tho-

22. Vide: E. von Ivànka, *Plato Christianus. Ubernahme und Umgestaltung des Platonismus durch die Väter.* Einsiedeln, 1964.

23. Vide: V. Lossky, *À l'image et à la resemblance de Dieu*, Paris, 1967, p. 50.

24. Vide: P. Hacker, *Westöstliche Mystik* (Review), pp. 41-42.

mas Aquinas God is primarily pure being, the main tenet of a Plotinian version of Neo-Platonism, as well as of a Christian one (which represents the reference point for Eckhart), is that God is ultimately pure consciousness.[25] Therefore, argues Hacker, one should draw a comparison between them only in this respect. In other words, one should not go into the problem of real being but should try to collate only their statements about pure consciousness. And here the analogies really are remarkable. For instance, Śaṅkara maintains: "All the modifications—those of the cause, the effect and so on—exist only /in the case/ that before them exists their foundation—their own nature /in the form of/ *ātman*, or pure consciousness."[26] And Eckhart says the following: "Intelligere est altius quam esse" (Rational consciousness is higher than Being).[27] And elsewhere he says, "Wesen ist sîn vorbûrge, vernûnfticheit ist der tempel gotes" (Essence is his foothill, the ability to cognize is the temple of God.)[28]

In full correlation with the tradition of apophatic theology of Pseudo-Dionysios, that serves as a foundation for Eckhart's teaching, this higher cognition, or Divine light (usually we find in Eckhart's works the term *ungemischte lieht,* or, unmixed light), which supports the existence of all the things of the world, coincides for the soul with its 'nothing' *(niht),* that is, with the throwing of all qualities and attributes.[29] The metaphor of 'invisible light', which

---

25. H. Ebeling. *Meister Eckharts Mystik. Studien zu den Geisteskämpfen um die Wende des 13, Jahrhunderts,* Aalen, 1966, p. 97.

26. Śaṅkara, Commentary on *Īśopaniṣad,* IV: *sarvā hi kāryakaraṇādivikriyā nityacaitanyātmasvarūpe sarvāspadabhūte satyeva bhavanti* /.

27. Meister Eckhart, *Lateinische Werke,* Stuttgart, Band 5, Seite 42, no. 1.

28. Meister Eckhart *Deutsche Werke,* Stuttgart, vol. I, p. 150, no. 1.

29. Of course, one should not overlook the fact that the essentially Christian mysticism of Eckhart differs from Śaṅkara's teaching at least

imperceptibly spreads through endless space, is one of the favorite similes of Śaṅkara when he discusses attributeless Brahman. When all objects are removed, when the veil of attributes and relations is thrown off, argues Śaṅkara, "and the foundation, /which is nothing else but/ knowledge itself, is not perceived any more, it happens—just as in the case of light, /which spreads through empty space, and so is not seen/—only because there are no objects that can be illuminated, and not because it does not exist according to its own nature."[30]

And still, even though *ātman,* or the higher Brahman, is not attainable by the *pramāṇas,* Advaita indicates that there is a means that helps one at least to go in the right direction, while moving towards it. This specific means does not provide a guarantee that the aim will be achieved, but it certainly helps one to come closer to this essentially elusive entity. Among all the *pramāṇas*—the instruments of cognition—one enjoys an exclusive role. In Śaṅkara's words, "even if it seems that in many spheres the reasoning is well-founded, still, in the sphere we are talking about now, it cannot be beyond reproach of the lack of foundation, since one cannot know this hidden nature of everything existing without the sacred texts *(āgama),* telling about the binding /of *saṃsāra*/ and liberation."[31] The evi-

---

in one decisive respect. As shown by the end of the 19th century by H. Denifle, according to Eckhart's system even in the unity *(Unio)* of an individual soul with God, this soul—even having totally lost its attributes—still remains a particular entity and never entirely dissolves in the higher reality. Vide: H.S. Denifle, *Die deutschen Mystiker ders 14. Jahrhunderts, Beitrag zur Deutung inrer Lehre (Hrsg. von O. Speiss).* Freiburg, 1951, S. 152 ff.

30. Śaṅkara, Commentary on *Brahmasūtra,* II.3.18: *yathā vidyāśrayasya prakāśasya prakāśyābhāvādanabhivyaktiḥ na svarūpābhāvāttadvat /.*

31. Śaṅkara, Commentary on *Brahmasūtra,* II.1.11: *yadyapi kvacidviṣaye tarkasya pratiṣṭhitatvamupalakṣyate tathāpi prakṛte tāvadviṣaye prasajyata evāpratiṣṭhitatvadoṣāt anirmokṣastarkasya /*

dence of revelation is given to a man not only as a promise, but also as a path. Indeed, we have seen by now that an ordinary person cannot realize *ātman* through inference. The only way open to him is to draw closer to the moment of a sudden leap into the new reality—and take the help of axiomatic and rigid mythological texts. The function of Vedic sayings of a *pāramārthika* level (that is, from the standpoint of absolute truth) is unique: even though these *śruti* texts also cannot ensure the attainment of *ātman,* they do help an adept to stay in the vicinity of *ātman* by apophatically removing every attribute ascribed to it from the beginning.

Of course, many scholars paid attention to the role of *āgama* for Śaṅkara's conception; this theme was most thoroughly discussed in the previously mentioned book by K. Satchidananda Murty. However, it happens only too often that the heart of the matter is replaced by a sort of historical analysis—so that one mostly encounters reference to Brahmanic tradition, whose pressure was felt by the Advaitist. In my opinion, the specific part played by the evidence of revelation in Advaita, as well as the very opportunity to determine (at least roughly) the extent of *śruti* approach to *ātman*, are brought about by Śaṅkara's attitude to language.

Indeed, one cannot, according to Śaṅkara, "see the witness of seeing ... or think the essence of thinking.[32] And still, there is something inherent in the very nature of language, something that helps to reveal reality without giving it an exhaustive definition. There are ways and

---

nahīdamatigambhīraṃ bhāvayāthātmyaṃ muktinibandhanamāgama-mantareṇotprakṣitumapi śakyaṃ/.

32. Śaṅkara, Commentary on *Bṛhadāraṇyakopaniṣad,* III.4.2: *na dṛṣṭerdraṣṭāraṃ paśyeḥ . . . na vijñātervijñātāraṃ vijānīyāḥ.* To be precise, these are not the words of Śaṅkara himself, he is just citing the Upaniṣad; however, he is explaining that the division of one entity into two parts must be regarded here only as a concession to 'worldly' *(laukika)* speech patterns.

means to speak of—to speak around—this entity without assigning it to a specific category. We were not told (and so we cannot, in turn, tell) everything; that is why, according to Śaṅkara, we are always trying to catch this being at its word, to apprehend it through fragments, through scraps and broken phrases, where one can still discern the echo of the true word, unpronounced and ineffable.[33] Hence the bent of Indian tradition in general for metaphors, parables, curious etymologies; and Śaṅkara here is no exception. A present-day scholar would probably only smile condescendingly, encountering this kind of etymology: *upaniṣad* = *upa* (near) + *ni* (completely) + *sad* (weaken; approach; destroy), so that the whole term *upaniṣad* is supposed to mean something that weakens the bonds of birth, old age and death, allows one to approach Brahman and destroys *saṃsāra* (vide: Śaṅkara, *Upadeśasāhasrī, Padya-bandha,* I.25-26). Here one is obviously dealing with 'popular etymology', where words are explained not according to their actual historical origin, but according to their consonance. Still it is only during this kind of bringing words together—not only because of their sense, but also through listening to their inner resonance—that there might eventually emerge something that Boris Eikhenbaum, a prominent Russian literary scholar belonging to the 'Formal school', used to call 'side meanings'.[34]

---

33. One might remember in this connection also the hypothesis of anagrammatic structure of Vedic hymns, suggested by F. de Saussure, and later, by V. Toporov. This construction, according to them, is probably characteristic of Indo-European poetry in general. When we are dealing with anagrammatic structure, "the key word might be absent from the text, but it is essentially reconstructed by the whole of its sonorous structure . . . . And all the lines of the hymn give some reflection of this key word." Vide: V. Ivanov, *Ocherki po istorii semiotiki v SSSR,* Moscow, 1976, pp. 254-55.

34. All this is closely correlated with the teaching of A. Potebnia about the 'inner form' of a word, constituting the image, ultimately leading to some new knowledge. When this 'inner form' is cognized, we are dealing, according to A. Potebnia, with a poetic word, and when it remains unrevealed and operates only subconsciously, there emerges a

In European philosophy a somewhat similar attitude to language might be found in the later works by Heidegger, who believed in the advantage of an etymological and hermeneutical approach rather than a purely scientific one. His examination of Greek etymology (especially, in his work *Unterwegs zur Sprache*) led him to accept the fundamental tenet: "das Wort sei Wink und nicht Zeichen in Sinne der blossen Bezeichnung" (the word is a hint and not a sign in the sense of simple signification). That is, the word should be regarded as an indication, as a pointer, oriented towards the eternally elusive Being, and not as a label, providing this Being with a fixed definition.[35] A radical turn made by Heidegger in respect to language, which is regarded now not as a determination of reality, but as its own self-revelation ("Die Sprache *allein* ist es, die eigentlich spricht. Und sie spricht *einsam*."—The Speech is the *only one* which essentially speaks. And it speaks alone. Ibid., p. 265), demands from a person—and not only from a poet, but also from a philosopher—an ability to listen and to hear what is being prompted and suggested by language.[36] Perhaps, one should also see in

---

'prosaic word'. A.A. Potebnia, *Iz zapisok po teorii slovesnosti,* Kharkov, 1905. To my mind, extremely interesting in this respect are also the observations of O. Freidenberg; in her opinion, a metaphor functions as the means of forming a figurative sense. Incidentally, according to the scholar, the emergence of speculative notions mark the period of disintegration of mythological thinking, after which we are dealing with poetical and philosophical types of cognition separately. Vide: O.M. Freidenberg, *Mif i literatury drevnosti,* Moskva, 1978, (Part 2, Chapter 2).

35. Vide: M. Heidegger, *Unterwegs zur Sprache,* Pfullingen, 1959, p. 119.

36. "Der Mensch aber vermag nur zu sprechen, insofern er, der Sage gehörend, auf sie hört, um nachsagend ein Wort sagen zu können." (But man can speak only as far as he, belonging to Speech, listens to Her, so that he later can pronounce a word.). M. Heidegger, *Unterwegs zur Sprache,* p. 266. One should, by the way, pay attention to the intentional play on words in the German text: *gehörend* (belonging to) and *auf sie*

a different light the Vedic sayings of *pāramārthika* level relating to the identity of *ātman* and Brahman—sayings that are notoriously abounding in metaphors and parables. They were never meant to define the subject but rather to describe it, barely touching upon the topic, which was inevitably slipping away from the most diligent listener. A hermeneutical interpretation of language—primarily the language of *śruti*—has direct analogies with the teaching of the grammarian Bhartṛhari, as well as, in its own way, with that of the Mīmāṃsaka Kumārila. A comparison of Śaṅkara's views on sacred scripture with those of the Mīmāṃsakas will be made in the last chapter.

So the hierarchy of *pramāṇas* in Advaita is composed with due consideration of the dominant position of sacred scripture. From this angle Śaṅkara criticizes the opinion of the Lokāyatikas, who would not allow for the existence of any means of valid knowledge other than immediate perception. In Śaṅkara's words, "a person who is speaking about Brahman investigates the essence of the cause /of the world/ and the rest, basing himself on sacred scripture,

---

hört (listens to her, that is to Speech). Lately, several works have appeared dealing with Śaṅkara's Advaita-Vedanta and Heidegger's philosophy. This problem was extensively dealt with in the article by J. Mehta ("Heidegger and Vedanta: Reflections on a Questionable Theme," *International Philosophical Quarterly*, New York, 1978, vol. 18, no. 2). One might agree with the author that both these thinkers, each in his own way, were 'completing' entire epochs of particular philosophical traditions. In my opinion, the observations of J. Mehta on the notion of 'Being' in systems of Heidegger and Śaṅkara are rather interesting. However, he absolutely overlooks another essential aspect, rather important for both teachings—that of the philosophy of language, of the ontological role of language in the creation and self-revelation of the world. The same bias is characteristic of a recent publication by John Grimes (J. A. Grimes, *Quest for Certainty: A Comparative Study of Heidegger and Saṅkara,* New York, 1989), which otherwise gives a detailed account of some ontological problems in Heidegger's *Sein und Zeit* and Śaṅkara's Advaitic works. (The only shortcoming is that the author made use only of the English translation, while for Heidegger, as I have tried to show, the nuances of his language are important in themselves.)

and so he does not have to accept everything according to perception, while the opponent, who ... bases himself solely on the examples of perception, must accept everything according to experience; and here is the advantage of the former."[37] One must admit that the Lokāyatikas' standpoint was really extremely vulnerable in this respect, since, having refused to accept any criterion of true knowledge and existence other than *pratyakṣa,* they were forced to accept *all* perceptions (including illusions and dreams) as equally valid and equally significant. It goes without saying that this distinction was surely in practice, but the opponents of the materialists readily seized the opportunity to use this gnoseological oversight in their polemics. For instance, Vācaspatimiśra in his Commentary on *Sāṃkhyakārikā* notes that for a Lokāyatika, who denies inference and the evidence of authority, there is no *pramāṇa* which could help him to realize whether one or another observer is mistaken.[38]

Since we are examining here not only the concrete polemics but also the *opposition* between systems, we might touch in brief upon a 'theory of the distinction of errors' *(vibhrama-viveka)* in Advaita. Except Lokāyata, all the other philosophical schools in India were discussing the problem of valid knowledge. First of all, one might investigate—but now from a gnoseological angle—the Advaita concept of the levels of reality and cognition. Indeed, besides the level of ultimate truth *(pāramārthika)* and that of phenomenal practice *(vyāvahārika),* entirely depending on the higher Brahman, Advaita distinguishes also the level of appearance *(prātibhāsika).* The latter

37. Śaṅkara, Commentary on *Brahmasūtra,* II.2.38: *apica āgamabalena brahmavādī kāraṇādi svarūpaṃ nirūpayatīti nāvaśyaṃ tasya yathādṛṣṭam eva sarvamabhyupagantavyam iti niyamo 'sti / parasya tu dṛṣṭāntabalena . . . yathādṛṣṭam eva sarvamabhyupagantavyam ityamastyatiśayaḥ /.*

38. One might find this passage in his Commentary on the 5th *kārikā.* Vide also: G. Tucci, *Linee di una storia del materialismo indiano,* p. 95.

level incorporates manifold mistakes and errors of perception, which can be 'removed' as unreal even within the limits of this world. Actually, the level of *prātibhāsika* is just as unreal in comparison with ordinary practice and cognitional activity, as this latter level is unreal and illusory in comparison with the higher reality. Parenthetically, one might note that exactly because of that the illusions of perception (a shell as silver, a rope as a snake) constitute quite apt metaphors in the course of examining the levels of *vyāvahārika* and *pāramārthika.* And it is on account of the close connection between Advaita gnoseology and its ontological foundations that the 'distinction of errors' is represented there not in a psychological sense, but rather in a logical and a methodological one. Indeed, both parts of the equation (namely, the shell and the silver) depend upon recollections[39] and so even the practically acceptable version ('this is a shell') cannot be actually defined as real *(sat).* Therefore, the most one can say about the level of phenomenal practice is that it is can be determined neither as real nor as unreal *(sadasadanirvacanīya),* while the level of *prātibhāsika,* coinciding with the former in its ontological status, is detrimental only from the standpoint of practical convenience.

In the sūtra wholly devoted to the refutation of the Lokāyatikas' views (Commentary on *Brahmasūtra,* III.3.54), Śaṅkara specially dwells upon other gnoseological questions. He reminds the opponent that while some attributes of a living being (namely, external form, coloring, etc.) are accessible for sensuous perception, the others—for example, memory, reason and so on—cannot be perceived externally. And since the only criterion of valid knowledge in Lokāyata is *pratyakṣa,* one cannot entirely exclude the possibility that, even if one were to adhere to the basic notions of materialism, after the

39. As it is said in the preamble ot Śaṅkara's Commentary on *Brahmasūtra,* "The superimposition *(adhyāsa)* . . . is the manifestation later of something seen before, in the form of memory." *(adhyāsaḥ . . . smṛtirūpaḥ paratra pūrvadṛṣṭābhāsaḥ . . .).*

destruction of a concrete body the activity of cognition, inherent in it, could continue inside some other body. According to Śaṅkara, the possibility of such an inference testifies to the fact that the Lokāyatikas are unable to refute theoretically the notions of the orthodox tradition (as well as those of other heterodox systems) concerning *sāṃsāric* transmigrations. Still, from a formal standpoint, one has to admit that the reproach of the Advaitist is a bit unfair, since for the Lokāyatikas consciousness is considered to be an *attribute* of the body, and, according to Lokāyata, (incidentally, also according to Advaita itself) an attribute cannot exist separately from its bearer *(āśraya)*.

Referring to ordinary human experience, Śaṅkara distinguishes between the characteristics of the body and the attributes of consciousness. In his words, "consciousness may not be present while the body is still intact /say, immediately after death/.[40] Here Śaṅkara skillfully shows that the Lokāyatikas—even if one were to accept their initial tenets—cannot determine how a specific level of material, 'natural' organization might give rise to an attribute of consciousness. The materialists, to his mind, are unable to reveal the real nature of consciousness, since they would not accept any other primal principles besides the four elements, that are essentially inanimate *(jaḍa-bhūta)*. Finally, according to Śaṅkara, having originated from the elements and their compositions, consciousness could not immediately perceive them in any way. One of the main tenets of Śaṅkara in this respect runs as follows: "An action, oriented towards its own source, cannot be /thought about/without inner contradictions, since even hot fire cannot burn itself and even the most able actor cannot climb on his own shoulder."[41] This observation is

---

40. Śaṅkara, Commentary on *Brahmasūtra,* III.3.54: *vyatireka evāsya dehād bhavitumarhati tadbhāvābhavitvāt /.*

41. Śaṅkara, Commentary on *Brahmasūtra,* III.3.54: *tarhi . . . nataddharmatvamasnuvītasvātmani kriyāvirodhāt / nahyaghiruṣṇaḥ sansvātmānaṃ dahati /nahi naṭaḥ śikṣitaḥ sansvaskandham adhirokṣyati /.*

made in the *sūtra* quite incidentally, as a sort of a passing remark concerning Lokāyata, but it is not hard to notice how closely it is connected in its very essence with the Advaita notion of the foundation of consciousness, which cannot become its own object.

In spite of this significant digression of Śaṅkara, which found itself a place in the course of argumentation, one must admit that up to now this polemical opposing of the 'qualities of the body' to the 'attributes of consciousness' is in itself an indication that Śaṅkara's dispute is still carried on upon the level of *aparavidyā*. It is because of that reference is so often made here to ordinary experience, accepted by Lokāyata. Of course, if one were to regard the object of disagreement from the standpoint of the 'ultimate truth' of Advaita, it is quite clear that all manifold psychic attributes still remain characteristics 'connected with the body' *(deha-dharma)*,[42] that can never possibly relate to *ātman*.

In a *sūtra* directed against the materialists, a transition from the empirical level of discussion, where Śaṅkara was merely trying to expose the inner inconsistencies of their doctrine, to the ontological notions of Advaita, essentially opposed to materialism, is formally marked out by introducing the term *upalabdhi*. It is usually translated as 'perception', but it means not so much sensuous perception as a means of valid knowledge, but the very ability to cognize, to perceive, an ability identical with *ātman*. In Śaṅkara's words from this *sūtra*, "*ātman* is by nature the very essence of perception itself—thus is its nature established, which is different from the body; and *ātman* is eternal, since perception goes on eternally and the essence here is one and the same."[43] *Ātman*, entering as a living soul *(jīva)* all animated beings, is devoid of any attributes and therefore essentially self-identical. It can be only one

42. Vide : Śaṅkara, *Sarva-darśana-siddhānta-saṅgraha*, XII.44-47.

43. Śaṅkara, Commentary on *Brahmasūtra*, III.3.54: *upalabdhi-svarūpa eva ca na ātmetyātmano dehavyatiriktatvam/nityatvaṃ copalabdheḥ/ekarūpyāt.*

and the sole, since one can regard as manifold only its bodily reflections, which depend upon the limitations of *avidyā.* In other words, there is only one consciousness, which only appears divided due to nescience.

The role played by the body is explained in Advaita by its auxiliary functions, just like, for instance, the lighted lamp may assist perception but does not cause it. Morever, the assistance of the body is not even absolutely necessary: during its temporary inaction (for instance, during dreaming) various sensations might still arise.[44] Strictly speaking, here Śaṅkara is again slightly unfair towards Lokāyata: even according to Advaita, the state of dreaming *(svapna)* presupposes the activity of one of the body's instruments—*manas*—and this activity is considered to be based on former impressions.

A Buddhist philosopher Śāntarakṣita and his disciple and commentator Kamalaśīla further developed this latter argument against Lokāyata. They showed that after apparent interruptions, for example, after a deep sleep *(suṣupti)* or a swoon, the thread of consciousness is tied up again without any damage, though for the Lokāyatikas, taking into account the complete inaction of sense organs, such an interruption should be equivalent to death, while the resuming of the conscious activity would be identical to new birth.[45] However, according to the evidence of

---

44. Vide : Śaṅkara, Commentary on *Brahmasūtra,* III.3.54.

45. Śāntarakṣita, *Tattva-saṅgraha,* 1929:
If/the existence/of consciousness is not recognized
during dreams, bewilderment and similar states,
Then/they/should be death; and if one/recognizes/
the emergence/of consciousness again after them/,
death should not exist at all.
svapnamūrchādyavasthāsu cittaṃ ca yadi neṣyate /
*mṛtiḥ syāttatra cotpattau maraṇābhāva eva vā //*1929//
Tattva-saṅgraha by Śāntarakṣita, with Kamalaśīla's *Pañjikā,* Gaekwad's Oriental Series, no. 30, Baroda, 1926.

Kamalaśīla's Commentary on this *kārikā* runs as follows : "And if/the opponents would say :/ 'if it happened that consciousness completely left the body, it is assumed that consciousness originates again/when a person awakens/',then/we will add:/when/consciousness/is assumed to

ordinary experience, the unity of personal consciousness is not disrupted. For Śaṅkara, in the deep sleep *(suṣupti)* a soul for a period of time comes back to a peculiar state, in some respects rather close to unity with Brahman; but after awakening that person still remains the same, preserving former recollections and being guided by *śruti* injunctions.[46] The ultimate cessation of all former kinds of psychic activity (and not only in this embodiment, but also in the entire chain of transmigrations) is possible only after the attainment of higher knowledge *(vidyā)*. This notion of the unity of consciousness Advaita opposed to the Lokāyata notion which reduced consciousness to a mechanical conglomerate of sense organ functions.

In conclusion I would like to touch upon a point which Śaṅkara did not examine in any detail. Denying any criteria of real existence except *pratyakṣa,* the materialists naturally could not accept the existence of *adṛṣṭa* (lit.: unseen, imperceptible), which concept plays an important part in religious and philosophical systems. *Adṛṣṭa* is a kind of a residuum of former intentions and actions, that as an organizing principle immediately influences the destiny of a living being in subsequent embodiments. It was the denial of *adṛṣṭa* that led the Lokāyatikas to the conviction of the absurdity of any belief in *karma* and Īśvara, as well as to the conclusion that any sins or merits are virtually nonexistent. According to Śaṅkara's exposition, Lokāyata came to consistent hedonism and to complete denial of any moral obligations:

---

originate in this way, it means that death does not exist at all, since the unjustified conclusion would follow that the awakening is similar to the new beginning of consciousness in a dead man—and also since only inner self-consciousness is capable of immediately continuing in another embodiment."

Atha tatra tathābhūte nirmūlamapagatavijñāne dehe punarutpattiriṣyate vijñānasya tadā tatrotpattaviśyamānayam maraṇābhāvaḥ prāpnoti; mṛtasyāpi punarvijñānotpattiprasaṅgāt suptaprabuddhavat manobuddhereva janmāntarapratisandhane samārthyāt/.

46. Vide: Śaṅkara, Commentary on *Brahmasūtra,* III.2.9.

And how could something become real that was never
perceived,
like the horns of a hare?
That is why other /schools/ should not regard/as the
cause/
of happiness and unhappiness some
righteous or sinful/actions/.
But according to his own nature is a man happy or
unhappy,
and there is no other reason for that.[47]

Indeed, Śaṅkara has enough arguments that could be opposed to these tenets from the standpoint of traditional ethical and religious notions. He says: "If /as it is argued by the Lokāyatikas/there were no *ātman,* different from the body, any *śāstra* injunctions concerning the fruits/ of actions, that are reaped/ in the other world, would not be compulsory for anyone."[48] But in this *sūtra* of the Commentary it is the only remark that touches upon the ethical position of Lokāyata; and the plausibility of such an argument cannot even be compared with his detailed polemics about the ontological and epistemological foundations of rival systems.

2. *ADVAITA AND JAINISM*

In Śaṅkara's compendium, whose chapters are linked together by key problems—so that the exposition of a subsequent system is opened by the refutation of a former one—the third chapter starts with the critique of Lokāyata by Jaina philosophers. The pretext for the polemics is

47. Śaṅkara, *Sarva-darśana-siddhānta-saṅgraha,* II.3-4:
nityādṛṣṭaṃ kathaṃ satsyāt śaśaśṛṅgādibhissamam //3//
na kalpyau sukhaduḥkhabhyāṃ dharmādharmau parairiha /
svabhāvena sukhī duḥkhī jano 'nyannaiva kāraṇam //4//.

48. Śaṅkara, Commentary on *Brahmasūtra,* III.3.53: *nahyasati dehavyatiriktātmani paralokaphalāścodanā upapadyerankasya . . . /.*

provided by the previously mentioned problem of *adṛṣṭa*. Of course, *adṛṣṭa* plays an important part in the while structure of the universe, presented by Jainism, since the Jainas, though adhering to the heterodox current, still shared many traditional religious and philosophical tenets. In Śaṅkara's words, the Jainas realize that happiness and unhappiness cannot represent the nature *(svabhāva)* of *ātman,* since these attributes are transient; they are only signs that serve as indication of this 'unseen' force *(adṛṣṭa),* determining the destiny of a human being in accordance with his former actions (vide: *Sarva-darśana-siddhānta-saṅgraha,* III. 3). The Jainas acknowledged the general notion of a moral order, manifesting itself through the world structure. Unlike the Lokāyatikas, the followers of Jainism consider *ātman* to be distinct from the body, subject to transmigrations and capable of attaining ultimate liberation. All these notions, which cannot be substantiated by sense perceptions, are introduced into the system through reference to sacred texts, as well as through logic argumentation:

> Owing to perception, inference and sacred scripture,
> People who adhere to Jaina scripture clearly see both
> seen and unseen.[49]

Though in his works Śaṅkara does not touch upon the role of *pramāṇas* in Jainism, one might note here that these *pramāṇas* are not equally valid. In a certain respect Jainism is closer to Lokāyata than any other system, since, according to the Jainas, it is *pratyakṣa* that gives one the most clear and precise *(spaṣṭa, viṣada)* knowledge, that is, the most sound one. Other *pramāṇas*—recollection *(smṛti),* recognition *(pratyabhijñā),* induction *(tarka),* inference *(anumāna)* and evidence of scripture *(śruti, āgama)*—are considered to be indirect (literally, beyond

---

49. Śaṅkara, *Sarva-darśana-siddhānta-saṅgraha,* III.6 : *pratyakṣenānumānena paśyantyatrāgamena ca / dṛṣṭādṛṣṭam janāḥ spaṣṭamārhatāgamasaṃsthitāḥ //6//.*

the range of sight, *parokṣa*), because they function only through the use either of the 'middle term' (like inference), or of word combinations (like the evidence of authority), or else of memory impressions (like recollection). Therefore all these means of valid knowledge occupy a subsidiary place in relation to *pratyakṣa*,[50] the higher kind of which, however, is represented by the immediate intuitive cognition of Jaina saints, or *ārhatas*.

The system of the Jainas singles out several categories *(padārtha)*,[51] but the most important among them are only two: *jīva* (soul) and *ajīva* (inanimate object), since all the rest define the relations between these two classes and, according to Śaṅkara's interpretation, are ultimately dependent upon them.[52] The very existence of a cognizant soul is perceived directly through introspection.

All the *jīvas* are divided into liberated ones (lit.: perfect, accomplished ones; *siddha*); bound by *saṃsāra (baddha)*; and so-called hellish ones *(nārakīya)*.[53] Bound souls occupy a specific place inside the hierarchy of living beings according to the number of their sense organs, starting with plants, which have only the sense of touch, and winding up with human beings, demons and gods, who have at their disposal, besides five sense organs, also a sense integrator—*manas*. By their nature all souls are eternal and omniscient, and their size is determined by

---

50. Vide: Haribhadra, *Ṣaḍdarśanasamuccaya*, p. 85:
Immediate perception of an object directly—
only this is *pratyakṣa*,
All other /cognition/ is beyond the range of sight, when
one means grasping.
aparokṣatayā 'rthasya grāhakaṃ jñānamīdṛśam /
pratyakṣamitarajjñeyaṃ parokṣaṃ grahaṇekṣayā //.

51. They are: *jīva, ajīva, āsrava, nirjarā, saṃvara, bandha, mokṣa.*

52. Vide: Commentary on *Brahmasūtra*, II.2.33: *saṃkṣepastu dvāveva padārthau jīvājīvākhyau /.*

53. Vide: Śaṅkara, *Sarva-darśana-siddhānta-saṅgraha*, III.7.

the body. A soul is soiled by a kind of a fine matter *(karma)* that accrues to it in accordance with actions; the sources or means through which *karma* gets into the soul are called *āsrava*; the control over *karmas*, hindering their mixing with souls, is *saṃvara*, while the purification of the souls from *karma*, that is, the destruction of soiling, is *nirjarā*, which can lead directly to liberation *(mokṣa)*.[54]

The echoes of active polemics with Vedanta are easily discerned in Jaina works, starting with the 7th century AD. Samantabhadra, one of the prominent philosophers of the Digambara school in his work *Āptamīmāṃsā* (Deliberation on the attained)[55] criticized even the teaching of Advaita, probably implying, among others, the direct predecessors of Śaṅkara. Starting from the 10th century, Śaṅkara's Advaita was considered by the Jainas to be the only school of Vedanta worthy of their attention.

Serious contradictions separated the Jaina teaching from Buddhism. Śāntarakṣita and Kamalaśīla accused Jainism of being inconsistent and illogical (vide: *Tattvasaṅgraha*, 317-318). The Buddhists opposed the Jaina notion of reality, where one could find a combination of the constancy of substance with the manifoldness of its various states. In Śāntarakṣita's words,

That is why one has to accept /one of two possibilities/—

---

54. Vide: Śaṅkara, Commentary on *Brahmasūtra*, II.2.33; Haribhadra, *Ṣaḍdarśanasamuccaya*, pp. 79-84.

55. As one can see in this work (which is also known under the name *Devāgama-stotra*, or praise of God's scripture) about Advaita (*Śloka* 26)

There would not be any difference in actions, any
difference in the fruits/of actions/or in
the/existing/worlds;
It would be impossible/to find/any difference
between knowledge and nescience, as well as
any difference between the bonds /of *saṃsāra*/ liberation.

karmadvaitaṃ phaladvaitaṃ lokadvaitaṃ ca na bhavet /
vidyāvidyādvaitaṃ na syāt bandhamokṣadvaitaṃ tathā //.

Vide: Hajime Nakamura, *The Vedanta As Noticed in Mediaeval Jain Literature*, p. 187.

either that everything can be destroyed,
or that everything is eternal,
Since inclusion and exclusion cannot exist /simultaneously/ in one and the same entity.[56]

The reproach here is more or less justified. In the Buddhists' opinion, any consistent and well-founded philosophical system is confronted with an alternative: it must either accept the Buddhist view, according to which there is no immutable substance *(dravya),* since it is changing all the time together with its qualities or disappearing states *(paryaya);* or agree with the Advaitists that the eternal self-identical substance is not affected by the illusory evolution of its attributes.

From the standpoint of the opponents, the Jainas performed something of 'unlawful' operation: being dissatisfied both with the picture of the world reduced to a conglomerate of vanishing qualities, and with the image of an illusory universe, where the attributes are only temporarily superimposed upon some real foundation, they decided to combine the two attitudes. In the words of S. Dasgupta, "the solution of Jainism is thus a reconciliation of the two extremes of Vedantism and Buddhism on grounds of common-sense experience.[57]

Trying to bring together the notion of the stability of the world with that of its changeability, the Jainas formulated a concept of relativity (lit.: uncertainty, indefiniteness; *anekāntatva*) of everything existing. In their opinion, all definitions of reality are true from some particular point of view *(naya)* and in some specific sense. Therefore, argue the Jainas, any statement about reality should include a necessary addition, or, to be more precise, a modal expression—the word *syād*; that is, maybe, possibly. According to Śaṅkara's exposition, the Jainas apply to all their catego-

---

56. Śāntarakṣita, *Tattva-saṅgraha,* 321:
tato niranvayo dhvaṃsaḥ sthiraṃ vā sarvamiṣyatām /
ekātmani tu naiva sto vyāvṛttyanugamāvimau //321// .

57. S. Dasgupta, *A History of Indian Philosophy,* vol. 1, p. 175.

ries "the logics of the so-called seven parts /with respect to the expressions/: 'perhaps, it is not , perhaps, it is and is not, perhaps, it is/under certain circumstances'/, 'perhaps, it cannot be expressed in words', 'perhaps, it is and is not expressible', 'perhaps, it is not and is not expressible', 'perhaps, it is and it is not and is not expressible.' "[58]

In this way the Jainas flatter themselves on making use of—and exhausting—all possible judgements on reality, suggested by other systems. The Jainas maintained that every philosophical school had succeeded in grasping some important aspect of the existing universe; any system, to their mind, was true in a certain respect, but the most widely spread defect of these systems consisted in subsequent absolutization of this grain of true knowledge. Overcoming this inevitable one-sidedness of limited standpoints characteristic of the opponents, the Jainist philosophers believe in the feasibility of combining different notions of reality. In the words of a present-day scholar who sympathizes with Jainism, the all-embracing view of existence contributes towards correction of inevitable one-sidedness, and this view should be grounded in concrete experience, which harmoniously combines the notions of being and becoming, identity and difference, whole and particular.[59] Other scholars are also eager to acclaim the 'dialectical foresight' of the Jainas, who allegedly were inspired by the intuitive realization of the 'infinite complexity' of being.

To my mind, though, what is important here is the fact that in the eyes of the opponents—and primarily in the eyes of the Advaitins—the Jainas tried to conduct an exhaustive investigation within the framework of formal logic, organizing the data of sense perception. From this

58. Śaṅkara, Commentary on *Brahmasūtra,* II.2.33: *sarvatra cemaṃ sapta-bhaṅgīnayaṃ nāma nyāyamavatārayanti / syādasti syānnasti syādasti ca nāsti ca syādavaktavyaḥ syādasti cāvaktavyaśca syānnāsti cāvaktavyaśca syādasti ca nāsti cāvaktavyaśceti /.*

59. Vide: Y.J. Padmarajiah, *Jaina Theories of Reality and Knowledge,* Bombay, 1963, p. 58 f.

standpoint the famous 'relativity doctrine' *(syād-vāda)* of Jainism demonstrated rather an eclectic combination of mutually contradicting attributes ascribed to the objects. And though this type of approach proved to be fruitful for specifically logical constructions, in the sphere of ontology it did not allow the Jainas to transcend the simple determination of contradictions that were revealed in immediate perception. In the opinion of Hajime Nakamura, while examining the polemics between Vedanta and Jainism, one should take full account of the importance of the opposition between Advaita (which ultimately aimed at surpassing the bonds of formal logic) and Jainism (which tried to theorize within its rules).[60] One might remember that both teachings quite willingly use purely logical methods. The most impressive example is probably the use of 'reductio ad absurdum' through the introduction of *prasaṅga* or *atiprasaṅga,* that is, an unlawful or unjustified conclusion. But for Śaṅkara this kind of reasoning represents only a preliminary stage of actual polemics.

The main argument of the Jainas, according to Śaṅkara's exposition, runs as follows: "When during the /investigation/ of some object there emerges a definite knowledge that it is of a heterogeneous nature *(anekātmaka),* this knowledge cannot be just /slightingly/ rejected as a mere doubt."[61] In the words of N. Tatia, "the follower of Jainism as if demands the Vedantin to take another step and accept every experience as real, and criticises him for an a priori acceptance of the dictate of abstraction in his interpretations ... of experience".[62] So argues the scholar, who is obviously biased towards Jainism: when unity and

60. Hajime Nakamura, *The Vedanta As Noticed in Mediaeval Jain Literature,* p. 190 ff.

61. Śaṅkara, Commentary on *Brahmasūtra,* II.2.33 : *nanvanekātmakaṃ vastviti nirdhāritarūpam eva jñānamutpadyamānaṃ saṃśayajñānavannpramāṇaṃ bhavitumarhati*/.

62. Nathmal Tatia, *Studies in Jaina Philosophy,* Banaras, 1951, p. 175.

manifoldness are perceived at the same time, when identity and difference are equally justified by experience, both these aspects should be regarded as essentially true.

But these Jaina tenets are vehemently opposed by the Advaitist. Śaṅkara notes that the acceptance of this attitude leads to a situation in which the very knowledge of the Jainas becomes indefinite and unreliable. No statement may be regarded as authoritative if the means of valid knowledge, its objects, the cognizing subject, as well as the results of cognition, are considered devoid of definite characteristics. Moreover, since the categories introduced by the Jainas find specific verbal expression in their system, and their authors are not ready to resign themselves to an arbitrary interpretations of these tenets, the categories cannot ever become indefinite.[63] An indefinite statement cannot be placed in the foundation of ordinary human practice; and even injunctions concerning appropriate or inappropriate actions and the possibility of attaining ultimate liberation from *saṃsāra* inevitably lose their authoritativeness and incontestability if these injunctions are self-contradictory. "If in this teaching," argues Śaṅkara, "heaven and liberation /simultaneously/ exist and do not exist, are eternal and non-eternal, then, owing to this indefiniteness, the action/aimed at their attainment/ would also be impossible."[64] Finally, the Advaitist notes that one should not arbitrarily combine such opposing attributes *(viruddhadharma),* as reality and non-reality *(sadasttva)* in one and the same bearer *(dharmin).*[65]

---

63. Śaṅkara, Commentary on *Brahmasūtra,* II.2.33: *naiṣaṃ padārthānanı avaktavyatvaṃ saṃbhavati /.*

64. Ibid., II.2.33: *svargāpavargayośca pakṣe bhāvaḥ pakṣe cābhāvaḥ tathā pakṣe nityatā pakṣe cānityatā ityanavadhāraṇāyāṃ pravṛttyanupapattiḥ /.*

65. Vide: Bādarāyaṇa's *sūtra* (II.2.33): *ekasminnasaṃbhavāt* (Because of the impossibility in one), and its interpretation by Śaṅkara: *nahyekasmindharmini yugapatsadasattvādiviruddhadharmasamāveśaḥ saṃbhavati śītoṣṇavat /.* (Because of the impossibility of simul-

Indeed, on the level of phenomenal existence, where there prevails the relation of substance and its attributes *(dharma-dharmin-bhāva),* Advaita unswervingly follows the rule of *tertium non datur.* But even here it is not as simple as it looks at first sight. One might remember that in another part of the *Brahmasūtra* Commentary, where Śaṅkara's argumentation is not submitted to the tasks of concrete polemics with an opponent, we find a completely different remark. In the Advaitist's words, "consciousness is the very nature of this /soul/—just like light and heat are /the very nature/ of fire, since there is no separation into an attribute and its bearer.[66] Besides that, it is fairly well-known that Śaṅkara himself, referring to the Upaniṣadic texts, often gave different—even mutually contradictory—definitions of *ātman*, Brahman, the nature of *avidyā.* Does this necessarily mean that his approach to higher entities is essentially similar to the Jainas' relativism? Certainly not. The core of Advaita teaching is the concept that *ātman* is devoid of any attributes, but Advaita opposes Jainism primarily because it managed to organize all contradicting attributes (essentially *unavoidable* in the statement relating to *ātman*) in a strictly hierarchical sequence. The lower layer of this sequence is represented by the sayings of *śruti,* related to profane knowledge.

Already Bādarāyaṇa himself showed that there were different kinds of *śruti* texts: those relating to the higher Brahman, and others, oriented towards ritual injunctions or towards meditation on other, lower levels of reality. Lower *śruti* sayings, according to Bādarāyaṇa, should be understood either from the context *(prakaraṇāc-ca, sūtra*

---

taneous existence of such opposing attributes as reality and non-reality and so on in one and the same bearer, just as cold and heat /cannot exist together/.) This view point of Śaṅkara remains unchanged during the whole of his dispute with the Jainas.

66. Śaṅkara, Commentary on *Brahmasūtra,* II.3.29: *caitanyameva hyasya svarūpam agnerivauṣṇyaprakāśau /nātra guṇaguṇivi bhāgo vidyata iti/.*

I.2.10) or in connection with other sayings/or the Upaniṣads/ (*vākyānvayāt, sūtra* I.4.19). This concept was further developed by Śaṅkara, who distinguished two tiers of reality and, respectively, two kinds of *śruti* sayings.

Advaita was conceived as an accomplishment of the Upaniṣadic teaching, as its clarification and non-contradictory interpretation; Śaṅkara considered it quite possible to reconcile all sayings of sacred scripture. Hence all the pathos of Śaṅkara's exposition when he comments, for instance, on the fourth *sūtra* (first *adhyāya,* 1st *pāda*) of Bādarāyaṇa's work; he singles it out as a separate *adhikaraṇa* on the concert, harmony, coordination *(samanvaya)* of all *śruti* aphorisms. The sayings that are difficult to coordinate with the main concepts of Advaita are regarded by Śaṅkara as *anuvāda,* or sayings adding to, or pariphrasing something that had been previously explained in another context. These sayings should not be comprehended in a direct, literal *(mukhya)* sense; they occupy a lower, subordinate position, but still serve as metaphorical *(aupacārika)* approaches to their objects. "The subsequent part of the text," says Śaṅkara in the beginning of his Commentary on *Brahmasūtra,* "is exposed in order to show that, though Brahman is one and alone, the Upaniṣads teach about it being the aim of meditation and knowledge, either with the help of its connection with limitations—or without this connection."[67] The limitations (lit.: ingoing limitations; *upādhi*) here are the grains or specific combinations produced by *avidyā,* that hinder—but also determine and specify for the first time—the cognition directed towards Brahman.

According to the Advaitist, the contradiction of *śruti* texts, dealing with the definition of *ātman* (and Brahman), is only apparent. *The whole corpus of Vedic sayings*

---

67. Śaṅkara, Commentary on *Brahmasūtra,* I.1.11: *evamekamapi brahmāpekṣitopādhi saṃbandhaṃ nirastopādhisaṃbandhaṃ copāsyatvena jñeyatvena ca vadānteṣūpadiśyata iti pradarśayituṃ paro grantha ārabhyate* /.

can be divided into two main groups: the vyāvahārika and the pāramārthika ones. Their appropriateness depends on the previous instruction received by the adepts. It goes without saying that in the absolute sense no word can be related to *ātman,* but still the Advaitist ascertains that "texts teaching /about Brahman/ as devoid of any definitions cannot be surpassed by other ones",[68] that is, by texts teaching about it as having attributes *(saguṇa).* And should a doubt arise as to which level of knowledge is to be ascribed a particular *śruti* saying, "this question must be resolved by taking into account the context of the exposition."[69] Śaṅkara points out that *śruti* aphorisms of the lower *(vyāvahārika)* level have a corroborative *(anuvāda)* or metaphorical *(aupacārika)* meaning; they usually deal with the creation of the world; the perfections of Īśvara, or Saguṇa-Brahman, the attributes of the soul, its activity, size, etc.

Śaṅkara's attitude towards the two groups of sacred texts is clearly outlined in his polemics with the Jainas about the problem of the size of the soul *(jīva).*

The opponents' belief in the limited size of *jīva* Śaṅkara classifies as the second (after relativism) defect *(doṣa)* of their system. The Jainas maintained that *jīva* has the size of the body *(śarīra-parimāṇa),* completely fills this body and illuminates it from within like a lamp. Yet Śaṅkara shows that, owing to this dependence upon the body, the soul, which changes with every incarnation, cannot be omniscient and omnipresent by its very nature. And that means, he adds, that this soul cannot be regarded as eternal *(nitya),* since, according to the teaching of the Vedas, any entity that is subject to change, is essentially non-eternal (vide: Commentary on *Brahmasūtra,* II.2.34).

---

68. Śaṅkara, Commentary on *Brahmasūtra,* IV.3.14: *ato na viśeṣanirāka-raṇaśrutīnām anyaśeṣatvamavagantuṃ śakyate* /.

69. Ibid., I.1.11 : *evamihāpyādityamaṇḍale hiraṅmayaḥ puruṣaḥ sarvapāpmodayaliṅgātpara eveti vakṣyati* /.

Finally, Śaṅkara notes, the Jainas could not provide any satisfactory explanation for the fact that in each new incarnation the soul is capable of occupying a new body, different in size from the former one. One might presume, says the Advaitist, that according to the Jainas' teaching, the soul has some parts *(aṃśa)* that can contract or expand, or that the number of these parts can change. In any case, he goes on, "one cannot escape contradictions owing to its being subject to changes."[70] And even if the soul is in itself changeable, contracting and expanding 'like a piece of leather' *(carmādivat),* it is still unclear where one should look for the source of its constant renewing; indeed, in the Jainas' opinion, in spite of its ability to occupy space,[71] the soul is 'immaterial' (lit.: devoid of elements; *abhautika*) and therefore cannot derive its substance from gross elements.[72]

According to the Jainas' teaching, notes the Advaitist, the 'perfect' or 'liberated' *(siddha)* state of the soul is essentially its eternal state, which is constant and does not undergo any change. But real eternity stretches both ways: if it provides a key to the true nature of the soul, that means that all other—embodied—states of the *jīva* must necessarily correspond to this inner nature. Therefore, in Śaṅkara's eyes, the Jainist notion of *jīva* is clearly inconsistent. In the second chapter of his Commentary on *Brahmasūtra,* in the parts specially devoted to the dispute with the Jainas, Śaṅkara pursues polemics mainly along the lines of *vitaṇḍa*—that is, he tries to argue from their

70. Bādarāyaṇa's *sūtra* here runs as follows (II.2.35): "And even if /one were to admit the changes/of the attributes, one cannot escape contradictions, owing to changeability and so on" *(naca paryāyādapyavirodho vikārādibhyaḥ l.)*

71. According to the Jaina system, the soul is one of the five 'extending' (lit., occupying place, *astikāya*) entities. The other four similar entities are *pudgala* (body as a combination of atoms), *dharma, adharma* and *ākāśa* (space). Vide: Śaṅkara, Commentary on *Brahmasūtra,* II.2.33.

72. Vide: Śaṅkara, Commentary on *Brahmasūtra,* II.2.35.

own tenets. Later, however, when he is not so rigidly bound by the conventions of the polemics, the Advaitist also draws attention to the Jainas' open hostility towards Upaniṣadic tradition. For instance, in the third chapter of the commentary Śaṅkara says: "And there should be rejected all the theories /concerning the embodied soul/ that proceed from human reason . . . and that contradict the views of the Upaniṣads . . ./namely, the doctrine of the Jainas, according to which/ the soul jumps from the body into another, just like a parrot jumps from one tree on to another."[73]

On the whole, the Jainas' erroneous assumptions concerning the nature of the soul are brought about, in Śaṅkara's opinion, by their general concept of the indefiniteness of all knowledge concerning reality. And Advaita, which is not alien to different interpretations of the nature of *ātman,* arrives at a uniform and consistent concept of a human soul owing to the construction of a hierarchy of sacred texts dealing with this subject.

Ātman, entering as an inner soul into every living being, is mentioned in the Upaniṣads either as atomic in size *(aṇu)*, or as endless and omnipresent (*vibhu, sarvagata*). The notion of *jīva's* atomic size, which corresponds to the *vyāvahārika* level, is brought about, in Śaṅkara's words, on the one hand, by the difficulty of cognizing *ātman* properly (so that it is subjectively perceived as an infinitely small and evasive limit of cognition); and on the other, by its combination with 'ingoing limitations' *(upādhi).* While the first aspect can be overlooked right now as a sort of poetic licence, the second one surely calls for more thorough deliberation.

And really, why is it that *jīva,* according to Advaita, though, of course, only from the standpoint of 'practical', empirical needs, is of 'atomic size'? The core of the matter

73. Śaṅkara, Commentary on *Brahmasūtra,* III.1.1: *yāḥ puruṣamati-prabhavāḥ kalpanā /ḥ . . . jīva eva votplutya dehāddehāntaraṃ prati-padyate śuka iva vṛkṣāt vṛkṣāntaram /ityevamādyāḥ tāḥ sarvā evānādar-tavyāḥ śrutivirodhāt /.*

is that Advaita (and Vedanta in general) patterned its concept of *jīva,* suitable for using on the profane plane of knowledge, upon the notion of the soul presented by Sāṃkhya. In this latter system the soul is formed by a temporary combination of *puruṣa* (pure spirit, Self, *ātman*) and *antaḥkaraṇa* (lit.: inner organ), produced by *prakṛti,* or, nature, primal matter. This *antaḥkaraṇa* consists of *buddhi* (intellect together with will, ability to make decisions), *ahaṅkāra* (ego, the perception of one's individuality) and *manas* (reason or understanding, integrating the sense data). We will discuss the difference between the analysis of consciousness of Sāṃkhya and that of Advaita more thoroughly in the fifth chapter of the present work. But now one can still note that the alleged 'atomic size' of *jīva* is a reflection of the corresponding size of *buddhi,* which constitutes the main component of *antaḥkaraṇa.* The parameters of *antaḥkaraṇa,* which are superimposed on *ātman,* form the limitations which temporarily determine the size and other attributes of the soul. In Śaṅkara's words, "only owing to the combination with *buddhi* one might assume that the soul is of /a specific/size.[74]

Meanwhile, according to *śruti* sayings of the *pāramārthika* level, even infiniteness and omnipresence cannot be regarded as *jīva's* essential attributes. "Though one and the same *ātman,*" says Śaṅkara, "is hidden within all beings ... the *śruti* texts thus describe that immutable and eternally uniform *ātman:* there is a gradation in the manifestation of its divine /qualities/and power /caused by/ the gradation of consciousness *(citta)* /belonging to the souls/that limit this *ātman.*"[75]

---

74. Vide: Śaṅkara, Commentary on *Brahmasūtra,* II.3.29: *tasmāttad-guṇa-sāratvādbuddhiparimāṇenāsya parimāṇavyapadeśaḥ* / One might remember, incidentally, that it is in the same *sūtra* that we can find a passage to the effect that the soul cannot be regarded as a substance, that is, from the standpoint of its division into attributes and their bearer.

75. Śaṅkara, Commentary on *Brahmasūtra,* I.1.11: *yadyapyeka ātmāsarva-bhūteṣu . . . gūḍhastathāpi cittopadhiviśeṣatāratamyādāt-*

So one can easily see that even the question about the size of the soul transcends the limits of some particular disagreements and, to a certain extent, outlines the core of principal divergence between the ontological tenets of Advaita and Jainism. It is not by chance that Śaṅkara likens the concept of the Jainas concerning the changeability of the soul to the Buddhist negation of immutable *ātman* (vide: Commentary on *Brahmasūtra*, II.2.35). Both these systems, proceeding from empirical tenets, rejected the concept of a supernatural ontological reality, essentially opposed to all other worldly entities. And because of their acceptance of heterogeneity and inner chageability of the universe, they could dispense with the notion of Īśvara, or God the creator—the usual object of worship according to orthodox religious tradtion.

---

manaḥ kuṭastha-nityasyaikarupasyāpyuttarottaramāviṣkṛtasya tāratamyamaiśvaryaśakti-viśeṣaiḥ śrūyate . . .

CHAPTER V

Brahman as Being: Cataphatic Theology and the Boldness of Heretics

1. *ŚAṄKARA'S POLEMICS WITH SARVĀSTIVĀDA*

Probably only now, based on concrete text material, one might at last substantiate the thesis proposed in the very beginning of the book. According to this thesis, the apparent similarity of some notions and conceptual schemes of Buddhism and Advaita does not signify the typological affinity of these two teachings; neither does it prove the conjecture about the decisive influence of the Buddhist heresy upon Śaṅkara's system, since the latter always remained purely orthodox in its most essential foundations.

I have already mentioned that adherence to the accepted rules of polemics did not allow Śaṅkara to refer directly to sacred scripture during his disputes with heterodox opponents. Nevertheless, as shown above, logical inference here is merely the means to lead the listener to the notions of Advaita that cannot be revealed without their inner support in *śruti* sayings. I will try to clarify the mechanism operating here, taking as an instance Śaṅkara's polemics with probably the most rationalistic and, so to speak, 'naturalistic' school of Buddhism, namely, Sarvāstivāda.

In his Commentary on *Brahmasūtra* Śaṅkara mentions the followers of three Buddhist schools of thought, that is, the adherents of Sarvāstivāda, those of Vijñānavāda and those of Śūnyavāda. Arranging the Buddhist schools in this sequence, Śaṅkara deliberately avoids the problem of a historical evolution of Buddhism; he is obviously interested neither in chronology nor in determining the names and specific arguments of his opponents. The Advaitist presents the three systems as three equally possible interpretations of the initial teaching of the Buddha. One should not, of course, overlook the fact that when three Buddhist doctrines are posited in this way as synchronous and equally justified, their inevitable collision was certainly to the advantage of the orthodox opponent. Incidentally, though, the discrepancy in the notions of the main Buddhist schools is explained by Śaṅkara on a purely psychological basis: either as a testimony to the Buddha's demonic enmity towards all living beings, whom he had been ardently wishing to lead astray to their eventual perishing[1]—or as a result of insufficient understanding of the Tathāgata's teaching even by his closest disciples, who had been transmitting it in accordance with their comprehension.[2] The compendium ascribed to Śaṅkara gives a short synopsis of the Buddhist teaching, starting with Śūnyavāda and somewhat arbitrarily dividing Sarvāstivāda into the Vaibhāṣika and Sautrāntika schools.

As shown by the Advaitist, the Buddhists are classified under different sects in accordance with their interpretation of reality: Some maintain that everything exists

---

1. Śaṅkara, Commentary on *Brahmasūtra,* II.2.32: "The Buddha exposed for the sake of instruction three mutually contradictory doctrines ... having manifested thus either his own incoherent garrulity or his enmity towards all living beings, having erroneously assumed that they would be confused."

(trayam itaretaraviruddhamupadiśatā sugatena spaṣṭīkṛtamātmano 'sambaddhapralāpitvaṃ pradveśo vā prajāsu viruddhārthapratipattyā vimuhyeyur imāḥ prajā iti /.)

2. Śaṅkara, Commentary on *Brahmasūtra,* II.2.28: "Actually, having noticed the attraction of some disciples towards external objects and having taken it into account, /the Buddha/ proclaimed a teaching about /the existence/ of external objects. /But/ this is not the opinion of the Buddha /himself/." *(keṣāṃcitkila vineyānāṃ bāhye vastunyabhiniveśamālakṣya tadanurodhena bāhyārthavādaprakriyeyaṃ viracitā /nāsau sugatābhiprāyaḥ /.)*

(sarvo 'sti = sarvāstitva) hence the name /Sarvāstivāda /; others allow for the existence of consciousnes *(vijñāna)* alone; and there are some who claim everything to be void *(śūnya)*.[3] The general definition applied by Śaṅkara to all Buddhist schools is derived from the term *vināśa,* destruction, annihilation; it points out the core of the teaching, namely, the idea of the non-existence of *ātman* as a separate ontological reality. Therefore, Buddhism is determined by him as *vaināśika-mata,* which can be roughly rendered as a teaching about non-existence, destruction, or even a nihilistic teaching. The attitude of the Advaitist is further confirmed by the material of *Sarva-darśana-siddhānta-saṅgraha,* according to which:

> In all four Buddhist /schools/ there is agreement
> about inner consciousness,
> They disagree with each other about
> phenomenal existence.[4]

While going over Śaṅkara's arguments against the Buddhists, D. Ingalls compared his Commentary on *Brahmasūtra* with that of his younger contemporary, Bhāskara,[5] arriving at the conclusion that in all the passages where Bhāskara differed from Śaṅkara, the latter must have substantially deviated from the general Vedanta tradition. It is worth noting that the main lines of dispute against Sarvāstivāda teaching pursued by Śaṅkara (vide: Commentary on *Brahmasūtra,* II.2.18-27) practi-

3. Śaṅkara, Commentary on *Brahmasūtra,* II.2.18: *tatraite trayo vādino bhavanti kecit sarvāstivādinaḥ kecidvijñānastitvamātravādinaḥ anye punaḥ sarvaśūnyatvavādina iti* /.

4. Śaṅkara, *Sarva-darśana-siddhānta-saṅgraha*, IV.4.5: *caturṇamapi bauddhānāmaikyamdhyātmanirṇaya* / *vyāvahārikabhedena vivadante parasparam* //5//.

5. Vide: D.H.H. Ingalls, "Śaṅkara's Arguments against the Buddhists," *Philosophy East and West*, vol. 3, no. 4, January 1954, pp. 291-306.

cally coincide with those touched upon by Bhāskara—and therefore must have been derived from the same source.

Śaṅkara's attention is concentrated on the doctrine of 'dependent origination' *(pratītya-samutpāda),* that of 'momentariness' *(kṣaṇikavāda),* as well as the notion of 'uncomposite elements' *(asaṃskṛta-dharma).* Some of Śaṅkara's arguments against Sarvāstivāda, in particular, those concerning the notion of causality, apply to all other Buddhist schools.

As previously mentioned, 'everything exists' from the standpoint of Sarvāstivāda. The empirical world is regarded here as an aggregate *(samudāya, saṃhiti)* of elements. According to the Sarvāstivāda notion (as presented by Śaṅkara), these elements may be divided into two main classes: that of 'gross' elements and their derivations *(bhūta-bhautika)* and that of elementary mental states and their respective derivations *(citta-caitta).* The Sarvāstivāda teaching, though, is far from opposing them to each other: the phenomenal world, open to our perception is homogenous in the sense that all its constituents belong to one and the same plane of existence. Even when the Buddhists make use of the widely accepted notion of the so-called 'ultimate atoms' *(paramāṇu),* that allegedly join together to form the 'gross' elements *(bhūta),* they resort to it not for the sake of any naturalistic allusions but, rather, in order to find an opportunity to identify these minute particles with their corresponding qualities. In this way, for example, the atom of earth is regarded not as a substrate or bearer for the quality of solidity, smell, etc., but rather as a source of a particular sensation which arose from its contact with the organ of perception *(indriya);* in the ultimate sense it tends to be identified with this sensation (and hence with the quality as such). The Buddhists made a point of their denial of the existence of any permanent substance, that could form the substrate *(āśraya)* for transient and temporary attributes. Even the admission of ultimate atoms (the existence of which is surmised by inference, based on sense perception) was made mostly on moral grounds: by getting into the habit of regarding nature (including his own body) as a mere conglomerate of atoms, an adept gradually acquired an indifferent and detached attitude towards any natural phenomena.

According to the Buddhsit teaching, all simple phenomena are momentary *(kṣaṇika)* and so, on the other hand, the empirical world is to be regarded as infinitely heterogenous. Having existed just for an instant, discontinuous momentary objects give rise to corresponding perceptions; in the words of a Sautrānitika follower, cited in Śaṅkara's compendium. "Objectivity is verily an ability to be a cause."[6] Just as a forest is perceived as a whole only from a distance, but on approaching proves to be a conglomerate of different trees, any unity, which at first glance might seem undeniable—whether it is the uniformity of an external object or the unity of a consicous self—is in fact nothing but a conglomerate of momentary elements and mental states. According to Sarvāstivāda, all the elements are causally conditioned and can be classified under five groups *(skandha)*.[7] It should be borne in mind that the

---

6. Śaṅkara, *Sarva-darśana-siddhānta-saṅgraha,* IV.3.7:
... *viṣayatvaṃ hi hetutvaṃ* ... /.

7. There are five *skandhas.* The first *one is rūpa*, that is, form, shape. *Sarva-darśana-siddhānta-saṅgraha,* IV.4.12:

"*Rūpa skandha* is a combination of actual material elements".
(rūpaskandho bhavatyatra mūrtibhūtasya saṃhatiḥ /.)

The second is *vedanā,* sensation (of something pleasant, unpleasant or indifferent). The third is *saṃjñā,* image, idea; (six kinds of 'images' correspond to the five senses plus their integrator, or *manas*). The fourth is *saṃskāra,* an ability and readiness to accept the empirical world within the frames of definite mental constructions (*Sarva-darśana-siddhānta-saṅgraha,* IV.4.11:

"The combination of inner tendencies is called
the *skandha* of *saṃskāra*."
samskāraskandha ityukto vāsanānāntu saṃhatiḥ /.)

And the fifth is *vijñāna,* or self-consciousness (*Sarva-darśana-siddhānta-saṅgraha,* IV.4.10:

"The flow of the states of consciousness is called here
the *skandha* of *vijñāna.*"
jñānasantatirevātra vijñānaskandha ucyate /.)

skandhas do not have any separate ideal existence along with, or above, the empirical phenomena; they are essentially just conventional labels used for a more convenient classification of elements. In his Commentary on *Brahmasūtra* Śaṅkara exposes the Sarvāstivāda teaching in the following way: "Having come together, these *skandhas* form an inner consciousness *(adhyātma)* which is the source of all phenomenal practice."[8]

A starting point for Śaṅkara's polemics with Sarvāstivāda is provided by the Buddhist notion concerning the emergence of combinations *(samudāya).* In the Advaitist's opinion, such a combination cannot be accomplished without the purposeful activity of a conscious agent. Śaṅkara reminds the opponent that any spontaneous activity of unconscious elements, joining together of their own accord irrespective of the intentions of the agent, should be considered endless, since such an activity would constitute an indispensable attribute of the elements themselves.[9] However, this assumption would inevitably contradict the basic religious tenets of Indian tradition (including its heterodox versions) where ultimate liberaion is regarded as a complete cessation of activity.[10]

In this passage, as well as in many of the same kind, it leaps to the eye that Śaṅkara is inconspicuously trying to shift the center of discussion from the plane of psychology and epistemology to that of ontological problems. Indeed, from the Buddhists' point of view, any combination of elements was only an imaginary entity, resulting from a

---

8. Śaṅkara, Commentary on *Brahmasūtra,* II.2.18: *te 'pyadhyātmaṃ sarvavyavahārāspadabhāvena saṃhanyanta iti manyante* /.

9. Śaṅkara, Commentary on *Brahmasūtra,* II.2.18: "And because an assumption of independent activity would lead to /the conclusion/ about ceaseless /uninterrupted/activity" *(... nirapekṣapravṛttyabhyupagame ca pravṛttyanuparamaprasaṅgāt .)*

10. One might note, incidentally, that a similar chain of reasoning was often used in the Vedanta tradition against the notions of Sāṃkhya and early Vaiśeṣika.

mental construction *(kalpanā)*. In the words of a Vaibhāṣika adherent, referred to in *Sarva-darśana-siddhānta-saṅgraha,*

> A fivefold division in the form of action, substance, quality, kind and name
> Is a mental construction, that is, an illusory *(bhrānta)* vision; it is the very nature of body /phenomenon/.[11]

In the Buddhists' opinion, discontinuous elements are ever alternately flashing into existence, stamping their impressions upon the corresponding sense organs *(indriyas)* and evoking various visual, oral, tactile and other sensations. Though in his Commentary on *Brahmasūtra* Śaṅkara does not draw any distinction between the Vaibhāṣika and the Sautrāntika schools, one might note that the Vaibhāṣikas were in favor of the notion of some actual foundation for the perceptible elements. This foundation was supposed to move through 'three times' *(trikāla)*, namely, the past, the present and the future, but to reveal itself to perception for a mere moment. According to the Sautrāntikas, only momentary elements could be considered as essentially real. Anyway, from the Buddhist standpoint, the past could be considered real, certainly not because it somehow continued to exist in the present in a transformed, modified way, but because it constituted a *cause* for the present, because it was *significant* for the present.

According to Sarvāstivāda, the essence of the elements which form 'external objects' *(bāhyārtha)* is in their effectivity, that is, in their ability to arouse corresponding perceptions. In a particular sense, all empirical phenomena are to be regarded as causes *(hetu)* for other phenomena. The Buddhist term for 'perception' (*grahaṇa*, lit.:

---

11. Śaṅkara, *Sarva-darśana-siddhānta-saṅgraha,* IV.4.17:
nāmajātiguṇadravyakriyārūpeṇa pañcadhā /
kalpitaṃ bhrāntadṛṣṭyaiva śarīrabhavanātmakam //17// .

grasping) is traditional enough, though the meaning implied here is rather that of a superimposition or a contact between a perceived entity *(grāhya),* or an object, a corresponding organ or instrument of perception *(grāhaka)* and a resulting sensation or specific mental state.

According to Śaṅkara, the greatest defect of this Buddhist doctrine lies in its persistent denial of any permanent subject: "And even if the whole were possible as an object of enjoyment /or perception/, all the same, in accordance with your assumption there would not be any soul as a permanent enjoyer /or perceiver/."[12] Indeed, a distinctive feature of Buddhism is its denial of the traditionally accepted division of consciousness between the eternal *ātman* and the so-called 'inner organ' *(antaḥkaraṇa)* which plays the part of a natural, 'body' instrument of perception. In the Vaibhāṣikas' opinion, consciousness is concentrated in *manas* which is regarded simply as a sixth sense organ, coordinating the functioning of the other five *indriyas. Manas* is assumed to be a kind of a perpetual flow, a flux *(saṃtāna),* consisting of momentary and causally conditioned states of consciousness *(citta, vijñāna)* in relation to which all other phenomena (whether physical or mental) are just objects *(viṣaya).* It perceives external objects through the mediation of unconscious instruments *(indriyas).* In a sense, it actually animates perceptive operations, accompanying them as a kind of a dim self-consciousness *(sva-saṃvedanā).* Besides, it has its own specific object—mental states and operations *(buddhi, saṃjñā).* In the words of *Sarva-darśana-siddhānta-saṅgraha,*

> *Buddhi* is a composite consciousness,
> *manas* is an /elementary/instrument of perception.[13]

---

12. Śaṅkara, Commentary on *Brahmasūtra,* II.2.19: *api ca yadbhogārthaḥ saṃghātaḥ syāt sa jīvo nāsti sthiro bhokteti tavādhyupagamaḥ* /

13. Śaṅkara, *Sarva-darśana-siddhānta-saṅgraha,* IV.4.16: *samudāyikacaitanyaṃ buddhiḥ syāt karaṇaṃ manaḥ* /.

So in the Vaibhāṣika system, discontinuous and momentary *manas* assumes some of the functions of traditional *ātman.*[14] Besides that, it is used to bridge sense perception with a faculty of mental construction *(kalpanā)*. According to the notion of momentariness *(kṣaṇikavāda), manas* inevitably becomes different in each subsequent moment, being alternately identified with different mental states. That is why Śaṅkara draws attention to the fact that in Sarvāstivāda "enjoyment is only for the sake of enjoyment itself, without anyone striving for it. But then liberation must also exist only for the sake of liberation itself, and there will not be anyone aspiring to it."[15] This argument might be essentially interpreted in the following way: according to the Buddhist teaching, ultimate liberation is impossible as an ontological reality, indeed, as the only real entity above others; for the Buddhists there are only subsequent mental states, equally real and differing form each other only in their specific features. Then *along with* 'enjoyment' one can also speak of 'liberation' which conforms to certain conditions. A popular Buddhist simile, comparing a person to a necklace without any string running through it—that is, a person, devoid of any permanent self *(ātman)*—is actually extremely vulnerable, since with the loss of such a binding string one inevitably loses the awareness of *transition*, the awareness of crossing the border between a lower and a higher ontological plane. An empirical *manas*—just an

14. One is reminded here of the Sāṃkhya notion, according to which *manas* (which experiences pleasant, unpleasant or indifferent sensations) together with *buddhi* (the faculty of discernment and volition) and *ahaṅkāra* (ego-consciousness) form an internal, inner organ *(antaḥkaraṇa)*. The most important point is that the five *indriyas* and *antaḥkaraṇa* are essentially inanimate and gain consciousness only when they are illuminated by *ātman*, so that even introspection is explained by analogy with sense perception.

15. Śaṅkara, Commentary on *Brahmasūtra*, II.2.19: *tataśca bhogo bhogārtha eva sa nānyena prārthanīyaḥ /tathā mokṣo mokṣārtha eveti mumukṣunā nānyena bhavitavyam /.*

element completely at par with all the other elements—might be identified with its own subsequent states; therefore, to Śaṅkara's mind, it cannot pretend to assume the part of a real Self, *for the sake of which* these mental states are primarily evoked.

Śaṅkara's argumentation here evidently attains its goal. Any attempt to harmonize an empirical and phenomenological approach to reality with basic religious tenets of *karma* and ultimate liberation was doomed to inner contradictions. However, one might note that it was already Sarvāstivāda that outlined the direction of the further evolution of Buddhist notions, having assigned an exceptional place among other *skandhas* to the *skandha* of *vijñāna*. The former are regarded as dependent upon consciousness; in other words, while *vijñāna* is synonymous with *citta,* the three remaining *skandhas* are referred to as derivative mental phenomena *(caitta).* Even *rūpa* is to some extent conditioned by *vijñāna,* since it is the latter that ensures the recognition of sense data as 'external objects'. The Vijñānavāda system, which did away with the notion of the sixth sense organ (its place in the table of elements became occupied by empirical self, namely, the 'stained' *(kliṣṭa) manas)* and incorporated the category of 'pure consciousness' *(citta-mātra),* as a matter of fact, made concessions to the traditional notion of *ātman.*

Within the frame of Sarvāstivāda, an attempt to overcome a contradiction between its empirical postulates and some residual religious tenets manifested itself in the dividing of all elements into 'composite' *(saṃskṛta)* and 'uncomposite' *(asaṃskṛta)* ones. The former (the greater part of all elements) were considered to be conditioned and impermanent, while the latter (*pratisaṃkhyānirodha,* or, cessation by consciousness, *apratisaṃkhyānirodha,* or, extinguishing; and *ākāśa,* that is, space or ether were essentially unconditioned (*ahetuja,* lit.; not born from a cause) and eternal. A slight modification, brought to the notion of *asaṃskṛta-dharmas* by the Sautrāntikas, is connected with their conception of derivability of the existence of all elements from mental operations *(anu-*

meyatatva). In the Sautrāntika section of *Sarvadarśana-siddhāntasaṅgraha* one might find a definition, according to which

> An element of *ākāśa* ... is an ultimate atom,
> /Therefore,/ it should be only an idea, and is not to be considered
> as something other than that.[16]

And the same holds true with regard to the two kinds of cessation. While arguing with the Buddhists in this connection, Śaṅkara raised objections primarily to the Sautrāntika version: "They consider these three /entities/ to be unreal, a pure absence and impossible to define."[17] And according to the interpretation suggested by T. Stcherbatsky, "a cessation *(nirodha)* defines two kinds of eternal void which come after all powers of the universe are exhausted."[18] In his opinion, cessation here is equal to counterbalance and eternal rest of all *dharmas.* That is why it should be defined neither as identical with *skandhas,* nor as different from them.

Śaṅkara points out inner inconsistencies in the Buddhist notion of the two kinds of *nirodha.* Indeed, no cessation may ever take place inside the causal chain of phenomena, since the distinctive feature of *nirodha* is its being unconditioned by any natural cause. But no cessation is possible inside a separate element, since "it is impossible to see the destruction of existing /phenomena/ without any trace and definition because in all the states there is an /uninterrupted/ connection /which is revealed/

---

16. Śaṅkara, *Sarva-darśana-siddhānta-saṅgraha,* IV.3.5:
ākāśadhātur asmabhiḥ paramāṇuritīritaḥ /
sa ca prajñaptimātraṃ syād naca vastvantaraṃ matam //5// .

17. Śaṅkara, Commentary on *Brahmasūtra,* II.2.22: *trayamapi caitadavastvabhāvamātraṃ nirupākhyamiti manyante /.*

18. T. Stcherbatsky, *Buddhist Logic,* vol. 2, Leningrad, 1930, p. 92.

owing to recognition."[19] And, as Śaṅkara points out, even a limited meaning of the term recognition *(pratyabhijñāna)*, peculiar to the Buddhists, still ought to imply a change, occurring in some existing entity *(bhāva)*, radically opposed to the notion of total destruction, or non-being *(abhāva)*.

A cessation by consciousness, or *nirvāṇa*, is the supreme goal of the Buddhists' teaching. It equals the destruction of fundamental ignorance *(mūlājñāna, avidyā)*. The higher knowledge of *Advaita*, identical with *ātman*, is also connected with the ending of *avidyā*, but in Śaṅkara's system the latter is regarded as a universal potency *(śakti)*, dependent upon Brahman and giving rise to the individuation of different souls *(jīva)*. According to Advaita, the ultimate liberation occurs not only *through* the higher knowledge—it *is* nothing else but this very knowledge which existed prior to the creation of the universe. Roughly speaking, it is not only the purpose and the goal, but also the cause itself. Meanwhile, in Sarvāstivāda liberation is one of the elements of existence; it is not its initial foundation but only a prospective and desirable end.

It should be noted that Śaṅkara does not confine himself simply to drawing attention to some minute inconsistencies of the Buddhists' doctrine. The gulf between the

---

19. Śaṅkara, Commentary on *Brahmasūtra*, II.2.22: *nahi bhāvānāṃ niranvayo nirupākhyo vināśaḥ saṃbhavati sarvāsvapyavasthāsu pratyabhijñānabalenānavayyavicchedadarśanāt.* While in Advaita the possibility of recognition *(pratyabhijñāna)* is based on self-evidence, self-luminosity *(svayaṃprakāśa)* of *ātman*, because everybody is aware of his own self, where various perceptions are, so to speak, brought into a focus (the closest European analogy to this is, probably *transzendentale Apperzeption* suggested by Kant); the Buddhsits are always trying to divorce the act of perception from the recognition of the object. For instance, in the passage from Śaṅkara's Commentary cited above (and the text is offered from the standpoint of Sarvāstivāda), recognition implies simply a possibility of inference concerning the alleged connection of phenomena, in spite of all perpetual changes occurring in the chain of empirical events.

systems is far deeper. In Advaita, as well as in Sarvāstivāda, the ultimate liberation is placed beyond the causal chain of phenomena. Such a situation becomes possible only because of Śaṅkara's notion of the identity of liberation and eternal Brahman, so that ultimate liberation, which is regarded as the higher knowledge (or pure consciousness), precedes this chain and presupposes it. Hence all Śaṅkara's arguments, pointing out that if, according to Sarvāstivāda, liberation were to emerge through the higher knowledge, then it could not be regarded as 'not born from a cause' *(ahetuja);* while if liberation were a conditioned entity, emerging as a spontaneous product of the elements, this assumption would inevitably lead to the "conclusion that instruction about the path of liberation is meaningless."[20]

Both Advaita and Buddhism emphasize a deep inner affinity of the notions of *ākāśa* and liberation. The Buddhist practice of meditation encouraged an adept's mental identification of space and *nirvāṇa* as one of the subsidiary means leading to the attainment of liberation.[21] Just like *nirvāṇa, ākāśa* was considered to be eternal and, simultaneously, indefinable *(nirupākhya).* The Sautrāntikas, however, somewhat modified this approach to the notion of *ākāśa,* regarding it as a pure non-being *(abhāva)* and a mere absence of any obstacle *(niravaraṇa).*

Śaṅkara's Commentary on *Brahmasūtra* often presents *ākāśa* as a proper and apt metaphor of the higher Brahman devoid of any attributes (Nirguṇa-Brahman). Just as space seems to be divided and limited due to earthen jars placed in it and supposedly containing some portions of this space, but once again becomes completely uniform and homogenous after their removal, so the higher Brahman, essentially devoid of attributes, seems to be divided into separate selves owing to the limitations *(upādhi)* of

---

20. Śaṅkara, Commentary on *Brahmasūtra,* II.2.23: ... *mārgopadeśānarthakyaprasaṅgaḥ* /.

21. Vide, for instance: Johannes Bronkhorst, *The Two Traditions of Meditation in Ancient India,* Stuttgart, 1986, pp. 77-79, 82, 84-87.

avidyā.[22] So it is quite understandable why the very essence of Śaṅkara's argumentation is directed against the concept of *ākāśa* as non-being. Though this entity is considered to be essentially indefinable, it is, nevertheless, undeniably real. In Śaṅkara's opinion, this tenet finds a further confirmation, if one were to remember that *ākāśa* is the known substrate, or bearer, of an attribute of sound *(śabda),* or, to be more exact, the condition of its spreading; and, as Śaṅkara hastens to remind, "the usual practice of /the relation between/ a substance and its attributes is based on /their mutual/ reality."[23] In his painstaking efforts to secure ample grounds for the notion of *ākāśa* as a real, positive entity *(bhāvarūpa),* the Advaitist is even ready to resort to the writings of his opponents, where *ākāśa* is sometimes regarded as a 'foundation of the wind.'[24] One might add that in the cosmological picture suggested by Advaita, *ākāśa* is created by Brahman and, in its turn, gives rise to other 'gross' elements (vide, for instance: Śaṅkara, Commentary on *Brahmasūtra,* II.3.1-7).

Unlike the above-mentioned three 'unconditioned' elements, all the other phenomena in Buddhism are included in the general causal chain of events. The wheel of *saṃsāra,* responsible for subsequent reincarnations, is composed of twelve main causal links *(nidāna).* They are enumerated by Śaṅkara in the passage of his Commentary on *Brahmasūtra* which concerns his dispute with Sarvāstivāda about the problem of combinations.[25] *Avidyā,* being the first link

---

22. Vide: Śaṅkara, Commentary on *Brahmasūtra,* I.1.5; II.1.13, etc.

23. Śaṅkara, Commentary on *Brahmasūtra,* II.2.24: *vastvāśrayatvāt dharmadharmivyavahārasya* /.

24. Vide: Śaṅkara, Commentary on *Brahmasūtra,* II.2.24: *saugate hi samaye ...ityasminprativacanapravāhe pṛthivyādīnāmante "vāyuḥ kiṃ saṃniśrayaḥ" ityasya praśnasya prativacanaṃ bhavati "vāyurākāśasaṃniśrayaḥ" iti .*

25. Vide: Śaṅkara. Commentary on *Brahmasūtra,* II.2.19. The first one is *avidyā,* after it comes *saṃskāra* (lit., preparation), or predisposi-

in the chain, to some extent determines all the others. Nevertheless, one should be careful in order not to ascribe any ontological significance to the Buddhists' interpretation of *avidyā*. In the words of a present-day scholar, "though ignorance is the first to be named, it should not be interpreted as the only source or absolute origin of an individual. Nor does it have any cosmological sense."[26] *Avidyā* certainly does not play the part of the ultimate cause or uniting principle for a colorful mosaic of momentary events. The Buddhists are interested only in its epistemological aspect, manifesting itself in the ability to conceal the true nature of the world; and the ultimate truth, in the eyes of the Buddhists, implies the futility of any attempts to find an ontological principle behind a mere linking together of various pehnomena in the wheel of *saṃsāra*.

Both in Advaita and in Buddhism the notion of *avidyā* is immediately related to the problem of causality, though the latter finds exactly opposing solutions in both systems. In his exposition of the Sarvāstivāda standpoint Śaṅkara states: "When this sequence /of moments/, starting with ignorance *(avidyā)*, perpetually revolves like a water wheel, so that /its components /mutually determine each other,

---

tion entailing the appearence of the first moment of consciousness in a new incarnation; the latter starts with the emergence of *vijñāna* as the third link. It is followed by *nāmarūpa* (that is, *rūpa*, or shape, as a physical body, together with *nāma* which is composed of three mental *skandhas*. The fifth moment brings about the emergence of six fields *(ṣaḍāyatana)* of perception, or organs of sense (including *manas*). The sixth one is *sparśa,* or touching, namely, the contact between an *indriya,* its object and a state of perception. It is subsequently followed by *vedanā* (sensation), *tṛṣṇā* (lit.: thirst, yearning), *upādāna* (attachment), *bhāva* (existence on a specific plane of the empirical universe), *jāti* (birth) and *(jarāmaraṇa)* ('old age and death'). One might note that *saṃskāra* belongs to a previous incarnation, the last two moments to a future one, while the middle *nidānas* are concentrated in a present embodiment. *Avidyā* applies, more or less, to the whole wheel of existence.

26. S. Bhikshu, *A Survey of Buddhism,* Bangalore, 1976, p. 101.

the whole emerges by force of circumstances."[27] However, Śaṅkara immediately draws attention to the fact that even in this case a preceding *(pūrva)* moment will cause a succeeding *(uttara)* one, but the source of the uniform whole would still remain without any satisfactory explanation. In Śaṅkara's own opinion, "when one is speaking about the emergence of a pot, one assumes that there exists some other agent of this activity /besides the necessary operations for producing it, as well as besides the parts of the pot itself/. But if it be true, when one is speaking about the emergence of the pot, the originating cause is supposed to be the potter and other /agents/. Still, when one is discussing the emergence of the pot, one cannot usually see the potters who produced it, but can perceive only /something/ produced /by them/."[28] In accordance with the Buddhist doctrine of causality, there was really no need to introduce the notion of the spiritual entity *(ātman)*, going through innumerable incarnations, since the causal succession of events could still ensure the functioning of *karma* rules, even in the absence of any agent or support, bringing about the formation of the universe as a whole.

For Śaṅkara the problem of the emergence of *avidyā*, responsible for setting into motion the wheel of phenomenal existence, was equivalent to the notion of creation of the world by God. The task facing the Advaitist was a difficult one: he had to reconcile the *śruti* sayings about Brahman as the cause of the world with the orthodox notion of Brahman's immutability. On the one hand,

---

27. Śaṅkara, Commentary on *Brahmasūtra,* II.2.19: *tadevamavidyādikalāpa parasparanimittanaimittikabhāvena ghaṭiyantravadanisamāvartamāne 'rthakṣipta upapannaḥ saṃghāta iti cet* /.

28. Śaṅkara,Commentary on *Brahmasūtra,* II.1.18: *ghaṭasya cotpattirucyamānā ghaṭakartṛkā kiṃ tarhyantakartṛkā iti kalpyā syāt / tathā kapālādinām apyutpattirucyamānānyakartṛkaiva kalpyeta /tathā ca sati ghaṭa utpadyate ityukte kulālādīni kāraṇānyutpadyante ityuktaṃ syāt /naca loke ghaṭotpattirityukte kulālādīnāmapyutpadyamānatā pratīyate /utpannatāpratīteḥ* /.

Śaṅkara maintains: "But only a divided entity might have an effect, and origination exists because there are effects."[29] While, on the other, Brahman for him is an immutable and self-identical entity which is not obscured by fortuitous phenomena. According to Indian philosophical tradition, any division is a step towards disintegration, towards destructive chaos; meanwhile, Brahman is regarded as the efficient *(nimitta)* and material *(upādāna)* cause of the endlessly heterogenous, moving and changeable world. What was Śaṅkara's solution for this apparent contradiction?

It is fairly well-known that within the framework of religious and philosophical tradition of India one can find two main concepts of causality. The first one was suggested by the Vaiśeṣikas and the Buddhists; in their opinion, the effect is always a new production from the cause, it is ever emerging anew. Hence the name of the doctrine, *asatkāryavāda,* or the teaching that the effect is non-existent prior to its production by the cause. The adherents of the other concept (for instance, the Sāṃkhyayikas) maintained that the effect exists prior to its manifestation and only transforms from its latent state (in the cause) to the revealed, manifested one; this doctrine acquired the name of *satkāryavāda,* or the teaching that the effect really pre-exists in the cause. Śaṅkara, though clearly adhering to the latter doctrine, suggested his own version of *satkāryavāda* theory; later this Advaita version, fully developed by Śaṅkara's followers, got the name of *vivarta-vāda,* or the teaching of appearance. *Vivarta* enters the same semantic cluster of terms referred to in the previous chapter; it is synonymous with *māyā* (illusion), *avidyā* (ignorance), *adhyāsa* (superimposition). In other words, the core of the causality concept of Advaita is the notion that the effect, or the empirical world, is just an illusory appearance superimposed on the eternal *ātman-*

29. Śaṅkara, Commentary on *Brahmasūtra,* II.3.17: *nanu pravibhaktatvād vikāro vikāratvāccotpadyata ityuktam* /.

Brahman as its cause. The universe is identical with Brahman, since in the ultimate sense nothing ever happened to this immutable entity. So, from the *pāramārthika* point of view (that is, from the standpoint of the ultimate truth) the effects, originated by Brahman, are essentially only new names for something already existing, and the change does not take place at all. Ultimately, the effects are nothing else but new definitions of the eternal reality. That is why Śaṅkara interprets the passage of *Chāndogyopaniṣad* (IV.1.4) concerning metal objects by saying that the modifications *(vikāra)* of metal 'originate from speech',[30] implying that they are real not as separate and specific objects, but only to the extent of their participation in the nature of metal. In the words of Śaṅkara's Commentary on *Brahmasūtra*, "the modification originates from speech, it is merely a kind of name."[31]

Up to now we were interested in the correlation of Brahman and the world as knowledge *(vidyā)* and ignorance *(avidyā)*: their opposition in this respect was absolute, and in order to reveal it, one had to move *inwards*, taking off all futile, superimposed attributes from the ever-present foundation of Pure consciousness. However, now one needs to shift the angle of consideration, since the polemics against the Buddhists brings to the foreground the aspect of *reality*. The move that is needed here starts from the core *outwards*, and the reality of Brahman proves to be so powerful and strong that it shines through, illuminating by its inner light even the illusory appearance enveloping Brahman. So the manifold world, posited as *vivarta*, stays as if suspended between real and unreal, though its nature is obviously different from that of a mere error, a mere delusion of the senses.

As we have seen above, the world is manifested only because of the superimposition of attributes on some

---

30. Śaṅkara, Commentary on *Chāndogyopaniṣad,* IV.1.4: *vikārāḥ ... vācārambhāḥ* /.

31. Śaṅkara, Commentary on *Brahmasūtra,* II.1.14: ... *Vācārambhanaṃ vikāro nāmadheyam* /.

immutable entity, which is ineffable, indefinable, but still essentially real. And while Brahman—as if acquiring some attributes inside this illusory appearance (that is, being presented as *Saguṇa*)—is posited as the foundation of the world, there are immediately manifested only its attributes of *sat* (reality), in particular, its ability to fill space, to be omnipresent. In this way a transparent glass is obscured and colored by the object which is seen through it; and, one must add, it is only this coloring and obscuration which makes the glass perceptible to human eye for the first time. In Śaṅkara's words, "this superimposition, so defined, is called *avidyā* by the sages, while the affir mation of a true nature of something that is real by distinguishing / it from the superimposed things/ they call knowledge."[32] In this sense, the source of the world and of the differentiation of souls, the substrate which, unlike Brahman, is ever-changing and evolving, is *avidyā*, or *māyā*. And remembering *avidyā* during his polemics with the Buddhists, Śaṅkara actually shifts the angle towards the concept of Saguṇa-Brahman, though the transition to a different level of consideration is quite intentionally left unaccomplished. Anyway, it would be incorrect to assume that *avidyā*, or *māyā*, in Advaita is something unreal, since it certainly absorbs something of the reality of its ultimate origin, indeed, in Śankara's words "something perceived cannot be a mere non-being."[33]

One might note that the notion of *māyā-avidyā* in Advaita is one of the most interesting and original ideas of Śaṅkara. Actually, in Bādarāyaṇa's text the term *māyā* occurs only once (III.2.3) and the meaning implied is that of sorcery, illusion. Śaṅkara's interpretation of *māyā* became a pretext for violent attacks by many theistically-minded thinkers, including those of the Vedanta school.

---

32. Śaṅkara, Commentary on *Brahmasūtra*, I.1.1: *tametamevaṃlakṣaṇamadhyādsaṃ paṇḍitā avidyeti manyante / tadvivekena ca vastusvarūpāvadhāraṇaṃ vidyām āhuḥ /.*

33. Śaṅkara, Commentary on *Brahmasūtra*, II.2.28: *nacopalabhyamānasyaivābhāvo bhavitumarhati /.*

For example, Rāmānuja considered Śaṅkara's *māyā-vāda,* or the doctrine of *māyā,* to be a direct compromise with the Buddhist teaching. His famous seven arguments against the Advaita notion of *māyā* deal mainly with the problem of its receptacle *(āśraya)* and source.[34] While discussing Śaṅkara's concrete arguments against the Buddhist teaching, D. Ingalls also draws attention to the vagueness of this concept, regarding it as the most vulnerable spot in Advaita doctrine.[35]

However, the complaints of the later Vedantins concerning the alleged incomprehensibility of *māyā-avidyā* and its inaccessibility to *pramāṇas* are hardly valid. In Advaita this entity is indefinable in principle, and one can approach it only through opposing it to *ātman*, and, simultaneously, through regarding it as dependent upon this *ātman*. According to a popular simile, a person wishing to know *avidyā* would be like somebody trying to see darkness with the help of a burning torch. Even Rāmānuja himself had to admit that for Advaita the impossibility of understanding *avidyā* is rather an adornment than a defect.

Yet another aspect of this problem might be mentioned in this connection. The Advaitists after Śaṅkara usually distinguished between *māyā,* a creative power of Īśvara, and *avidyā,* an ignorance characteristic of an individual consciousness. Of course, it is no mere chance that Śaṅkara uses these terms completely interchangeably. Beginningless *(anādi)* (since time acquires meaning only with the

---

34. One can find this polemics in the very beginning of Rāmānuja's Commentary on *Brahmasūtra (Śrībhāṣya,* I.1.1). One might note, incidentally, that Viśiṣṭādvaita of Rāmānuja defended the reality of Īśvara's modifications *(vikāra),* which assumed the forms of individual souls and inanimate objects depending upon Brahman. So it is no wonder that the very term *māyā* is used by Rāmānuja beyond polemics with reference to *Śvetāśvataropaniṣad* (IV.9), where it "determines wonderful things" of the manifold, but by no means illusory, world.

35. Vide: D. H. H. Ingalls, *Śaṅkara's Arguments against the Buddhists,* p. 302.

emergence of the phenomenal universe), definable neither as real nor as unreal *(sadasadanirvacanīya), avidyā* continues to be the substrate of the world and the only means of our experience until the sudden rise of the higher knowledge. "The name and the form",[36] says Śaṅkara, "which constitute the seeds of all phenomenal existence and are formed by ignorance *(avidyā),* are as if indistinguishable from omniscient God; they cannot be defined either as real or unreal, and are mentioned in *śruti* and *smṛti* as Īśvara's potency *(śakti),* called *māyā,* or as *prakṛti.* But omniscient God is distinguished from them. Therefore, just as space is divided by limitation *(upādhi)* in the form of pots and so on, God is determined by the names and the forms produced by ignorance."[37]

On the whole, Śaṅkara's interpretation of causality as inalterable preservation of the substrate, which is regarded as immutable from the standpoint of the ultimate truth, is directed straight against the Buddhists. The main principle of causality common to all Buddhist schools was the notion of *pratītya-samutpāda,* or 'dependent origination'. According to Śaṅkara, it can be summed up in the following words: "With the emergence of the succeeding moment, the preceding one is obliterated."[38] Usually *pratītya-samutpāda* is described in terms of functional dependence: the effect here is not originated by the cause—

36. In contrast to the Buddhist teaching, for Śaṅkara the names and forms *(nāma-rūpa)* are the seed *(bīja)* of the future manifestation of the world, which becomes developed in the act of creation owing to Īśvara's grace (Vide: Śaṅkara, Commentary on *Chāndogyopaniṣad,* VI.3.2, VIII.14.1).

37. Śaṅkara, Commentary on *Brahmasūtra,* II.1.14: *sarvajñasyeśvarasyātmabhūte ivāvidyākalpite nāmarūpe tattvāṇyatvābhyām anirvacanīye saṃsāraprapañcabījabhūte sarvajñasyeśvarasya māyāśaktiḥ prakṛtir iti ca śrutismṛtyorabhilapyete / tābhyāmanyaḥ sarvajña Īśvaraḥ ... evam avidyākṛtanāmarūpopadhyanurodhīśvaro bhavati vyomeva ghaṭakarakādyupādhyanurodhi /.*

38. Śaṅkara, Commentary on *Brahmasūtra,* II.2.20: *kṣaṇabhaṅgavādino 'yamabhyupagama uttarasmin kṣaṇe utpadyamāne pūrvaḥ kṣaṇo nirudhyata iti /.*

there is nothing between them to suggest an interfusion of essence, and, therefore, no real connection between two successive moments of existence.

As for Śaṅkara himself, it is impossible for him even to imagine "the emergence of the effect which would not be colored by the essence of its cause."[39] In the first part of the second *adhyāya* of Śaṅkara's Commentary on *Brahmasūtra*, where the relation of the cause and the effect is investigated in connection with the main notions of Advaita, Śaṅkara writes as follows: "Though /everything/ is devoid of differences and does not exist prior to /its emergence/, there is some inclination (lit.: preference, *atiśaya,* for curds in milk and not in a clump of clay... . But then, owing to the existence of such an inclination, Asatkāryavāda doctrine is destroyed and Satkāryavāda doctrine is established /beyond doubt/ ."[40] Formally, this argumentation is directed against the Vaiśeṣikas, but its main points are to some extent applicable to the Buddhist teaching as well. Of course, a Buddhist could always argue that *atiśaya* must be interpreted rather as a certain combination of conditions which makes possible the emergence of the effect. However, it should be borne in mind that the core of Śaṅkara's reasoning does not boil down to anything like the Sāṃkhya notion of evolution *(pariṇāmavāda).*

T. Stcherbatsky drew attention to the fact that the notions of causality in Sāṃkhya and Buddhism were exactly opposed to each other and so could be regarded as mutually complementary: the former system virtually ignored the attributes, and development there was presented as a kind of perpetual changing within the substrate, namely, *prakṛti,* while in the latter, the attributes, which became

---

39. Śaṅkara, Commentary on *Brahmasūtra,* II.2.20: *hetusvabhāvānuparaktasya phalasyotpattyasaṃbhavāt* /.

40. Śaṅkara, Commentary on *Brahmasūtra*, II.1.18: *athāviśiṣṭe 'pi prāgasattve kṣīra eva dadhnaḥ kaścidatiśayo na mṛttikāyāṃ ... atastarhyatiśayavattva prāgavasthāyā asatkāryavādahāniḥ satkāryavādasiddhiśca* /.

as if destitute of any foundation, were intermittingly flashing into existence, being extinguished in the next moment. Śaṅkara's concept of causality might be posited above this duality, transcending its inevitable limitations. According to Advaita, the evolution *(pariṇāma)* continues in the domain to *avidyā*, while the real *(sat)* foundation of the world is the immutable Brahman, transferring a part of its own reality of *avidyā*. *Avidyā* represents the reverse side of Brahman, participates in its being and therefore is, in a sense, identical with it. In Śaṅkara's words, "Just as Brahman, /that is/ the cause, never ceases to exist in the three times, the universe, which is its effect, never departs from existence in the three times. But existence is only one. This is the additional argument for non-distinguishing of the cause and the effect."[41]

Śaṅkara indicates the inner core of the Buddhists' statements which unavoidably implies that existence is rooted in non-being *(abhāva)*, intermittingly swelling up into being by successive moments *(kṣaṇa)*; he is certainly right when he maintains that "a non-existence of the permanent cause leads to the assumption of something emerging out of nothing."[42] Nevertheless, it is worth pointing out that Śaṅkara's specific arguments brought up against this notion are valid only on the empirical level of knowledge. For example, he says: "If existence were to arise out of non-existence, the assumption of different causes would become meaningless, because non-being is beyond any attributes,"[43] or, in other words, any effect

41. Vide: Śaṅkara, Commentary on *Brahmasūtra*, II.1.16: *yathāca kāraṇaṃ brahma triṣu kāleṣu sattvaṃ na vyabhicaratyevaṃ kāryamapi jagattriṣu kāleṣu sattvaṃ na vyabhicarati ekaṃ ca punaḥ sattvam ato 'pyananyatvaṃ kāraṇātkāryasya* /.

42. Śaṅkara, Commentary on *Brahmasūtra*, II.2.26: ... *yataḥ sthiramanuyāyikāraṇamanabhyupagacchatām abhāvādbhāvotpattiriti* ... /.

43. Śaṅkara, Commentary on *Brahmasūtra*, II.2.26: *yadyabhāvādbhāva utpadyeta abhāvatvāviśeṣāt kāraṇaviśeṣābhyupagamo 'narthakaḥ syāt* /.

could arise anywhere, which contradicts ordinary experience.[44]

It leaps to the eye that an objection of this kind is a double-edged weapon which could easily be turned against Śaṅkara's own Advaita; indeed, Śaṅkara himself is far from ignoring this circumstance. "If an effect were to emerge from immutable cause, anything could arise anywhere, because of the identity /of the cause/" argues the Advaitist from the viewpoint of Savāstivāda adherents.[45] An entity indeterminable in its essence and devoid of any attributes can be called either *bhāva* or *abhāva*; its reality is only arbitrarily postulated by the Advaitist—*owing to his reference to śruti texts.* This is probably the reason why the problem of causality is considered by Śaṅkara in the section of his Commentary on *Brahmasūtra* which deals with the investigation of Brahman as the material cause *(upādāna)* of the world. So when Śaṅkara maintains that the terms 'origination' *(utpāda)* and 'annihilation' *(nirodha)* determine the two states called 'beginning' and 'end' of an entity which is intermediate between them,[46] this statement should be considered not only as an argument directed against the Buddhist doctrine of momentariness *(kṣaṇikavāda),* but also in a more general way, as Śaṅkara's evidence concerning the grade (or level) of the reality of phenomenal world which, according to Advaita, is not definable as 'real' or 'unreal' *(sadasadanirvacanīya).* In Śaṅkara's words, "the state of the manifested names and forms *(nāmarūpa)* differs from that of the unmanifested ones. Therefore, though the effect remains identical with the cause even before the creation, from the stand-

44. Vide: Śaṅkara, Commentary on *Brahmasūtra,* II.2.20-21.

45. Śaṅkara, Commentary on *Brahmasūtra,* II.2.26: *kūṭasthāccetkāraṇātkāryam utpadyeta aviśeṣāt sarvaṃ sarvata utpadyeta* /.

46. Śaṅkara, Commentary on *Brahmasūtra,* II.2.20: ... *utpādanirodhaśabdābhyāṃ madhyavartino vastuna ādyantākhye avasthe abhilapyete iti* ... /.

point of the difference of the states the effect is regarded as non-existent before /the act of/ creation". And further on: "Because it is accepted in the world that something exists when it is manifested through names and forms, so, conceding to ordinary views, we say that the world did not exist before its manifestation through names and forms."[47]

The notion of causality is closely connected with the relation of substance and its attribute *(dharma-dharmi-bhāva)*. The Buddhists deny the reality of such a relation; in their opinion, the substance is identical with its attributes and might be reduced to them, so that the only reality are primary elements, qualities *(svalakṣaṇa)*, which appear from the non-being only in order to return to it a moment later. In Advaita *dharma-dharmi-bhāva* permeates all the phenomena of the empirical world. In the worlds of Śaṅkara, which seem to be directed specially against the Buddhists (though, in fact, they were said in a totally different context), "the quality which leaves its substance would lose its essence of being the quality."[48] The relation of substance and attribute in Advaita is regarded as a more limited application of the relation of origination, or that of cause and effect. In this way the relation is once again connected with the creation of the world by Brahman—which is interpreted here not as a *temporal* event (such an interpretation, in Śaṅkara's opinion, is, after all, nothing else but a concession to common sense) but rather as a *temporary* qualitative determination of Brahman through pehenomenal characteristics. In other words, all the limitation ascribed to Brahman are

47. Śaṅkara, Commentary on *Brahmasūtra,* II.1.17: *vyākṛtanāmarūpatvād dharmād avyākṛtanāmarūpatvaṃ dharmāntaraṃ tena dharmāntareṇāyamasadvyapadeśaḥ prāgutpatteḥ sata eva kāryasya kāraṇarūpeṇāyasya /... nāmarūpavyākṛtaṃ hi vastu sacchabdārthaṃ loke prasiddham / ataḥ prāñnāmarūpavyākaraṇādasadivāsīdityupacaryate /.*

48. Śaṅkara, Commentary on *Brahmasūtra,* II.3.29: *guṇatvam eva hi guṇinamanāśritya guṇasya hīyeta /.*

conditioned by *avidyā,* which is understood not only as personal ignorance but as a sort of universal evolution.[49] That is why, for example, the definitions of a living soul *(jīva),* which is considered to be atomic in size, active, etc., are valid only on the profane level of discussion.[50]

Jīva is radically different from the rest of the world; its reality is absolute and without reserve. In Śaṅkara's words, "the eternity of this /soul/ is known from *śruti* through the absence of modifications and the absence of origin of immutable Brahman which /may exist/ as Brahman and as individual soul".[51] *Jīva,* falsely identifying itself with the attributes of intellect *(buddhi)* and the like, has in Śaṅkara's system on ontological status similar to that of Īśvara; the ascribing of attributes to the individual soul or to the personified God starts along with the mythologically interpreted history of the evolving of *avidyā.*

Meanwhile, the immutable foundation of transient attributes is Brahman itself; its constant presence, according to Śaṅkara, explains the identity of the agent of perception and memory. The corresponding passage of Śaṅkara's commentary on *Brahmasūtra* runs as follows: "And how could there emerge a conviction that I had /earlier / seen that and see this /now/, if there were no seer *(drāṣṭṛ)* who was the same before and afterwards?"[52]

A Sarvāstivādin, recognizing only the reality of momentary qualities, resorts to the notion of conformity or similarity *(sārūpya),* which is understood as a sort of co-

---

49. Śaṅkara, Commentary on *Brahmasūtra,* II.3.18.

50. Vide: Śaṅkara, Commetnary on *Brahmasūtra,* II.3.29; 3.40.

51. Śaṅkara, Commentary on *Brahmasūtra,* II.3.17: *nityatvaṃ hyasya śrutibhyo 'vagamyate tathājatvamavikāritvam avikṛtasyaiva brahmaṇo jīvātmanāvasthānaṃ brahmātmanā ceti* /.

52. Śaṅkara, Commentary on *Brhamsūtra,* II.2.25: *kathaṃ hi ahamado 'drāksaṃ idaṃ paśyāmi iti ca pūrvottaradarśinyekasminnasati pratyayaḥ syāt* /.

ordination between successive mental states. For Śaṅkara, however, the possibility of establishing one and the same subject of the preceding moment and the succeeding one is ensured by the single and unified nature of *ātman*: "Perhaps, sometimes a doubt may arise regarding the external object ...whether it is the same /thing/ or merely similar to it. But there is never any doubt regarding the perceiving /subject/, whether it is I or merely /somebody/ similar to me, because one feels a certain identity /represented in the words/: 'I, who saw it yesterday, remember it today'. Therefore the teaching of the nihilists /who deny *ātman*/ is inconsistent."[53]

To sum up briefly the most important points of Śaṅkara's dispute with Sarvāstivāda, one should first of all mention his objections against the Buddhist notion of causality, as well as his criticism of the denial of *ātman*. In both cases the main line of polemics is strengthened by the Advaitist's conception of a permanent foundation which is itself immutable but still capable of bringing about illusory modifications. One is greatly tempted to present Śaṅkara as a kind of an objective idealist philosopher. Indeed, after S. Radhakrishnan it became almost universally accepted to interpret all Śaṅkara's arguments against the Buddhists in this light.[54]

To my mind, however, the essence of Śaṅkara's dispute is not exhausted by the arguments valid on the empirical level of reasoning; otherwise one would be forced to admit that the Advaitist did not bother himself with considering

---

53. Śaṅkara, Commentary on *Brahmasūtra,* II.2.25: *bhavedapi kadācidbāhyavastuni ... tadevaṃ syāttatsadṛśaṃ veti saṃdehaḥ / upalabdhari tu saṃdeho 'pi na kadācidbhavati sa evāhaṃ syāṃ tatsadṛśo veti /ya evāhaṃ pūrvedyuradrākṣaṃ sa evāhamadya smarāmīti niścitatadbhāvopalambhāt /tasmād apyanupapanno vaināśikasamayaḥ /.*

54. One is especially prone to regard Śaṅkara in this way in view of such passages as, for example, the often-cited instance of a seed which is dying but still remains partly preserved in a sprout. Vide: Śaṅkara, Commentary on *Brahmasūtra,* II.2.26: *anupamṛdyamānānāmevānuyāyināṃ bījādyavayavānāmaṅkurādikāraṇabhāvaḥ ... /.*

seriously the Buddhist notion of causality and so the controversy would lose much of its meaning because of the substitution of the initial postulates. Actually, Śaṅkara's chief object was the use of critical argumentation for the sake of gradual approach to ontological concepts of Advaita, where causality is directly linked with the notion of Brahman as the foundation of the phenomenal world, as well as with the idea of creation.

2. *ŚAṄKARA AND MAHĀYĀNA BUDDHIST SCHOOLS*

As mentioned above, many scholars investigating Indian religion and philosophy maintain that Mahāyāna Buddhism and Śaṅkara's Advaita virtually coincide in their main concepts. Undoubtedly, this point can be substantiated. One might note, for example, that through Gauḍapāda's mediation Śaṅkara could incorporate into his own system a Buddhist notion of *māyā* which had not been minutely elaborated in the Upaniṣads. Mahāyāna doctrines were probably the initial source of the concept of levels of reality and knowledge. Last but not least, Advaita is certainly close to Buddhism in its notion of the higher reality as ineffable, inexpressible in words, lying beyond any definitions. Probably because of these similarities, even such an astute Buddhologist as O. Rozenberg was of the opinion that "a precise differentiation between Brahmanism and Buddhism is impossible to draw."[55]

Still, the present work is based on a completely different approach. One can find indirect support for this approach in the fact that Śaṅkara himself fought all his life against Buddhist 'heresy'. The fact is that similar notions of different schools are seldom really identical. In the history of philosophy one cannot usually compare systems, simply superimposing them on each other at their coinciding points. Usually the relationship here is more complicated:

---

55. O. O. Rozenberg, *Problemy buddiyskoy filosofii*, Petrograd, 1918, p. 258.

even analogous ideas are included in different pictures of reality, placed on different planes. Therefore, while examining Śaṅkara's Advaita and Mahāyāna teachings, one should every time re-examine the coordinates of similar concepts, taking into account their place in different systems, as well as the part assigned to them.

The polemics with Vijñānavāda and Śūnyavāda was so important for Śaṅkara that he devoted to it not only special sections of his commentary on *Brahmasūtra* (II.2.28-32), but also some passages of the commentary on *Bṛhadāraṇyakopaniṣad* (I.4.7; II.3.6; IV.3.7), where polemical attacks are far more rare.

While going over the Sarvāstivāda arguments supporting the theory of momentariness *(kṣaṇikavāda),* Śaṅkara already examined the possibility of transmitting the impulse *(vyāpara)* from the preceding moment to the succeeding one (Commentary on *Brahmasūtra*, II.2.20). If it be held, contends the Advaitist, that in this way an earlier moment continues until the emergence of the subsequent moment, the cause and effect would become simultaneous,[56] and so the difference between them would be obliterated. This is rather a curious charge to be made, since to some extent it corresponds to the views of Vijñānavāda. This Buddhist school considers the object of perception and perception itself to be simultaneous, thus fusing together the content and the act of cognition, that is, νόημα and νόησις. The fact actually signified that only one moment *(kṣaṇa)* was left here, since, according to Buddhist tenets, all successive moments should be regarded as heterogenous, so that any coinciding events were posited as identical. While exposing the views of Vijñānavāda in his Commentary on *Brahmasūtra,* Śaṅkara says: "Besides, in accordance with the rule of joint perception, there is a non-distinction of the object and /its/ cognition, since they cannot be perceived apart from each other. And this

56. Vide: Śaṅkara, Commentary on *Brahmasūtra,* II.2.21: *athotarakṣaṇotpattiḥ yāvattavadavatiṣṭhate pūrvakṣaṇa iti brūyat tato yaugapadyaṃ hetuphalayoḥ syāt* /.

could not have taken place if they had been different in their nature.... Also for this reason there is no external object."[57]

Within the frame of Buddhism Vijñānavāda was a natural enough development of its empirical and phenomenological premises. But at the same time this school became something of a landmark in the emerging rapprochement between Buddhism and the initial tenets of orthodox philosophy. True, many contact points could be noted between Advaita and Vijñānavāda,[58] but that only forced Śaṅkara to be even more severe in his irreconcilable dispute with the Buddhists.

Vijñānavāda accepted only one of the known five *skandhas,* that is, the *skandha* of *vijñāna* (consciousness). In Śaṅkara's compendium one finds the following statement, made from the standpoint of Yogācāra, or Vijñānavāda:

> The nature of consciousness is indivisible, /but/
> those who see only dimly
> Distinguish as if separately—something perceived
> *(grāhya),*
> the perceiver *(grāhaka)* and the perception
> *(saṃvitti).*[59]

---

57. Śaṅkara, Commentary on *Brahmasūtra,* II.2.28: *apica sahopalambhaniyamānabhedo viṣayavijñānayor āpatati / nahyanayorekasyānupalambhe 'nyasyopalambho 'sti /... tasmādapyarthābhāvaḥ /*

58. It is quite easy to compare, for example, Śaṅkara's words concerning Vijñānavāda: "According to this teaching,all worldly practice, connected with the valid means of knowedge, the objects of knowledge and the results of cognition, is going on through the superimposition of inner forms upon consciousness" (*tasmiṃśca vijñānavāde buddhyārūḍhena rūpeṇāntastha eva pramāṇaprameyaphalavyavahāraḥ sarva upapadyate* / (Commentary on *Brahmasūtra,* II.2.28)—and an almost literal reiteration of this concept from the standpoint of Advaita (Commentary on *Brahmasūtra,* II.3.30).

59. Śaṅkara, *Sarva-darśana-siddhānta-saṅgraha,* IV.2.4 / *avibhāgo hi buddhyātmā viparyasitadarśanaiḥ / grāhyagrāhakasaṃvittibhedavānivalakṣyate //4//* .

'Consciousness', or *vijñāna* (a synonymous term used here is *buddhi,* is quite a polysemantic word in Buddhist teaching; it may mean either different, specific states of empirical consciousness, or pure consciousness, devoid of any attributes. On the whole, the Vijñānavādins accept the table of elements suggested by Sarvāstivāda, though all its components are regarded now as derived from consciousness. Therefore, any external object is considered in Vijñānavāda to be originated by consciousness.

The Buddhists explain their position thus: any perception should have some similarity *(sārūpya)* with its object, since it does appear as some concrete perception, for instance, as the perception of a column, a wall or any other sense object. "But on this assumption any image of the object /can be explained/ only on the base of consciousness," goes on the Yogācārin, an imaginary opponent of Śaṅkara, "since /these images/ are contained within /consciousness/ and so any concept about the real existence of external object is useless."[60] Since the objects are given to us only in perception, it is more 'economical'—as if cutting off everything superfluous by Occam's razor—to think of them as identical with perception, without setting oneself the task of attempting to clarify what might have caused these perceptions. Anyway, this attitude perfectly agrees with the Buddhist tenets that aim primarily at quite a practical goal, namely, the specific restructuring of this consciousness for the sake of liberation.

---

60. Śaṅkara, Commentary on *Brahmasūtra,* II.2.28: *aṅgīkṛte ca tasminviṣayākārasya jñānenaivāvaruddhatvādanarthikā bāhyārtha-sadbhāvakalpanā.* A similar tenet about the identity of consciousness and its content, suggested from the standpoint of Vijñānavāda, can be found in Śaṅkara's Commentary on *Bṛhadāraṇyakopaniṣad,* IV.3.7: "So, having assumed in this consciousness some impurity in the form of a perceiver and something perceived, they think about purifying it; some /Buddhists maintain that / this consciousness, being set free from the /duality of / the perceiver and the perceived, stays pure and momentary." *(evaṃ tasyaiva vijñānasya grāhyagrāhakākāratāmalaṃ parikalpya tasyaiva punarviśuddhiṃ parikalpayanti tad grāhya-grāhakavinirmuktaṃ vijñānaṃ svacchībhūtaṃ kṣaṇikaṃ vyavatiṣṭhata iti kecit /.)*

In order to refute this Buddhist thesis, Śaṅkara makes use of a Bādarāyaṇa's *sūtra* (II.2.28), which runs as follows: "There is no non-existence /of the objects/ because of /their/ perception."[61] Indeed, perception not only constructs the image of the object for consciousness, it is also one of the valid means of knowledge *(pramāṇa)*. One might remember that within the limits of phenomenal existence in Advaita all methods of logical reasoning are fully justified, all means of knowledge are valid and all worldly and traditional religious practices are quite legitimate (vide: Śaṅkara, Commentary on *Brahma-sūtra,* II.1.14). "Only the applicability or non-applicability of *pramāṇas* can definitely resolve the question about the possibility or impossibility of existence," says Śaṅkara.[62] Moreover, now when it is convenient for this new turn of the polemics, the Advaitist, without a shade of hesitation, identifies perception as such *(upalabdhi)* with sense perception *(pratyakṣa)* as one of the valid means of knowledge. One might note that even the *verification* suggested by Śaṅkara is feasible only on the plane and within the limits of ordinary worldly practice. Only in this empirical sphere "all ordinary people *(laukika)* perceive the column, the wall and so on, just like the objects /of consciousness/."[63] I might add that the conscientious determining of the domain, where such a reasoning is really valid, is essential and does credit to Śaṅkara: one is being surreptitiously reminded that, even from the Advaita standpoint, no *pramāṇa* can be directly related to *ātman*.

Now we can trace the line of the polemics still further. To Śaṅkara's mind, the Buddhist tenet that the object does not exist because it is similar to the corresponding percep-

61. *nābhāva upalabdheh* /.

62. Śaṅkara, Commentary on *Brahmasūtra,* II.2.28: *yataḥ pramāṇa-pravṛttyapravṛttipūrvakau saṃbhavāsaṃbhavāvadhāryete* ... /.

63. Śaṅkara, Commentary on *Brahmasūtra,* II.2.28: *upalabdhiviṣa-yatvenaiva tu staṃbhakuṇyādīn sarve laukikā upalabhante* /.

tion is absolutely inconsistent, since one can hardly imagine similarity with something that just never existed at all. The Advaitist argues: "And even / the Buddhsits themselves / perceive the images that reflect something external just as everyone else does but /they still/ deny the external object by inserting the word *vat* (as if) in the phrase 'as if external'. Otherwise, why should they say: "as if external".[64]

From the formal point of view Śaṅkara's position much better corresponds to common sense; and in comparison with Vijnānavāda views, it seems much more 'realistic'. In the words of S. Dasgupta, "that Śaṅkara had some realistic views is proved by his own avowal when he was criticising consistent idealists /of the Vijñānavāda school./"[65] However, on more careful consideration the main tenets of the opposing systems seem not so remote from each other.

First of all, one should specify the position of the Buddhists. For instance, Vasubandhu never really defended the thesis of absoulte identity of the objects and their perceptions. In his opinion, it is only pure consciousness *(vijñapti-mātratā)* that has higher reality, and this pure consciousness undergoes some inner transformations *(vipāka).* On this stage of transformation the acquired tendencies, or directions of evolution, are separated into the perception of psychic states *(manana)* and the projection of consciousness outwards, which is manifested as the perception of objects *(viṣaya-vijñapti).* Therefore, the external world is only *ultimately* brought about and conditioned by consciousness, and so, also from the Buddhist standpoint, we do not have any right to directly identify it with subjective perceptions. Vasubandhu maintains that the object is different from its cognitive image, although it

64. Śaṅkara, Commentary on *Brahmasūtra,* II.2.28: *te 'pi hi sarvalokaprasiddhāṃ bahiḥ avabhāsamānāṃ saṃvidaṃ pratilabhamānāḥ pratyākhyātukāmāśca bāhyamarthaṃ bahirvaditi vatkāraṃ kurvati / itarathā hi kasmād bahirvaditi brūyuḥ /.*

65. S. Dasgupta, *A History of Indian Philosophy,* vol. 2, p.2.

is pure consciousness lying in the foundation of the world that is divided into subject and object.

Scholars have repeatedly stressed a remarkable similarity between the views of Vasubandhu and those of a later Advaitist Prakaśānanda (latter part of the sixteenth century), the propounder of the school *dṛṣṭi-sṛṣṭi,* or the doctrine, according to which perception is ultimately equal to creation. In his own Commentary on *Brahmasūtra* a Vedantin Bhāskara criticizes not only the Buddhists, but also Śaṅkara; he accuses the latter of succumbing to the influence of Dharmakīrti. Śaṅkara was undoubtedly quite well acquainted with the ideas of late Vijñānavāda; in the very text of his commentary on *Brahmasūtra* one finds hidden citations or, perhaps, reminiscences from Diṅnāga[66] and Dharmakīrti.[67] To my mind, the alleged affinity of Śaṅkara's Advaita with late Vijñānavāda, which was interested primarily in logical and epistemological problems, is largely overrated. However, one could easily show many striking similarities between some theoretical notions of Śaṅkara and Vasubandhu.

---

66. Vide: Śaṅkara, Commentary on *Brahmasūtra*, II.2.28: *yad antarjñeyarūpaṃ tad bahirvad avabhāsate* /. "The inner form of knowledge is manifested as if externally" and, for instance, the words of Diṅnāga, referred to in Śāntarakṣita's *Tattva-saṅgraha,* 2082:

yad antarjñeyarūpaṃ tu bahirvad avabhāsate /
so 'rtho vijñāna rūpatvāt tat pratyayatayāpi /.

67. There is almost literal coincidence in the exposition of the Buddhist thesis concerning 'concomitant perception' by Śaṅkara (Commentary on *Brahmasūtra,* II.2.28) and by Dharmakīrti:

According to the rule of concomitant perception /there is/
non-distinguishing of a blue-black color
and the thought of it;
distinguishing is produced by erroneous consciousness,
/which/ appears as if divided.
sahopalambhaniyamād abhedo nīlataddhiyoḥ /
bhedaśca bhrāntavijñānair dṛśyate 'ndāvivādvaye /.

About that and other similar instances vide: K. Kunjunni Raja, *On the Date of Śaṅkarācāya and Allied Problems,* pp. 134-35.

From the Vijñānavāda standpoint, all human perceptions are similar to dreams; in other words, they are illusory. The Yogācārins were rather sarcastic about the 'naive' concepts of the Vaibhāṣikas, who, having agreed with the general homogeneity of all perceptions, were forced to assume that even dreams correspond to some real objects. S. Dasgupta explains Śaṅkara's criticism of Vijñānavāda by the facts that, unlike the Yogācārins, the Advaitist was sure that the objective world, open to human consciousness, was posited actually and independently.[68] And indeed, continuing his discussion on the level of profane knowledge, Śaṅkara points out that the characteristics of dreams and the waking state are completely different, since any object perceived in dreams, magical illusions, mirages, etc. can be appraised as unreal after waking or after the cessation of the illusion.[69]

We have already seen that in his Commentary on Gauḍapāda's *Māṇḍūkya-kārikā* Śaṅkara was inclined to share the opinion of his teacher, according to which ordinary perceptions, as well as everyday human activity, are similar to illusions or dreams. While acknowledging this fact, S. Dasgupta hastens to add that the explanation lies in the evolution of Śaṅkara's views—from his early enthusiasm for Buddhism to the increased and noticeable 'realism', characteristic of his Commentary on *Brahmasūtra.*[70] To my mind, though, one can hardly agree to this kind of interpretation; indeed, in other passages of his Commen-

---

68. Vide: S. Dasgupta, *A History of Indian Philosophy,* vol. 2, p. 30.

69. Śaṅkara, Commentary on *Brahmasūtra,* II.2.29: "But for somebody who awakened the object that had been perceived in dreams can be negated: 'My perception of contacts with important people was false; my mind was engrossed in drowsy inactivity, and therefore this error emerged.' So /he says, having awakened / ." *(bādhyate hi svapnopalabdhaṃ vastu pratibudhasya mithyā mayopalabdho mahājanasamāgama iti nahyasti mama mahājanasamāgamo nidrānlānaṃ tu me mano babhūva tenaiṣā bhrāntirudbhūveti* /.)

70. Vide: S. Dasgupta, *A History of Indian Philosophy,* vol. 2, p. 29.

tary on Bādarāyaṇa's text, where purely polemical reasons are set aside, Śaṅkara says: "Prior to the realization of /the identity of/ *ātman* and Brahman all actions may be regarded as true—just like the actions in a dream before waking up."[71] This is yet another proof not only of the assertion that logic is a double-edged weapon and the genre of *vitaṇḍa* allows for some liberties and distortions in the course of the polemics, but mainly of the fact that logical argumentation *(tarka)* in Advaita plays a subsidiary part and is subordinated to a more general task. Śaṅkara's goal can be revealed only from the context of his discussion; and here the comparison of dreams and ordinary practice reflects quite an auxiliary topic, being just a rebuke directed at the opponent who was bold enough to doubt the injunctions of *śruti,* as well as the possibility of combining these injunctions with the proclaiming of absolute identity.

Coming back to the *sūtra* under discussion, one might note that the term which defines illusions or magic sorcery is *māyā.* It is really a key word in this argumentation, and that allows us to interpret the purport of the Advaitist's reasoning in a slightly different way, tying it up with a new level of reality.

It is generally believed that the Advaita doctrine of *māyā* had its closest correspondence in the notion of predisposition, or tendency *(vāsanā),* in Vijñānavāda. T. Stcherbatsky used to translate this latter term as 'biotic force', implying natural inclination or temperament. In Śaṅkara's Commentary on *Brahmasūtra,* in the passages dealing with Buddhism, the notion of *vāsanā* means some latent inclinations or tendencies of development that are formed before the birth of a living being and favor certain kinds of perceptions, so that it is quite unnecessary and superfluous to look for external objects as their source. In the words of a Yogācārin, presented by Śaṅkara in his

---

71. Śaṅkara, Commentary on *Brahmasūtra,* II.1.14: *sarvavyavahārāṇāmeva prāgbrahmātmavijñānātsatyatvopapatteḥ /svapnavyavahārasyeva prākprabodhāt* /.

Commentary, "It is known that the manifoldness of knowledge is brought about solely by the tendencies, since...one might easily assume the existence of manifold knowledge originated by the tendencies even in the absence of the object, /for instance, in dreaming and other similar states/, but one cannot assume the existence of manifold knowledge only from objects in the absence of tendencies."[72]

However, the Advaitist quickly objects that without assuming the existence of objects, the tendencies would lack any source. Śaṅkara's reasoning runs as follows:"And even if these /tendencies/ are beginningless, this infinite regress would be devoid of foundation, just like a blind man, /who is being led/ by another blind man, so that ordinary human practice becomes completely shattered."[73] Still, one should not interpret this argument literally. For Śaṅkara, the only source of human activity is ever-active, ever-divided and manifold *avidyā,* "since the fact that the soul is manifested as an agent and enjoyer is brought about by ignorance."[74] Therefore, the source and condition of the activity of the soul lies in all the created universe, and this universe embraces the 'instruments' *(karaṇa)* of the soul, that is, its sense organs *(indriya), manas, buddhi* and so on, the activity of which incidentally continues even in dream. It also embraces external objects, the residue of former *karma* etc. The very process of phenomenal practice is beginningless in itself, but it still depends upon the permission and mercy of a personified God, or Īśvara, who "supervises over every kind of activity, staying in all the

72. Śaṅkara, Commentary on *Brahmasūtra,* II.2.28: *apica ... vāsanānimittameva jñānavaicitryam ityavagamyate / svapnādiṣvantareṇāpyartham vāsanānimittasya jñānavaicitryasya ... apyābhyāmabhyupagamyamāna / antareṇa tu vāsanāmarthanimittasya jñānavaicitryasya bhayānabhyupagamyamānatvāt /.*

73. Śaṅkara, Commentary on *Brahmasūtra,* II.2.30: *anāditve 'pyandhaparamparānyāyena apratiṣṭhaivānavasthā vyavahāralopinī syānnābhiprāyasiddhiḥ /.*

74. Śaṅkara, Commentary on *Brhamasūtra,* II.3.40: *avidyāpratyupasthāpitatvāt kartṛtvabhoktṛtvayoḥ /.*

beings; he is the inner witness *(sākṣin),* who grants his consciousness /to all/ .... Liberation can come through knowledge—and only by his grace."[75] Representing a sort of personal emobodiment of *karma,* Īśvara allocates the fruits of actions according to the efforts of living beings, just as rain contributes to the growth of greenery, the possibility of which is ultimately inherent in the plants.[76]

However in spite of the apparent similarity between the functioning of *māyā-avidyā* in Advaita and the origination of inner tendencies *(vāsanā)* in Vijñānavāda, Śaṅkara finds a way to oppose the senseless infinity of ever-originating states. Once again I would like to ask the reader not to trust excessively the outward arguments of the Advaitist. The infinite regress of the causal chain in the phenomenal world is broken off, but not owing to its foundation in real objects, as the ingenuous quibbles of Śaṅkara's dispute seem to imply. In Advaita the regress is brought to an end only through the notion of *creation.* The notion allows us to realize that any restless activity of *avidyā* is by no means self-originated—and therefore must eventually come to a close.

Nevertheless, Śaṅkara maintains that the freedom and personal striving of a man are not depreciated by the fact that eternal Brahman resides in him as his innermost self and immutable basis. It is rather the other way round—the presence of eternal Brahman, who created the world and numerous souls, ensures both the stability of the existence of the universe and the very possibility of its dissolution for a liberated person. In Śaṅkara's words, "the effort of a striving agent gains meaning, transforming the cause into the shape of the effect. For we have said already that every specific effect is burdened with the

---

75. Śaṅkara, Commentary on *Brahmasūtra,* II.3.41: ... *karmādhy-akṣātsarvabhūtādhivāśāt sākṣinaścetayiturīśvarāt ... tadanugra-hahetukenaiva ca vijñānena mokṣasiddhirbhavitumarhati /.*

76. Vide, for instance: Śaṅkara, Commentary on *Brahmasūtra,* II.3.42.

essence of the cause *(kāraṇasyātmabhūta)* and that anything, not existing already in the cause, cannot be produced."[77] Therefore, all that is ever demanded of the soul in Advaita is the ability to come to the realizaiton of its own essence; and the overcoming of the restless activity of phenomenal practice is possible only because this activity initially contains within itself the eternal inactivity of *ātman.*[78] The Buddhists are not interested in the way this causal chain was originated; dealing with its *present* states which are full of former tendencies, their teaching claims to have shown the Path of leaving behind the bonds of *saṃsāra* ties.

Now, having had at least a glimpse of the regular symmetry of the 'beginning' and the 'end', inherent in the very structure of the universe, according to Advaita, let us examine the functioning of the same argument 'from infinite regress' in a slightly different context. I mean the problem of the nature of consciousness in Mahāyāna schools of Buddhism and in Śaṅkara's Advaita.

In the opinion of the Vijñānavādins, the very possibility of ultimate liberation lies in the inner nature of consciousness, which is regarded as self-luminous *(svayaṃprakāsa)* and self-evident *(svayaṃsiddha).* As is said in Śaṅkara's Commentary on *Bṛhadāraṇyakopaniṣad* from the standpoint of Vijñānavāda, consciousness is similar to a lamp, which, "though it cannot be illuminated by something else, illuminates both itself and an earthen pot /that does not

---

77. Śaṅkara, Commentary on *Brhamasūtra,* II.1.18: *yataḥ kārya-kāreṇa kāraṇaṃ vyavasthāpayataḥ kārakavyāpārasyārthavattva-mupapadyate /kāryakāro 'pi kāraṇasyātmabhūta evānātmabhūtasyā-nārabhyatvādityabhāṇi /.*

78. Vide: Śaṅkara, Commentary on *Brahmasūtra,* II.3.40: "Activity is not inherent in the soul by its own nature, otherwise it would have led to the impossibility of liberation. Were the *ātman* active by nature, it could not be liberated from activity, just as fire /cannot escape / heat." *(na svabhavikaṃ kartṛtvamātmanaḥ saṃbhavati anirmokṣaprasaṅgāt /kartṛtvasvabhāvatve hyātmanno na kartṛtvānnirmokṣaḥ saṃbhavati agnerivauṣṇyāt /.*

emit any light at all /."[79] True, this definition of consciousness does not differ much from the image suggested by Advaita. Probably the only difference is that Śaṅkara was well aware of all the latent difficulties and hidden traps. First of all, as we remember from the analysis in the preceding chapter, pure consciousness in Advaita can never turn to grasp its own nature, can never become its own object. Then how can there be self-luminous and self-evident consciousness which is acknowledged by the Advaitist? In Śaṅkara's words, "as soon as consciousness emerges, there is no more striving to know its witness, and therefore there is no danger of infinite regress, which would have been inevitable if consciousness were grasped by something different from its own nature—or by other consciousness."[80] The witness *(sākṣin)* of consciousness, mentioned here, is essentially different from all other components of a cognitive act; that is, of course, *ātman,* which is devoid of any attributes. Only this *ātman* can be truly regarded as self-evident and self-luminous, or directly perceptible *(aparokṣa).*

Anticipating further analysis, I would like to say that this means of avoiding the senseless infinity of regress was partly suggested by the Pūrva-Mīmāṃsā attitude to the nature of consciousness. The notion that the existence of consciousness does not need any verification by some other cognition was borrowed by Śaṅkara from Kumārila's teaching. However, according to Pūrva-mīmāṃsā, every act of cognition gives its own knowledge (for instance, the perception of color), which simply does not need any corroboraton by other *pramāṇas* that have their own

---

79. Vide: Śaṅkara, Commentary on *Bṛhadāraṇyakopaniṣad,* IV.3.7: *tasmāt pradīpo'nyāvabhāsyo'pi sannātmānaṃ ghaṭaṃ cāvabhāsayati* / There is also a simile of this kind in the Commentary on *Brahmasūtra,* II.2.28.

80. Śaṅkara, Commentary on *Brahmasūtra,* II.2.28: *vijñānagrahaṇamātra eva vijñānasākṣino grahaṇākāṅkṣānutpādādanavasthāśaṅkānupapatteḥ* /.

objects and functions. Meanwhile, Śaṅkara emphasizes the fact that there is absolutely no need to resort to a new cognitive act in order to grasp the well-known perception 'I am'. The infinite regress of reflection is cut short because it is ultimately based upon the immutable *ātman.*

And vice versa: when the Buddhists refused to postulate the existence of *ātman* as an *a priori* reality, they at once stumbled over logical and gnoseological difficulties. On the one hand, the notion of changeable and momentary *vijñāna* could not shield their conception from the reproach of the inevitability of infinite regress, linking together causally conditioned states of consciousness that incessantly originate each other. On the other hand, it is easy to notice that even the key concept of a self-luminous and self-evidence consciousness was partly undermined "because of the assumption of differentiation of / attributes/ of consciousness in the form of origination, destruction and momentariness."[81]

Even the common receptacle of consciousness *(ālaya-vijñāna),* which is regarded by the Vijñānavādins as the base and source of inner tendencies *(vāsanā),* is devoid of a permanent form, since it grows and changes along with the changes in empirical consciousness of various living beings; besides, it is, of course, momentary. If one were to return to the classification of *vijñāna* by Vasubandhu, one might remember that *ālaya-vijñāna* is supposed to include three stages of the development of cognition.[82]

Because of this inner heterogeneity of *ālaya-vijñāna,* Śaṅkara denies the possibility of its connection with liberation. Even more than that: he believes that it cannot

---

81. Śaṅkara, Commentary on *Brahmasūtra,* II.2.28: *Vijñānasyotpattipradhvaṃsānekatvādiviśeṣavattvābhyupagamāt* /.

82. *Ālaya-vijñāna* is folded up into the pure consciousness *(vijñānamātratā)* of the saint. In this latter state it is called the primary element *(dhātu)* of all merits. Vide: Sthiramati's Commentary on the treatise *Triṃśika* by Vasubandhu, as well as the analysis of that passage by S. Dasgupta (S. Dasgupta, *A History of Indian Philosophy,* vol. 2, p.22).

ever constitute the base of *saṃsāra*. In Śaṅkara's words, "in the absence of one /subject/, binding and connecting the three times, the immutable witness of all objects, the worldly practices of memory, recognition and the like are impossible."[83] And if *ālaya-vijñāna* were to be acknowledged as something permanent, continues the Advaitist, in this case the main distinctive feature of Buddhism would disappear, that is, its doctrine of momentariness, while *ālaya-vijñāna* itself would become quite similar to the orthodox notion of *ātman*. (One might note in parentheses that actually *ātman* is close to the twentieth element from the Vijñānavāda table, namely, to pure cognition *(citta-mātra),* though even the latter remains for the Buddhists only one of the possible cognitive states.) Śaṅkara does not mention it in his polemical works, and so it is difficult to say what his opinion was about the identifying of this pure cognition with the reality, 'thatness' *(tathātā)* of the world in the Buddhist *Laṅkāvatāra-sūtra*, as well as in the teaching of Vasubandhu.

As regards Śūnyavāda, this teaching as favored with only a few phrases in Śaṅkara's Commentary on *Brahma-sūtra*. According to the Advaitist, "there is no attempt to refute Śūnyavāda, since it contradicts all the means of valid knowledge."[84] In the Commentary on *Bṛhadāraṇyako-paniṣad* Śaṅkara explains: "the Mādhyamikas maintain that consciousness is hidden, that it is devoid of any parts /in the form of/ the perceiver and the perceived, and that it is just void *(śūnya)*—like all external objects, pots and the like."[85] This Buddhist school is presented in more

83. Śaṅkara, Commentary on *Brahmasūtra*, II.2.31: *nahi kālatraya-saṃbandhinyekasminnanvayinyasati kūṭasthe vā sarvārthadarśini ... smṛtipratisandhānādivyavahāraḥ saṃbhavati /.*

84. Śaṅkara, Commentary on *Brahmasūtra,* II.2.31: *śūnyavādi-pakṣastu sarvapramāṇavipratiṣiddha iti tannirākaranāya nādaraḥ kriyate /.*

85. Śaṅkara, Commentary on *Bṛhadāraṇyakopaniṣad*, IV.3.7: *tadapi vijñānaṃ saṃvṛtaṃ grāhyagrāhakāṃsavinirmuktaṃ śūnyameva ghaṭādibāhyavastuvadityapare mādhyamikā ācakṣate /.*

detail in *Sarva-darśana-siddhānta-saṅgraha,* where Śaṅkara says from the standpoint of the Mādhyamikas:

There is no real *(sat),* no unreal,
no real and unreal,
and there is nothing that is different from the two /possibilities /.[86]

Somewhat later the compendium sums up the argumentation of some imaginary Śūnyavādin:

It is established that the essence is void,
since it is /free from the four approaches.[87]

In his works Śaṅkara clearly interprets the Buddhist notion of void or emptiness *(śūnya)* as mere absence, non-being. One might even think that he was hardly fair in his examination of the opponents' doctrine. This is the opinion shared by most Buddhologists and historians of philosophy.

According to F. Whaling, Śaṅkara could not really understand the motives of the Buddhists' attitude to *śūnya*: "He sees it from without where it seems to indicate emptiness; had he seen if from within it would have also mean fullness."[88] This kind of reproach is actually just an echo of the warning made by D. Conze, who maintained that the notion of *śūnya* can be grasped only from within the Buddhist *Weltanschauung*, that is, only with regard to the soteriological context of the teaching.[89] For instance, that is how emptiness is defined by Nāgārjuna:

---

86. Śaṅkara, *Sarva-darśana-siddhānta-saṅgraha,* IV.1.7: *nasannāsanna sadasannacobhābhyāṃ vilakṣaṇam /.*

87. Śaṅkara, *Sarva-darśana-siddhānta-saṅgraha,* IV.1.10: *catuṣkoṭivinirmuktaṃ śūnyaṃ tattvam iti sthitam /.*

88. F. Whaling, *Śaṅkara and Buddhism,* p. 13.

89. Vide: E. Conze, *Buddhist Thought in India,* Michigan, 1967, pp. 244-249.

Liberation /emerges/ from the destruction
 of the impurity of action,
And impurity of action / proceeds/
 form mental construction.
These /forms of mental construction start/
 from worldly manifoldness;
While worldly manifoldness
 disappears in emptiness.[90]

On the whole European scholars were inclined to accept the idea of a positive character of *śūnya*, representing a kind of general background of the world, so that emptiness meant for them something rather like ineffability, impossibility of being grasped by verbal means. Examining the spectrum of opinions on this matter, T. Stcherbatsky wrote: "And if Prof. Keith and Prof. M. Walleser suppose that Nāgārjuna stops at negation or denies even the empirical reality of the world, it is only because his real aim, the positive counterpart of his negativism...had escaped their attention."[91]

It is perfectly clear that this kind of interpretation naturally leads to the thesis that Advaita and Śūnyavāda are identical in their innermost foundation; and one might remember that such a thesis was quite popular with S. Dasgupta, S. Radhakrishnan and other astute scholars. Indeed, apparently the question of whether the higher entity is positive or negative ultimately depends upon the angle of consideration, since the Buddhist *śūnya* is neither more nor less real than the higher Brahman in Śaṅkara's teachng. In Śaṅkara's compendium it is said from the standpoint of the Mādhyamikas:

---

90. Nāgārjuna, *Mādhyamika-kārikā*, XVIII.5:
karmakleśakṣayānomokṣaḥ karmakleśa vikalpataḥ /
te prapañcātprapañcastu śūnyatāyāṃ nirūḍhyate //5//.

91. T. Stcherbatsky, *The Central Conception of Buddhism*, Calcutta, 1956, p. 52.

Ātman does not have any general or individual
attributes,
therefore, it does not exist;
Hence /there follows/ the non-existence of objects,
and so consciousness does not exist either—
That is the Mādhyamikas' argumentation concerning
general emptiness.[92]

This kind of reasoning is quite in conformity with Śaṅkara's own words: "Someone who sees in *ātman,* which is bliss, even a small separation from the impossibility of being somehow defined, is not free from the dread of *saṃsāra.*"[93]

The scholars who, for some reason or other, do not feel inclined to identify Advaita and Buddhism, continue to reason further on the following lines. Indeed, the absolute truth *(paramārthasatya)* of the Mādhyamika teaching—as well as the higher reality in Śaṅkara's system—lies beyond the sphere of discourse, language and empirical practice. However, the Buddhists' dialectic was supposed to fulfill a primarily destructive function in order to refute the opponents' views by the means of *reductio ad absurdum (prasaṅgāpādānam).* If Vijñānavāda refuted the independent and real existence of the objective world, and Mādhyamika opposed any kind of conceptualization *(vikalpa),* the system of Śaṅkara was oriented ultimately on the self-identity and absolute validity of the higher reality, which is exactly for this reason assumed to be free of any attributes. According to T. Murti, who to some extent shares similar opinions, Advaita and Buddhism

---

92. Śaṅkara, *Sarva-darśana-siddhānta-saṅgraha,* IV.1.17-17 1/2:
jātivyaktyātmako 'rtho 'tra nāstyeveti nirūpite /
vijñānamapi nāstyeva jñeyābhāve samutthite //17//
iti mādhyamikenaiva sarvaśūnyaṃ vicāritam /.

93. Śaṅkara, Commentary on *Brahmasūtra,* I.1.19: *yadaitasminnānandamaye alpamapyantaramatādātmyarūpaṃ paśyati tadā saṃsārabhayānna nivartate /.*

could not mutually borrow ideas and doctrinal concepts from each other, since each of them had quite a different background of traditions, as well as a differnt concept of reality.[94]

On the whole, one can easily enough sympathize with the real purpose of similar statements; still, there is a definite need to substantiate them with more detailed argumentation. My proposal is to approach the opposition of Advaita and Śūnyavāda from a slightly different angle. Let us, while examining the theory of two truths, which is similar in both systems, focus our attention not on the higher, absolute truth and its corresponding reality, but rather on the profane truth.

One should specify, however, that the very correlation of the two truths—the higher and the lower—was understood in a rather peculiar way. Nāgārjuna says in the *Kārikās:*

> Two truths are indicated in the Buddhists' teaching concerning *dharma:*
> The truth connected with the world *(loka-saṃvṛti)* and the truth from the higher standpoint *(paramārtha).*[95]

However, the higher truth in Mādhyamika, which is often equated with the emptiness *(śūnyatā)* of the world, can be comprehended also as an indication that all worldly phenomena are inter-dependent and inter-related. The refusal to look for some ontological reality over and above the interlinking of phenomena—the reality which could be separate from them but still could determine their exis-

---

94. Vide: T.R.V.Murti, *Saṃvṛti and Paramārtha in Mādhyamika and Advaita Vedānta: The Problem of Two Truths in Buddhism and Vedānta.* Dordrecht, 1973, p. 10.

95. Nāgārjuna, *Mādhyamika-kārikā,* XXIV.8:
eve satyd samupāśritya buddhānāṃ dharmadeśana /
lokasaṃvṛtisatyaṃ ca satyaṃ ca paramārthataḥ //8//.

tence—this refusal is probably close to the initial orientation of the Mādhyamikas' teaching, since, by the Buddhists' own avowal, they were actually looking for some middle *(mādhyama)* way between the extremes of nihilism and eternalism. In Nāgārjuna's words, for instance:

> This entity *(ātman)* cannot exist separately
> from the states of consciousness,
> But these states cannot exist without the self,
> which gives them unity;
> /but still/ they are not anything even when they are together.[96]

Incidentally, it is only in this way that one can explain the thesis of the identity of *saṃsāra* and *nirvāṇa,* since otherwise this Mādhyamika concept remais incomprehensible. These two truths or, perhaps, these two realities are completely superimposed over each other—just like two mutually convertible figures in *geṣtaltpsychologie*.

In his Commentary on *Mādhyamika-kārikā* by Nāgārjuna (it is called *Prasannapada,* or, Clear words) Candrakīrti gives his own interpretation of profane truth *(saṃvṛti-satya)* in Śūnyavāda. First of all, in accordance with its etymology, this truth conceals the real nature of things, forcing people to invent some general entities that are supposed to accompany ordinary phenomena; in this aspect *saṃvṛti* is identical with ignorance, or erroneous intellectual concepts. Besides that, *saṃvṛti* reflects the interdependence of phenomena, their ability to become 'causes' (of course, in the specific Buddhist meaning of the term) of each other. Finally, *saṃvṛti* is equated with ordinary worldly practice, being just some conventional, convenient *(saṅketa)* knowledge. In Nāgārjuna's words,

---

96. Nāgārjuna, *Mādhyamika-kārikā,* X.16:
ātmanaśca satattvaṃ ye bhāvānāṃ ca pṛthak pṛthak /
nirdiśanti na tān manye śāsanasyārthakovidān //16//.

Those, who do not know the difference between
these two truths,
Do not know the profound meaning of the Buddha's
teaching.[97]

The Mādhyamikas (as well as some later Advaitins who did not succeed in drawing a definite line between their own system and Buddhist conceptions; an example is the Vedantin Śrīharṣa)[98] regarded *saṃvṛti* as essentially erroneous, but still temporarily acceptable knowledge. By no means did they consider it to be an intermediate, interposing reality. One might add that in this respect they were willingly supported by the Jainas, as well as by the Mīmāṃsaka Kumārila.

In Śaṅkara's Advaita the correspondence of *saṃvṛti* is provided by the lower, profane knowledge (*aparavidyā*, or *vyāvahārikavidyā*). It tallies with ordinary worldly practice, *vyavahāra*. Both this knowledge and the world of experience as a sort of intermediary being, situated between the higher reality and a simple sense error, are posited within the framework of *avidyā*. One can see that in Buddhism the world, which is essentially homogeneous, is fastened together by causal dependence; it is structured by the interdependence and interrelation of phenomena. This concept is vulnerable to criticism—if only because it presupposes a general picture of reality in which the components are rooted in each other, abiding in each other. (In Indian logic this position was defined by the term *anyonyāśraya*). The inevitable consequence of it was infinite regress *(anavasthā)* and vicious circle *(cakraka)* in

97. Nāgārjuna, *Mādhyamika-kārikā*, XXIV.9:
ye 'nayor na vijānanti vibhāgaṃ satyayordvayoḥ /
te tattvaṃ na vijānanti gaṃbhīraṃ buddhaśāsane //9//.

98. In this respect Śrīharṣa was probably influenced by Kashmir Śaivism especially by the teaching of Abhinavagupta. Both of them maintain that any perception of differences cannot be essentially true, though Śrīharṣa stops at this tenet, while Abhinavagupta insists upon the absence of differences in the higher reality.

reasoning. Besides mere logical faults, there looms the danger of the impossibility of ultimate liberation. Furthermore, when a relation between two entities is examined in Advaita, it is never posited as an equal relationship; one must also take into account the vector of dependence—a precisely defined direction that determines the relationship. In other words, when two entities are connected with each other in some way, one of them should be higher and independent of the other. That is why Advaita regards *avidyā* as *śakti*; the emphasis is laid here not only on its creative power,[99] but primarily on its *dependence (paratantratā)* upon eternal Brahman.

Just as in Śūnyavāda, the higher *(pāramārthika)* truth in Advaita is related to the essentially ineffable *(anabhilāpya)* reality. However, in Śaṅkara's opinion, though we cannot speak about Brahman directly and literally, there is still a way to *indicate* its presence symbolically *(lakṣyārtham).* In the words of Śaṅkara's Commentary on *Brahmasūtra,* "Brahman is known in two aspects: in one as having limitations owing to various attributes of the universe, which is produced by names and forms, and in another as devoid of all attributes and opposed to that."[100] Both these approaches are represented in two groups of the Upaniṣadic saying: strictly speaking, all sacred texts are contained within the sphere of *avidyā*, but even inside the corpus of *śruti* texts there is a differentiation into the aphorisms "from the standpoint of the ultimate truth" and those "from the standpoint of worldly practice."

---

99. Padmapāda, the closest of Śaṅkara's disciples, notes in his subcommentary on the main work by the Advaitist that *avidyā* is interpreted by Śaṅkara as some power or potency, which forms the inanimate world *(jaḍātmikā avidyā śaktiḥ)* and constitutes its foundation *(upādāna).* Padmapāda, *Pañcapādikā, The Vizianagram Sanskrit Series,* 1891, p. 4.

100. Śaṅkara, Commentary on *Brahmasūtra,* I.1.11: *dvirūpaṃ hi brahmāvagamyate nāmarūpavikārabhedopādhiviśiṣṭaṃ tadviparītaṃ ca sarvopādhi vivarjitam* /.

The key sentence elucidating Śaṅkara's polemics with the Buddhists runs as follows: "No saying of the sacred scripture may be rejected, but, on being heard, it should be definitively added to the rest of the *śruti* texts, even if the latter are non-contradictory with each other and form an integrated whole."[101] That is why, according to Advaita, *the secondary (vyāvahārika) group of śruti texts is of no less importance than the primary (pāramārthika) one*—and hence all the *śruti* sayings relating, for instance, to creation, which starts as a mere pastime *(līlā)* of God,[102] to the origin of *māyā-avidyā* and the like, are to be wholly accepted.

These sayings, which seem quite subsidiary at first glance, are used to shift the emphasis of consideration; they accomplish a cataphatic function of describing Saguṇa-Brahman (Īśvara), or God the creator. It is to these texts that Śaṅkara turns for support when he opposes the doctrines which could be basically interpreted as a kind of psycho-technique. It is not by chance that Śaṅkara now stresses the importance of this group of *śruti* sayings: according to him, this is the only proper attitude for a person who aspires after liberation, since it gives one an opportunity to get hold of something transcending one's own being, something that started at a specific time-point (as long as the notion of time continues to make sense for this person). In Christianity, for instance, the same sort of guarantee, which prevents it from degenerating into just a moral theory or a psychoanalytical therapy, is provided by faith in the real incarnation, death and resurrection of Christ. In the words of the Danish religious philosopher Søren Kierkegaard, "men Vanskeligheden er at blive Christen, fordi enhver Christen kun er det ved at være naglet til det paradox at have begrundet sin evige Salighed paa

101. Śaṅkara, Commentary on *Brahmasūtra,* II.3.17: *nacakvacidaśravaṇamanyatra śrutaṃ varayitumarhati /śrutyantaragatasyāpi aviruddhasyādhikasyārthasya sarvatropasaṃhartavyatvāt /.*

102. Vide: Śaṅkara, Commentary on *Brahmasūtra,* II.1.33.

Forholdt til noget Historisk." ("But the difficulty is in becoming a Christian, since every Christian remains as such only as long as he is nailed to a paradox—the necessity to base his eternal bliss on some historical event.")[103]

Only with the help of *vyāvahārika śruti* aphorisms, which ultimately have only metaphorical meaning—but despite this should be accepted fully and seriously—an adept may regard his way to liberation as a way to something that really exists and existed before him; thanks to that, his own transition to the higher reality would not appear to him as just a remoulding and restructuring

103. S. Kierkegaard, *Afsluttende uvidenskabelig Efterskrift til de philosophiske Smuler. Mimisk-pathetisk-dialektisk Sammenskrift, Existentielt Indlaeg af Johannes Climacus.* Søren Kieerkegaard. *Samlede Vaerker.* Volume 10 (Andet halvbind). København, 1962, p. 244. In his work *Sygdommen til Døden (Sickness unto Death)* Kierkegaard says that it is absolutely indispensable to tie the thread of reflection with a knot of paradox, since otherwise the needle of reason might go back and forth forever: reflection would not 'sew' anything together. Attention to this problem was by no means accidental for Protestantism, where the stress was laid on personal effort, on one's inner, subjective experience. After Kierkegaard (and largely, *in the wake of* Kierkegaard) the realization of the dangers of a phenomenological approach to religious experience was manifested in the teaching of a Swiss theologian Karl Barth, who emphasized the importance of Christology. Soon, however, the Protestant *dialektische Theologie* gave rise to a slightly different approach to these problems. Since revelation here is regarded as a sort of breach inside eschatological time, as a sign of Christ's presence and contemporaneity with every true believer, the guarantees of the fulfilment of this promise are provided by the unreserved reliance upon the Word of the *New Testament*. To my mind, it is here that one should look for the core of the famous concept of *Entmythologisierung* (De-mythologization) suggested by Rudolf Bultmann (and not in the 'modernization' of the *Bible* interpretation, as is often believed). In this way the tradition of hermeneutics, used for the interpretation of Christian revelation (the foundation of which was laid by Friedrich Schleiermacher) was continued in this century. One might also remember that during the last years of his life Heidegger admitted that the sources of his later hermeneutical investigations could be found not in his classical philological education, but rather in the works by Schleiermacher, as well as in his own exercises on the exegetics of sacred scripture.

within his own consciousness. Śaṅkara writes in his Commentry on *Bṛhadāraṇyakopaniṣad:* "If someone maintains that the calming of consciousness is really the goal of men, /we would say:/ it is not so, since there should be a base for the fruits /of actions/; indeed, for a person who is pierced by a thorn, the fruit would be the calming of pain /when it is removed/, but if he were to die from this thorn, it would be impossible to achieve the calming of this pain."[104] Of course, it is quite clear that Śaṅkara is speaking here not only about the cessation of present earthly incarnation: the Buddhists shared the orthodox notion concerning transmigration. Still, Śaṅkara considered the Buddhists' orientation on a simple 'calming down' of consciousness to be groundless and even pernitious. To his mind, such an orientation was not substantiated for them by the ontological guarantees of ultimate liberation.

The restraint and auserity of Advaita in comparison with Buddhism are plainly manifested in its efforts to organize and differentiate the stages of ascent to the higher turth. In Śaṅkara's words, "it is the primary cause (*mūlakāraṇa,* lit., the root cause) itself which like an accomplished actor creates all the effects up to the last one by pronouncing the first words of all phenomenal practice,"[105] that is, Brahman is first of all to be comprehended as the origin of the world. Only on the higher stage (when the way is already accomplished and, so to speak, lies behind an adept) one might maintain that "in this *ātman* there is no entering,"[106] one might speak about its being

104. Śaṅkara, Commentary on *Bṛhadāraṇyakopaniṣad,* IV.3.7: *yadapi tasya vijñānasya nirvāṇaṃ puruṣārthaṃ kalpayanti tatrāpi phalāśrayānupapattiḥ kaṇḍakaviddhasya hi kaṇḍakavedhajanitaduḥkhanivṛttiḥ phalam /na tu kaṇḍakaviddhamaraṇe tadduḥkhanivṛttiphalasyāśraya upapadyate ... /.*

105. Śaṅkara, Commentary on *Brhamasūtra,* II.1.18: *tathā mūlakāraṇameva ā antyātkaryāttena tena kāryakāreṇa naṭavat ... vyavahārasya pratipadyate /.*

106. Vide: Śaṅkara, Commentary on *Brahmasūtra,* IV.3.14: *na punarbrahmāgamanam upapadyate /;* Commentary on *Brahmasūtra,* I.1.4: *naca tadātmanaṃ praveśaḥ saṃbhavati /.*

ungraspable, ineffable, devoid of attributes. "Without the realization of the other entity, Śaṅkara warns his opponent, one cannot deny ordinary practice, established in accordance with all means of valid knowledge."[107] And, in the words of the Advaitist, anyone who perceives objects in a usual way, but arbitrarily interprets his perceptions, "would become similar to a person, who is eating but still asserts: I am not eating and I am not satisfied."[108] Therefore, the *pāramārthika* level presupposes a preceding ascent to this higher reality, and this ascent, according to Śaṅkara, is simply impossible without reference to Upaniṣadic sayings. As we recall, these sayings form a hierarchic sequence; while going up these steps, one should not skip over stages: each of the sayings—even those that are only indirectly hinting at the nature of Brahman—should be understood and accepted in turn. The need for sacred texts loses its validity only for the adept who succeeds in attaining his goal.[109]

Only *after* this qualitative leap and dissolution in the higher Brahman does consciousness reveal its inner essence as self-evident and self-luminous. From Śaṅkara's standpoint, the Buddhist assertion that consciousness is

---

107. Śaṅkara, Commentary on *Brahmasūtra,* II.2.31: *nahyayaṃ sarvapramāṇaprasiddho lokavyavahāro anyattattvamanadhigamya śakyate ... /.*

108. Ibid., II.2.28: *yathā hi kaścidbhuñjāno ... brūyānnāhaṃ bhuñje na vā tṛpyāmīti /.*

109. As long as Meister Eckhart has already been mentioned, I would like to cite yet another of his aphorisms, which is referred to by an Italian semiotic, Umberto Eco, in his book *The Name of the rose* (U. Eco, *Il nome della rosa*). These words, presented without any translation or even attribution, constitute the main semantic center of the concluding passage of the book; they run as follows: "En muoz gelîchesame die leiter abewerfen, sô er an ir ufgestigen." ("it is necessary to throw away the ladder as soon as one has climbed on it"). Historians of philosophy would be certainly reminded in this connection of a no-less-expressive passage from *Logiko-Philosophische Traktat* of Ludvig Wittgenstein.

always manifested in this form is clearly not conscientious and is based on the mixing up of different levels of perception, as well as on the opponents' efforts to reduce the ontological aspect of the problem to a psychological one.

CHAPTER VI

Brahman in Language and Ritual: Freedom and Moral Duties

1. *ADVAITA AND PŪRVA-MĪMĀṂSĀ*

Now we can go beyond the limits of the direct opposition of openly hostile systems and investigate the relation of Advaita with the closest of its counterparts belonging to the sphere of orthodoxy. The differences here often seem eroded: many of the notions and conceptions coincide and some of them are frankly borrowed from similar systems. Nevertheless, that only means that one should be even more attentive and careful while drawing the line of demarcation between similar ideas.

Śaṅkara's Advaita, which was also called Uttara-Mīmāṃsā, or later, subsequent Mīmāṃsā, fully shared the notion of Pūrva-Mīmāṃsā (first, earlier Mīmāṃsā) about the absolute validity of Upaniṣadic sayings. In both these orthodox teachings the sacred texts are regarded as the root or source of any human knowledge (the conception of *veda-mūlatva*, formulated for the first time in *Mīmāṃsā-sūtra* of Jaimini).[1] When speaking about their similarity,

1. The tradition of Pūrva-Mīmāṃsā, as well as that of any other Indian philosophical school, had its own teachers and disciples. Its basic text is *Mīmāṃsāsūtra* by Jaimini, who was probably a contemporary of Bādarāyaṇa. This text became a foundation for a commentary (*Bhāṣya*) of Śabara (*ca.* fourth to fifth century AD), which in its turn inspired a sub-commentary by Prabhākara (seventh to the beginning of the eighth century), who wrote a work entitled *Bṛhati*. Another prominent Mīmāṃsā philosopher, Kumārila, wrote three sub-commentaries on Śabara's *Bhāṣya;* these three texts, written in about the seventh century, were

one should remember the concept of *veda-prāmāṇyam,* that is, the assertion that the Vedas can be a valid *pramāṇa;* this concept is undoubtedly essential both for Mīmāṃsā and for Advaita.

One of the differences between the systems is, of course, quite obvious. It is fairly well known that Pūrva-Mīmāṃsā regarded the sacred texts primarily as a dependable means to force a man to perform necessary rites. As for Śaṅkara, he emphasized the importance of the Vedas for the knowledge of Brahman. In his words, "the texts of *śruti* describe according to his own nature ... the *puruṣa* who is taught about by the *upaniṣads.*"[2] In Śaṅkara's Commentary on *Brahmasūtra* his polemics with the adherents of Pūrva-Mīmāṃsā is most thoroughly represented in the fourth *sūtra* of the first *pāda* of the first *adhyāya.* The heart of the matter is formulated in the following way: Advaita seeks the *knowledge* about already existing, real entity, that is, Brahman; while Mīmāṃsā aims at the *injunctions* about something which has to be done in the future (a definite, usually a ritual, action).

Moreover, following his line of reasoning, Śaṅkara notes that the rites are "ordered for a person who is prone to vices like passion and hate, /as well as/ to ignorance."[3] True, in this passage from his Commentary on *Bṛhadāraṇyakopaniṣad* the Advaitist implies primarily some specific kinds of ritual actions that are prescribed in special circumstances. But somewhat later he determines the general position of Advaita: "The injunction to perform

---

Śloka-vārttika, Tantra-vārttika and *Ṭupṭīkā.* Kumārila's sub-commentaries deal in detail with all the chapters of Jaimini's *Sūtras,* as well as with Śabara's Commentary. *Śloka-vārttika* became the most important of Kumārila's works; it also exercized the most profound influence upon the teaching of Śaṅkara.

2. Śaṅkara, Commentary on *Bṛhadāraṇyakopaniṣad,* III.9.26: *aupaniṣadasya puruṣasya ākhyāyikato—śrutyā svena rūpeṇa—nirdeśaḥ kṛtaḥ* /.

3. Śaṅkara, Commentary on *Bṛhadāraṇyakopaniṣad,* I.3.1: *avidyārāgadveṣādidoṣavato vihitatvāt* /.

some action is not observed for somebody who has realized the true nature of the higher *ātman,* except, /perhaps/, the efforts /that are directed / towards complete peace. The knowledge of *ātman* presupposes the destruction of the very cause of action, that is, the knowledge of various means /to attain this goal/, such as /the knowledge / of gods and like .... Indeed, for somebody who is firmly assured /in his own self/ in Brahman, devoid of size, non-dual, non-divided by time, space and so on, there is no performance of rites."[4]

Still, even this more or less obvious discrepancy between Śaṅkara's teaching and Pūrva-Mīmāṃsā needs somewhat greater accuracy. First of all, an indifferent observer or an outsider might think that the contradiction here is not that glaring. Indeed, one cannot but agree that the most important thing for the Advaitist was his relying on sacred texts. And so, as long as this essential condition is fulfilled, all the rest might be just a matter of the degree of understanding or the stage in the adept's ascent. If, for instance, in the beginning he is more concerned about ritual actions taught by Mīmāṃsā, later he might move quite naturally to higher knowledge, proposed by Advaita.

Nevertheless, to my mind, the teaching of Śaṅkara does not allow for this kind of conclusion. Though Indian tradition used to combine Pūrva-Mīmāṃsā and Advaita as a pair of kindred systems, Advaita cannot be regarded as a simple addition to Mīmāṃsā, or as its natural continuation.

Let us examine once again, more attentively, the notion of sacred texts in both schools of thought. The Advaitist differs from the Mīmāṃsā followers not only in his conception of the aim of Vedic texts, but also in his attitude towards the correlation of their parts. However, now the

4. Śaṅkara, Commentary on *Bṛhadāraṇyakopaniṣad,* I.3.1: *na paramātmyāthātmyavijñānavataḥ samopāyavyatirekeṇa kiṃcitkarma vihitamupalabhyate / karmanimittadevatādisarvasādhanavijñānopamardena hyātmajñānaṃ vidhīyate ... / na hi deśakālādyanavacchinnāsthūlādvayādibrahmapratyayadhāriṇaḥ karmāvasaro 'sti /*

two groups of Upaniṣadic sayings are singled out in quite a different way than in Śaṅkara's polemics with the adherents of heterodox schools. According to the traditional classification, the content of Vedic texts is divided into injunctions *(vidhi),* prohibitions *(pratiṣedha),* magic incantations *(mantra),* names *(nāma)* and the so-called explaining passages *(arthavāda).* Singling out the *arthavāda* sayings (they mainly consist of Upaniṣadic texts as contrasted to the ritualistic sayings of the *brāhmanas)* is usually connected with the works of the grammarian Bhartṛhari; one may find the description of these parts of the Vedas in the commentary *Vṛtti* on his treatise *Vākyapadīya.*[5]

Since the prohibitions might be also interpreted as injunctions about abstention from actions, the main kinds of Vedic texts remain the sayings *vidhi* and *arthavāda.* The texts related to the knowledge of Brahman certainly fall under the category of *arthavāda*; and Śaṅkara himself shows a decided preference for this group of texts. In the words of the Advaitist, "the horizon of reality of *ātman*-Brahman is knowledge and /therefore/ it does not depend upon injunctions. Though imperative verbs /which induce one to action/ in the Upaniṣads do get within this horizon, they are inapplicable there, just like the sharpness of a razor /is useless/ when it becomes blunt striking the stone, since the essence of this horizon, /that is, Brahman,/ is the reality which cannot be accepted or rejected."[6] Or, as he specified even more definitely in his Commentary on *Bṛhadāraṇyakopaniṣad,* "the reason for the authorita-

---

5. Especially the commentary on the first part of *Vākyapadīya: Brahmakāṇḍa,* 8. About this vide, also: W. Halbfass, *Studies in Kumārila and Śaṅkara,* Reinbek, 1983, pp.44, 77.

6. Śaṅkara, Commentary on *Brahmasūtra,* I.1.4: *yathābhūtabrahmātmaviṣayam api jñānaṃ na codanātantram / tadviṣaye liṅādayaḥ śrūyamāṇa 'pyaniyojyaviṣayatvāt kunṭhī bhavantyupalādiṣu prayuktakṣurataikṣṇyādivat / aheyānupādeyavastuviṣayatvāt /. Viṣaya (viṣayatva here)* means, of course, not an object, but rather objective field or horizon, that is, the sphere of the cognition of Brahman.

tiveness or non-authoritativeness of a saying does not consist in the fact that it describes /some/ object or /a proper/ action ... but in its ability to produce definite and fruitful knowledge."[7]

For Jaimini, Prabhākara or Kumārila the most valid are the sayings of the sacred scripture which immediately prompt an adept to action, that is, definite injunctions *(vidhi),* usually connected with rites. In his commentary on *Brahmasūtra* Śaṅkara says from the standpoint of Pūrva-Mīmāṃsā adherents: "Beyond their connection with injunctions, one cannot ever show the slightest indication that Vedic sayings have a purpose."[8] Other parts of the Vedas, in particular, the *arthavāda* texts, according to the Mīmāṃsakas, have only auxiliary meaning. When possible, they should be added to injunctions, and the role they play boils down to the propedeutical function of persuasion. In other words, the Upaniṣadic sayings, explanatory and illustrative, 'superfluous' in their impracticality, (and which are generally classified *as arthavāda*) are intended for spiritually immature adept, who is not yet ready to accept the grim picture of the world according to Mīmāṃsā, the picture that leaves no place for God or for the absolute unity of God and *ātman,* where ultimately there is only duty *(dharma),* regarded as an unswerving performance of ritual actions.[9] It goes without saying that

7. Śaṅkara, Commentary on *Bṛhadāraṇyakopaniṣad,* I.4.7: *na vākyasya vastvanvākhyānaṃ kriyānvākhyānaṃ vā prāmāṇyāprāmāṇyakāraṇam ... niścitaphalavadvijñānotpādakatvam /*. Somewhat later Śaṅkara refers in his commentary to a saying from the *Chāndogyopaniṣad* (VII.1.3), which runs as follows: "I am only the knower of the mantras, and not the knower of *ātman,* and /therefore/ I grieve." *(mantravidevāsmi nātmavitso 'haṃ ... śocāmi ... /.)*

8. Śaṅkara, Commentary on *Brahmasūtra,* I.1.4: *na kvacidapi vedavākyānāṃ vidhisaṃsparśamantareṇārthavattā dṛṣṭopapannā vā /.*

9. However, here one needs a certain clarification. In Śabara's words, "dharma is the meaning which links a man to higher fulfillment." *('so'rthaḥ puruṣaṃ niḥśreyas ena saṃyunakti') (Śābara-bhāṣyam,* XVI.

for Śaṅkara the *arthavāda* texts cannot ever be considered just auxiliary or subsidiary. "And if some people maintain /like the followers of Prabhākara /", says the Advaitist, "that there is no part of the Vedas telling about an object as such, except the injunctions that /induce/ one to actions or to their avoidance, as well as some additional parts / joining these injunctions/, then /we would say that / it is not so, since the *puruṣa* of the Upaniṣads cannot be subsidiary to something else."[10]

Mīmāṃsā was formed on the peak of Brahmanism as a religion of sacrifice, being its self-reflection and a means of philosophical comprehension. It clearly formulated its approach to the structure of the world, according to which the entire universe can be easily perceived in its spatial-temporal relations. In other words, the universe is not conceived as an outer envelope or a shell, hiding some higher entity which is the foundation of the world and its ultimate justifiction. The whole cosmos as nature, encompassing living beings, gods and people, is not based on anything beyond its own structure and mechanism. In the words of Raymundo Panikkar, according to this picture of the world, "This ultimate structure is not to be regarded as 'another' or 'deeper' 'thing' or substance; it is in fact sacrifice, which is, precisely, the internal dynamism of the universc, universal *ṛta*, cosmic order itself .... Sacrifice is the act that makes the unverse."[11] Along with that, for an ordinary man deeply engrossed in everyday life, ritual action (*yāga*) is a symbol of the higher significance and

---

11-12.) Besides that, *dharma* has its cause or characteristic *(lakṣaṇa)* in Vedic sayings *(Śābara-bhāṣyam,* XVI.8). Therefore, *dharma* cannot be reduced to rites as such *(yāga),* but is revealed—or gains significance—in ritual actions.

10. Śaṅkara, Commentary on *Brahmasūtra,* I.1.4: *yadapi kecidāhuḥ pravṛttinivṛttividhitaccheśavyatirekeṇa kevalavastuvādi vedabhāgo nāstīti tan na / aupaniṣadasya puruṣasyānanyaśeṣatvāt /.*

11. R. Panikkar, *The Vedic Experience,* Poona, 1958, pp. 352-353.

order; it is this action which gives meaning and dynamic tension to ordinary life. Francis D'Sa, a scholar who investigates primarily the tradition of Pūrva-Mīmāṃsā, writes that according to it, "such a sacrifice is not so much a ritual as a cosmic and communitarian action which makes and maintains cosmos as community."[12]

So the *dharma* of each individual being, the following of proper injunctions, is something, which, according to Śabara, "puts a man in contact with the higher fulfillment." And this higher fulfillment *(niḥśreyasa)*, or the aim of man *(puruṣārtha)*[13] is comprehended in Pūrva-Mīmāṃsā as the source of permanent bliss, usually identified with heaven (*svarga*). Actually, there is no need for persuasion in order to make one strive for bliss; the anticipated pleasure beckons and impels a man, waking in him a passionate thirst (*lipsā*). Still, the higher bliss is more problematic and evasive in this respect, since it is only outlined in some distant perspective, and does not immediately follow the performance of the act which is ordered by injunctions. However, the unavoidable connection between the action and bliss is demonstrated in an additional definition of *dharma* as something, which is "revealed in Vedic sayings and has a characteristic of inducing one to action";[14] here the validity of the higher ful-

---

12. Francis, X. D'Sa, *Śabdaprāmāṇyam in Śabara and Kumārila*, Vienna, 1980, p. 20.

13. On the one hand, it is the common goal, towards which all people naturally strive, while on the other it is something significant both for an individual and for the sake of one's destiny. In Śabara's words, "that in which a man finds pleasure, /that is,/ that significant thing, which when accomplished, originates pleasure, is the aim of man." (*yasmin prītiḥ puruṣasya yasmin kṛte padārthe puruṣasya prītirbhavati sa puruṣārthaḥ padārthaḥ* /. (*Śābara-bhāṣyam,* IV.1.2.2.) According to the interpretation of Francis D'Sa, pleasure *(prīti)* is something which is defined as being capable of attracting people. (Frances X. D'Sa, *Śabdaprāmāṇyam in Śabara and Kumārila*, p.21.)

14. Jaimini, *Mīmāṃsāsūtra,* I.1.2: *codanālakṣaṇo 'rtho dharmaḥ* /.

fillment acquires a solid guarantee owing to the connection of *dharma* with sacred scripture.

One might note from this text that the sayings of the Vedas (*vedavacana*) are defined in the teachings of Jaimini and Śabara by the term *codanā*, which literally means impact, or compelling. The adherents of Mīmāṃsā regard in this way both direct injunctions and prohibitions, as well as all the other Vedic texts which explain why some specific action should be performed. Kumārila directly identifies *codanā* with the word of revelation (*śabda*) (Vide: *Ślokavārttika, Codanāsūtra,*), which ultimately helps him not only to link the injunctions with the general corpus of Vedic texts, but also to arrive at the concept of the word in Pūrva-Mīmāṃsā.

As noted before, Mīmāṃsā regards injunctions (*vidhi*) as the sayings with the greatest validity among all the Vedic texts; they are usually presented in the imperative tense.[15] This naturally follows from the concept of the activity of the word, which is supposed to affect its listener, thanks to the so-called 'energy of becoming' (*bhāvanā*).[16] Indeed, according to the semantic tradition popular in various Indian philosophical schools, every phrase generates a sort of new sense impulse, which cannot be reduced to the simple addition of the meanings of its components, or separate words. This energy manifests itself primarily in the main active core of the phrase, that is, its verb, and is revealed in triple form: as a syntactic anticipation of the implied meaning (*ākāṅkṣā*); as a phonetic continuity (*saṃnidhi),* which actually forms the unity of the phrase; and as the logical sequence of the whole sentence (*yogyatā*),

---

15. To be more precise, they are presented in the imperative, optative, desiderative, as well as in the gerundive form.

16. In the interpretation of F. Edgerton, "the heart of each injunction is the efficient-force, the *bhāvanā*. This word is a noun of action from the causative of the root *bhū*, 'to come into being', and means accordingly 'a causing to come into being', a bringing-about, tendency to produce something; or as I have rendered it, 'efficient-force'." F. Edgerton, *Mīmāṃsā Nyāya Prakāśa,* New Haven, 1929, p. 5.

which allows one to conclude something about the meaning of the phrase. Owing to this triple correspondence, which is fused together in a united 'energy of becoming', the active influence of injunctions embraces not only the ritual itself, but also the acquisition of 'heaven' through ritual actions.

According to Mīmāṃsā, in the injunction itself there is latently present *śabda-bhāvanā,* or the force which induces the appearance of something new, while in the case of the performance of the prescribed action there is generated the energy of *artha-bhāvana,* which allows for the inevitable attainment of the fruit of action. In other words, having exposed himself to the inner energy of the injuction, an adept inevitably gets the result of the action, that is, the higher fulfillment, or 'heaven' (*svarga*). But that necessarily means that what is omitted from this moving towards *svarga* is personal striving, since from the moment of one's exposure to the efficient force of injunction, the process takes place on an impersonal basis, as if automatically. Therefore, according to Mīmāṃsā, the Vedic injunction, or *vidhi,* is determined by its own effort, and is by and large its own *ratio sufficiens,* while the sacred scripture is certainly absolutely valid and unconditioned. Of course, Śaṅkara would have gladly agreed with the latter statement, but still the Advaitist's idea of the eternity of *śruti,* as if that of man's dependence upon Vedic sayings, was quite different. According to his profound conviction, "the sacred texts do not hinder /people/ and do not induce /them to act/ by force, like slaves."[17]

Actually the notion of the eternity of Vedic texts and the Word in general (the notion of *śabda-nityatā*) was reduced by Śabara and Kumārila to the concept of the eternity of syllables *(varṇa-nityatā)* as the smallest separate particles of revelation. This reduction was brought about by the wish to dissociate themselves from the doctrine of *sphoṭa-vāda,* characteristic of the grammarians (primar-

17. Śaṅkara, Commentary on *Bṛhadāraṇyakopaniṣad,* II.1.20: *na tu śāstraṃ bhṛtyāniva balānivartayati niyojayati vā /.*

ily, of Bhartṛhari). Kumārila, who was probably closest to the actual concept of the eternity of *śruti* sayings, still could not accept the grammarians' doctrine concerning the reality of some absolute sound entity (*sphoṭa*) lying *over and above* the pronounced syllables, though manifested through them. In order to realize his motives, it is enough to remember that the very pathos of Pūrva-Mīmāṃsā was directed towards a sort of *positivist* denial of any reality, existing as a background of manifold phenomena, producing them and determining their very being.

To my mind, the concept of Pūrva-Mīmāṃā in this respect is curiously reminiscent of the Buddhist attitude to existence. It certainly was not accidental that one of the main reasons for divergence between Advaita and Mīmāṃsā was the concept of the omniscient and omnipotent Brahman as the creator of the universe. In Mīmāṃsā, where the world is wound up like a clockwork mechanism by prescribed action, that is, by rite, there is no longer any necessity for the creator, who is supposed to have thought out and arranged the structure of this world. Kumārila denies the existence of an omniscient person (this notion is called *asarvajñatva*), since, according to him, this person could become comprehensible only to some other omniscient personality, and so on. The argument from infinite regress (*anavasthā*) is also used by him to refute the possibility of the existence of an omnipotent creator (the notion of *asraṣṭṛtva*). Besides, maintains Kumārila, it remains unclear why an omnipotent person should wish to create something. As we may remember in this connection, according to Śaṅkara, the world starts as a mere play or pastime (*līlā*), as a pure creative impulse of Īśvara.

Meanwhile, in philosophical systems that acknowledge the transcendentality of the higher reality—for instance, in Advaita—the central part is played by thinking in analogies,[18] by recourse to myths, parables, metaphors, symbolic language in general. In Mīmāṃsā, where action

18. Vide: the work by H. Brückner about the role of a graphic example *(dṛṣṭānta)* in Śaṅkara's system. However, the scholar unwar-

was taking place inside the obvious spacial-temporal relations, we can see a sort of drying-up of the initial symbolical definition of the role of the word, whose sphere was narrowed down to the limits of ritual practice. The Mīmāṃsā language was shaped after the rigid forms of *vidhi*, so that attention was paid mainly to the simple correspondence between the word and its denotation. The focus upon the pragmatic result led to an intellectual situation in which even the notion of the initial eternity of syllables was replaced by the teaching about the simple beginninglessness *(anādi-nityatā)* of the pronounced syllables, which manifested itself in an uninterrupted teachers' tradition *(guru-śiṣya-paramparā)*. This picture not only directs against Mīmāṃsā its own argument, accusing the opponents of infinite regress in their reasoning; what is really important is the fact that it perfectly corresponds to an image of an immature adept, who is being passively led and induced by the impersonal commands of injunctions, an adept who feels himself to be just a small and insignificant cog in the complicated mechanism of the universe.

Everything would have been probably different had Mīmāṃsā chosen in its philosophy of language the sayings of the *arthavāda* type. The possibilities here are much richer. It was Bhartṛhari who noted that there are three main kinds of explanatory sayings *(arthavāda)*: the first is *guṇavāda*, or attributive shifting of meaning from one object to another (for example, when one says, "The sun has become a sacrificial pole"); the second is *anuvāda*, or corroborating with other words somethings already said or implied; and the third is *bhūtavāda*, or the reference to

---

rantedly narrows the sphere of the use of analogy and therefore arrives at some unjustified conclusions concerning the allegedly logical foundation of Śaṅkara's reasoning used for proving the validity of Vedic sayings. (H. Brückner, *Zum Beweisverfahren Śaṃkaras. Eine Untersuchung der From und Funktion von dṛṣṭānta im Bṛhadāraṇyakopaniṣadbhāṣya und Chāndogyopaniṣadbhāṣya des Śaṃkara Bhagavatpāda*, Berlin, 1979.

some well-known fact or occurrence (usually some event described in the Vedas). Besides that, *arthavāda* sayings may express praise or blame, or give a description of some heroic deed or some former event. It is fairly difficult to guess what would have been the direction of Mīmāṃsā evolution, had this system chosen for the base of its *śabda-prāmāṇyam* notion (the doctrine of the validity of Vedic texts) the *arthavāda* portions of the Vedas. In this case we would be probably dealing with a *Weltaschauung* resembling the *dhvani* doctrine of Ānandavardhana,[19] or with a system similar to Śaṅkara's Advaita.

Śaṅkara never considered Vedic sayings to be a kind of auxiliary instrument designed to bring an immature and dependent adept to perform necessary action; the goal of *śruti* is by no means that of inducing or enlightening a lazy or dumb disciple. In his opinion, all *śruti* sayings form an integrated and organic whole: one might pull by any thread—if it is done seriously and by right procedure—the whole illusory intertwining of the universe might become undone and dissolve, so that the true core of being, or *ātman,* might shine through and reveal itself. That is why the Bādarāyaṇa's *sūtra* (I.1.4) concerning the inner *harmony* and *concert* of all sacred texts is interpreted by Śaṅkara in his Commentary in the following way: "since in all the Upaniṣads the aphorisms follow each other, being oriented towards this goal (that is, *ātman)* and explaining only it."[20]

Moreover, if one were really to discuss the hierarchical structure of Upaniṣadic sayings, it becomes quite clear

19. Incidentally, the esthetical teaching about *dhvani,* or figurative allusion of poetic expression, was evolving in close contact with Kashmir Śaivism. At the beginning of the eleventh century Abhinavagupta wrote a commentary entitled *Locanā* (lit.: an eye) on the treatise *Dhvanyāloka* (The light of *dhvani*) by Ānandavardhana, composed in Kashmir before the end of the ninth century.

20. Śaṅkara, Commentary on *Brahmasūtra,* I.1.4: *sarveṣu hi vedānteṣu vākyāni tātparyenaitasyārthasya pratipādakatvena samanugatāni* /.

that according to Advaita, its base is formed by injunctions and prohibitions that represent some auxiliary conditions of attaining liberation, while the summit is manifested by the so-called great sayings (*mahāvākya*) of the Upaniṣads. The latter group of sayings is composed of the celebrated maxims *Tat tvam asi* (Thou art that), from *Bṛhadāraṇya-kopaniṣad,* III.9, *Chāndogyopaniṣad,* VI.8.7, etc.; *ayamātma brahma* (This *ātman* is Brahman), from *Bṛhadāraṇyakopaniṣad,* II.5.9, etc. These most significant sayings are 'useless' and devoid of any pragmatic meaning; they lead, strictly speaking, nowhere and teach no one, they only help to shift the angle of consideration, focusing attention on *ātman.* As for the portions of *śruti* which call to the knowledge of *ātman,* they are only apparently similar to injunctions; "their aim", writes Śaṅkara, "is to be the means of detachment from the objects towards which one is naturally attracted."[21] The same motive of a *shifting* can be found in his Commentary on the *Bhagavad-gītā,* when the Advaitist speaks about the necessity to become firm, steady (*sthira*), fixed in inner concentration: "the glance of the eyes /should be/ drawn towards the base."[22]

Such an angle-shifting presupposes a different notion of the function of language. Instead of the descriptive function, which provides for maintaining fixed and uniform correspondences between the object and meaning, priority is given to the evocative function. Even if the word does not directly create the world, as suggested by the grammarians, only the word is capable of revealing the true nature of the world. Legends and incantations, metaphors and epithets, irony and pathos—everything is used in order to create a colorful appearance, which bears a likeness to the world and, therefore, becomes a 'reflection of a reflection'

---

21. Śaṅkara, Commentary on *Brahmasūtra,* I.1.4: *svābhāvi-kapravṛttiviṣayavimukhīkaraṇārthānīti brūmaḥ* /.

22. Śaṅkara, Commentary on the *Bhagavadgītā,* VI.13: ... *cakṣuṣoḥ dṛṣṭisaṃnipātaḥ* /.

of the higher reality, hidden under empirical phenomena. That is why (and not fearing the danger of rationalistic argumentation to sacred scripture) Śaṅkara so passionately opposed the 'drying-up reasoning' *(śuṣka-tarka)*[23] of the logicians, as well as of the Mīmāṃsā adherents.

In the third chapter I raised the question of the reasons for Śaṅkara's keen attention to language. But the matter under discussion was mainly the poetical language of *śruti* and its part in the realization of the higher Brahman devoid of attributes (Nirguṇa-Brahman), that is, in the terms of apophatical theology. Probably the most concise expression for this correspondence can be found in the following *śruti* text: "Since the gods appear to like the indirect (*parokṣa,* lit., beyond the range of sight) and hate the direct /name/."[24] According to Śaṅkara, however, the word has also another—cataphatic—role, which becomes apparent in the gradual approach to God and Creator of the world, or Īśvara (Saguṇa-Brahman).

In order to comprehend this, one should remember a great European scholastic who lived more than four centuries later than Śaṅkara. For Thomas Aquinas, the possibility of knowing God is based on the notion of 'analogy of being' *(analogia entis),* that is, gradually manifests itself from the being of the created universe. The nature of God is profoundly different from the nature of the world, but 'various things might in a different way participate in the likeness of God's essence. God Himself is the primary

23. The term itself was introduced by Bhartṛhari *(Vākyapadīya,* I.34). Śaṅkara makes use of it in his Commentary on *Brahmasūtra,* II.1.11; II.2.6, etc. Vide also *Bhāgavata-purāṇa,* 12.20; XI.18.30. One recalls that in the teaching of Bhartṛhari the word is regarded as an inner seed *(bīja)* of being, which illuminates every cognition of an object with its own light. This notion is directly opposed to the concept of Nyāya, where the word is considered mostly as an outward, accidental envelope for thought and cognition.

24. *Bṛhadāraṇyakopaniṣad,* IV.2.2: *parokṣapriyā iva hi devāḥ pratyakṣadviṣaḥ /.*

model."[25] In other words, the universe is a kind of ladder of existing things, created owing to God's permission and mercy in order to facilitate man's ascent to God. Quite a similar notion of the hierarchical organization of the world surfaces in Śaṅkara's system, as soon as his interest shifts in the direction of Īśvara, or God the creator (and, incidentally, one of the main points of dispute between Advaita and Pūrva-Mīmāṃsā). In the words of the Advaitist, "among those having a body, starting with the people and ending with /Saguṇa-/Brahman, owing to a certain gradation of happiness from bodily /objects/, there is also the gradation of those who enjoy them. And owing to that, there is a certain gradation even of duty. And owing to the gradation of duty, there is gradation of persons. It is known that the gradation of persons is determined by their abilities, predilections and the like."[26]

---

25. Thomas Aquinas, *Summa theologiae,* I. q. 44, 3c. Of course, it is not by chance that some analogies with a 'regular' Christian theology (unlike those with an 'illegitimate' breach of the mystics) appear in Advaita only on the level of Saguṇa-Brahman (Brahman, having attributes), that is, on the level of the personified Īśvara. According to some modern neo-thomistic versions of Christianity, god's plan for the world consists in entrusting all beings to his own goodness, which is manifested as their own aim. It is done, certainly, not for the growth of this goodness, for that is impossible, but in order to stamp upon all these beings some likeness with this good. The existence (*esse*) of every thing and every being has its own place inside a hierarchy of different levels of existence, while the form (*forma*) is something which every time determines a specific level of *esse*—that is, determines also the greater or the lesser likeness to God (Vide: Henry Chavannes, *L'analogie entre dieu et le monde, selon saint Thomas d'Aquin et selon Karl Barth,* Paris, 1969, pp.64-65). Incidentally, according to the apt remark of H. Chavannes, the notion of *analogia entis* in Thomas Aquinas is based mainly upon the doctrine of close resemblance (or inner likeness) of cause and effect.

26. Śaṅkara, Commentary on *Brahmasūtra,* I.4: *manuṣyatvādārabhya brahmānteṣu dehavatsu sukhatāratamyādadhikāritāratamyam / tataśca taddhetor dharmasyāpi tāratamyaṃ gamyate / dharmatāratamyādadhikāritāratamyam / prasiddhaṃ cārthitvasāmarthyāvidvattādhikṛtamadhikāritāratamyam /.*

It goes without saying that in Śaṅkara's system many notions had completely different meaning from those of Christianity—the parallels here should not lead us too far. For example, in Advaita the ontological status of Īśvara and that of an individual soul are similar, their consciousnesses are in some respect commensurable; however, the possibility of a direct relationship here is hindered, since the *ātman* of man is obscured by the veiling power of *avidyā*. Therefore, the beginning of the way to Brahman calls for inserting an intermediary link, an analogy, between the creator and the living soul (*jīva*). If one were to follow the suggested comparison with creative activity, perhaps it would be more apt to resort to a modern interpretation of art, according to which the artist and the spectator are essentially equal in their creative activity, but need a concrete analogy in the form of an art object, so that they can relate to each other.[27]

One is reminded in this connection of a well-known hypothesis of the adherents of the 'Neo-Humboldtian' approach in linguistics, in particular, of the theory of E. Sapir and B. Whorf. In its general outline the doctrine maintains that the world really exists for us only as long as it is reflected in language, since it is language which

---

27. This kind of interpretation we find, for example, in Jean-Paul Sartre:"L'acte imageant, pris dans sa généralité, est celui d'une conscience qui vise un objet absent ou inexistant à travers une certaine realité que j'ai nommé ailleurs *analogon* et qui fonctionne non comm un sign mais comme un symbole" ("The act of imagination taken in its generality, is the act of consciousness which aims at an absent or nonexistent object through a certain reality that I defined elsewhere an *analogon*—this reality functions not as a sign but as a symbol.") (The passage is taken from Sartre's work on Flaubert entitled *Idiot de la famille;* some excerpts from it can be found in the article "L'acteur." Vide: J.P. Sartre, *Un théâtre de situations,* Paris, 1973, p. 199.) There is a passage dealing with the notion of analogy *(analogie)* in Sartre's work *L'imaginaire,* where one finds the following explanation: "Si le mot devient l'image mentale, il cesse de jouer la part d'un simple signe" ("And if the word becomes a mental image, it ceases to play the role of a simple sign.") (J.P. Sartre, L'imaginaire), Paris, 1940, p. 112).

preconditions the type of thinking, as well as the very culture of a given people. According to B. Whorf, nature is divided into separate classes and categories owing to the suggestions of language; the manifold kaleidoscope of impressions is organized by our consciousness, that is, primarily by the language system that structures all our experiences and events. A somewhat similar doctrine was propounded by a German linguistic scholar, Leo Weisgerber, who regarded language as a sort of an 'intermediate world' between consciousness and reality.[28]

In Advaita, Brahman creates the world and in the beginning of each world cycle he gives it the Vedas;[29] in other words, Īśvara creates a hierarchy of being, resembling steps leading to liberation. The merit, and even duty, of an adept is to meet these efforts half-way, creating, in his turn, a sort of poetic analogy of being. The pattern for these poetical works is provided, of course, by the sacred texts of *śruti.* Then the sayings of the *anuvāda* type, or reiterations of something said before, become promptings for an aspiring adept; a scholastic treatise gives enough place for discussions about figurative *(gauṇa)* meaning (vide: Śaṅkara's Commentary on *Brahmastura,* I.1.4), while the most prominent philosopher quite naturally turns out to be also one of the greatest poets of his time. It is the creative character of language, taken to its utmost limit and using every possibility of skillful interpretation or expansion of meaning, that supplies a brilliant and striking likeness to Īśvara's own theurgical play *(līlā)* of creation.

This interpretation may seem a bit arbitrary and therefore somewhat distant from the actual content of Śaṅkara's works. However, some indirect indications speak in favor

---

28. Vide: L. Weisgerber, *Von den Kräften der deutschen Sprache III. Die Muttersprache im Aufbau unserer Kultur.* Düsseldorf, 1957; L. Weisgerber, *Zweimal Sprache,* Düsseldorf, 1973.

29. According to the sayings of *Bṛhadāraṇyakopaniṣad,* II.4.10, from Brahma, like clouds of smoke, spread the Vedas, the Purāṇas, mythological tales and images, and various arts given to man as well as to all the universe.

of this interpretation. First of all, one might remember that Pūrva-Mīmāṃsā, which was oriented toward the impersonal commands of the injunctions, vigorously refuted the notion of God the creator. Secondly, it is quite easy to notice that even the structure of the first four *sūtras* of Bādarāyaṇa's text[30] circle around these problems. For instance, in the second *sūtra* we find a definition of Brahman as the creator of the world; it is called "/the one,/ from which the origination of this /universe/ and so on" *(janmādya-yataḥ)* (I.1.2); meanwhile in the next *sūtra* we find a passage concerning the connection between Brahman and the revelation of the Vedas. It is interesting to note that this *sūtra* (I.1.3) can be interpreted in two different ways: the Sanskrit text *śāstrayonitvāt* might be translated either as "/Brahman is omniscient /, since /it is/ the source (lit., *yoni,* or *womb*) of the *śāstras*" or as "/Brahman cannot be known without the Vedas/, since the *śāstras* are the source /of its knowledge./" Śaṅkara, who gives both interpretations one after the other, is not even slightly bewildered or confused by this double meaning; it seems that this kind of ambiguity perfectly corresponds with his own intentions. Actually, he is using here a purely poetical figure—what is known in Indian literature tradition as *vakrokti*, or 'double speech'.[31] One might say that Śaṅkara's own philosophical works, in spite of their unmistakable scholastic tinge, were modelled mainly after the pattern of rather ornamentative exposition of *śruti* texts.

The same pattern was used for many of his poetical metric works. In the famous hymn which is included in the

---

30. It is the first four *sūtras* of Bādarāyaṇa's text and Śaṅkara's Commentary that are undoubtedly the most important (and to some respect even decisive) for understanding the Advaitist's main work. The sub-commentary by Padmapāda *(Pañcapādikā)* is confined simply to their interpretation; they supply the only base of consideration for the exposition of *Sarva-darśana-siddhānta-saṅgraha* by Mādhava.

31. To be more precise, that is *śleṣavakrokti,* or ambiguous evasive speech, ambiguous play of words; the term was introduced by Rudraṭa in his treatise *Kāvyalaṅkāra* (poetical ornamentations), though it sporadically surfaces in some earlier works on poetics.

collection *Śivānandalaharī* the praise of Śiva is read through a skillful word play in the description of a thunder-cloud. The first version runs as follows:

> O you, pouring down merciful water, capable of removing
> burning heat,
> Used by the clever/peasants/ for getting crops,
> assuming strange shapes,
> Attended by dancing peacocks, hidden among other clouds,
> surrounded by the blazes of lightning,
> Auspicious, dark rain cloud—you are always passionately
> thirsted after by the *cātaka* bird!

However, the same chain of words could be understood in a different way:

> O you, sending down the *amṛta* of mercy, who has power to stop painful torments,
> Venerated by the wise for the sake of getting the fruit of knowledge, assuming various forms,
> Followed by the dancing *bhaktas,* living on top of the mountains, you with tangled flowing hair,
> Auspicious, blue-throated /Śiva/,—you are always passionately
> desired by my mind, which is like a *cātaka*
> bird'.[32]

32. Śaṅkara, *Śivānandalaharī*, 52:
kāruṇyāmṛtavarṣiṇaṃ ghanavipadgrīṣmacchi dākarmaṭhaṃ
vidyāśasyaphalodayāya sumanaḥsaṃsevyamicchākṛtim /
nṛtyadbhaktamayūram adrinilayaṃ cañcajjaṭāmaṇḍalaṃ
śaṃbho vānchati nīlakaṃdhara sadā tvāṃ me manaścātakaḥ//52//
One might say that it is certainly not the only example among the poetical works of the Advaitist; as for the simile likening Śiva with a blue-throated peacock, it is developed further on, in verses 53 and 54. What is noteworthy is that this simile is just hinted at by verse 52 where both of its parts (Śiva and a peacock) are already there but presented without a direct correspondence and comparison.

So, according to Śaṅkara, "the sacred texts themselves can speak about an entity which is not yet known only by resorting to ordinary words and meanings,"[33] and yet, in his opinion, human argumentation must be attentive not only to the content of scared texts, but also to poetical and even rhetorical means used by *śruti.* The language is ultimately one and the same: besides the immediate, direct meaning, it offers to the listener the whole aura of additional meanings encircling it. Incidentally, that was also the reason why Ānandavardhana considered it quite possible to make the notion of *dhvani*, originally used only in poetical speech, embrace the ordinary language as well.

2. *THE PROBLEM OF THE HUMAN SOUL: ADVAITA AND ITS CLOSEST COUNTERPARTS*

The concept of the individual soul *(jīva)* is very convenient for summing up the main notions of Advaita, as well as for examining its place in the cultural tradition of India. In Śaṅkara's teaching it became a point of contact between metaphysics and ethics, as well as an example of interconnectedness with other problems. Were one to consider an ontological relationship of God, the soul and the world, and the dependent issue of creation (whether regarded as evolution or not), in other words, the inevitable problem of causality; were one to investigate the source of self-consciousness and the cognitive faculty, the means of knowledge and the criterion of their validity; or were one to consider ethical problems arising in connection with the relative independence of a person within the limits of his accumulated karma, as well as his relation to ritual injunctions and traditional orthodox beliefs,—all this in one way or another is connected with the concept of the individual soul. Finally, the same conglomerate of problems borders the issue of the conditions and methods of correct perception and assimilation of sacred texts.

---

33. Śaṅkara, Commentary on *Bṛhadāraṇyakopaniṣad*, II.1.20: *na ca laukikapadapadārthāśrayaṇavyatirekeṇāgamena śakyamajñātaṃ vastvantaramavagamayitum* /.

A specific attitude of Advaita towards the main part of its canon, that is, to sacred scripture (primarily to the Upaniṣads), was manifested in the special methods of assimilation. These methods (based on Buddhist means of working with a canonic text) were *śravaṇa, manana* and *nididhyāsana.* The *śarvaṇa* (lit., listening to, hearing) implies that the comprehension of Upaniṣadic sayings has its only purpose and goal in Brahman; it can be accomplished with the help of six 'examinations' that contribute to the closer definition of the meaning of texts. *Manana* (thinking over) means the use of proper arguments in order to get rid of apparent contradictions between *śruti* sayings. *Nididhyāsana* (deep meditation) is the removal from the adept's consciousness of everything superfluous and the concentration of his mind on Brahman. True, in his Commentary on *Bṛhadāraṇyakopaniṣad* Śaṅkara hastens to explain that even these thoroughly considered methods do not have any absolute value and may be useful only at preliminary stages of the ascent to Brahman. That is why the scholarly skills of an adept are directly linked there to simple human merits—like love of one's neighbors, of God or of all living beings in general (Vide: Śaṅkara, Commentary on *Bṛhadāraṇyakopaniṣad,* II.4.5).

In the opinion of Sengaku Mayeda, Śaṅkara's treatise *Upadeśasāhasrī* gives the most detailed illustration on the relations demanded by Advaita between a teacher and disciple. To his mind the metrical part of the treatise *(Padya-bandha)* is a concise manual for an adept, while the prosaic one *(Gadyabanda)* represents primarily instruction for a teacher. "The three *prakaraṇas* of the Prose Part, says the Japanese scholar, "can, in content, be regarded as illustrating respectively the stage of hearing *(śravaṇa),* the stage of thinking *(manana)* and the stage of meditation *(nididhyāsana),* which constitute the three Vedantic stages to attainment of final release *(mokṣa).*"[34]

34. Sengaku Mayeda, Introduction to *Śaṅkara's Uadesasāhasrī,* p. 66. One must note that the principle of approaching the structure of this treatise was borrowed by Mayeda from the introduction by Paul

As for K. Satchidananda Murty, he discovered in *Upadeśa-sāhasrī* an indirect exposition of the *anvaya-vyatireka* method, which belongs to the standard set of components absolutely necessary for the correct accomplishment of 'hearing' *(śravaṇa)*.[35]

When he speaks about specific conditions that should be met during the adepts's preparation for the realization of Brahman, Śaṅkara—quite on the same plane—mentions both moral merits, strengthened by corresponding emotional states and stable habits, and clarity of vision, which is brought about by persistent intellectual exercises. Finally, the same commendable patterns of emotions and thoughts continue to function for quite a long time, accompanying the whole initial stage of the adepts's acquaintance with the sayings of revelation. In his commentary to the first *sūtra* of Bādarāyaṇa's text, Śaṅkara maintains that immediately after the hearing of sacred scripture the disciple can rely in his ascent on the four values that pre-

---

Hacker, written to his German translation of *Upadeśasāhasrī* (Vide: "Upadeśa-sāhasrī von Meister Shankara," *Aus dem Sanskrit Übersetzt und Erläutert vol Paul Hacker*. Bonn, 1949, S. 7-9). Later the interpretation by Sengaku Mayeda was favorably mentioned by Tilmann Vetter, who made use of it while trying to prove the existence of content coherence in *Gadyabandha,* as well as examining the meaning of the whole work. Vide: Tilmann Vetter, *Studien zur Lehre und Entwicklung Śaṅkara,* (III. *Upadeśasāhasrī, Gadyabandha* II), S. 76-77.

35. Vide: K. Satchidananda Murty, *Revelation and Reason in Advaita Vedānta,* pp. 152-53. *Anvaya-vyatireka* is quite a well-known logical method, based onthe ascertainment of invariable concomittance of the presence and the absence of two entities. In Advaita it is used for distinguishing *ātman* from non-*ātman*, as well as for specifying the meaning of these terms (Vide: G. Gardona, "On Reasoning from Ānvaya and Vyatireka in Early Advaita," *Studies in Indian Philosophy,* Ahmedabad, 1981, p. 87). For instance, this method can be used for substantiating *śruti* sayings about *ātman,* since it opposes the invariable presence of the witness of all cognitive acts to the possible absence of its objects. W. Halbfass showed that in *Upadeśasāhasrī* (*Padyabandha,* XVIII.96; XVIII.176; XVIII.178; XVIII.180; XVIII.189) *anvaya-vyatireka* often corresponds to the notions of *vyabhicāra-avyabhicāra,* that is, to the so-called 'deviation', 'possibility of being

pare the soil for the arousal of the very "desire to know Brahman" *(brahma-jijñāsā)*. The four values, or conditions are "distinguishing between the eternal and non-eternal reality, indifference towards enjoyment in this world and in the other world; acquisition of peace, self-control, concentration and the like; and desire for liberation."[36]

Let us examine now why it is that Advaita insists upon the necessity to precede the realization of the content inherent in sacred scripture by prerequisites for its correct assmilation. Or, putting the same question from another angle, is it really possible that the correlation of different stages in the ascent towards liberation is somehow previewed in the very nature of the individual soul? What are these 'preliminary conditions' of attaining *mokṣa*; what lies in their foundation?

To Śaṅkara's mind, *jīva* is eternal, it is beginningless and it cannot be destroyed. The Advaitist maintains that one cannot really speak about its creation (nor any creation at all) in the absolute sense, since ultimately everything is Brahman, devoid of any parts or attributes, Brahman, whose nature is immutable. Therefore, one might say that *jīva* is eternal and beginningless, but this reality is the reality of *jīva as* Brahman, and not as some separate and independent entity; this reality is completely revealed only with the dissolution of the soul in its initial source. The human mind, staying on the level of profane knowledge (*aparavidyā*) can grasp this situation only through the concept of the cycles of creation, according to which the soul periodically separates, divides itself from the higher Brahman and after some time is destroyed in the universal fire of *pralaya*. And if for Rāmānuja, for

---

removed', or 'inevitable presence' (W. Halbfass, *Studies in Kumārila and Śaṅkara*, pp. 58-59).

36. Śaṅkara, Commentary on *Brahmasūtra*, I.1.1: *nityānityavastuvivekaḥ ihāmutrārthabhogavirāgaḥ śamadamādisādhanasampat mumukṣutvaṃ ca* /. The third position in the list is given to the six merits, which are not enumerated fully. They are *śama*, peace; *dama*,

instance, the eternity of *jīva* is brought about by its irreduciable reality as a separate atom of substance, for the Advaitist, the eternity of the soul is caused by its being ultimately identical with Brahman.

Both these Vedantins were adherents of the causality doctrine called Satkāryavāda, according to which the effect always pre-exists in the cause. In Rāmānuja's opinion, the cause of the origination of souls is Brahman, in the sense that the whole might be regarded as the cause of its parts. Brahman here is a substrate of changes, actually evolving into the world, just as clay is transformed into earthen pots, and milk into curds. The God of Rāmānuja is evolving and growing from a homogeneous unity into the manifoldness of objects and separate souls (which He already contains within himself potentially). This version of the Satkāryavāda doctrine is usually called *pariṇāmavāda*, or the teaching about evolution, modification *(pariṇāma)*. Besides Viśiṣṭādvaita of Rāmānuja it is characteristic, for example, of Sāṃkhya. In the words of Rāmānuja from his treatise *Vedārthasaṅgraha,* "Brahman, whose body /is formed/ by animate and inanimate beings, who in his gross form is divided by distinctions of names and forms, is presented in the effect. This disunited and gross state of Brahman is called the creation."[37]

I have already mentioned that Śaṅkara adhered to a different version of Satkāryavāda, which later became known as *vivartavāda.* In Śaṅkara's words, "/Brahman/ manifests through the unthinkable power of its real essence these unmanifested /before/ names and forms, different from its own nature, being the seed of the world, supported by its essence, described neither as having its essence nor different from it, and known by their own

---

self-control; *uparati*, renunciation; *titikṣā,* fortitude; *samādhana,* power of concentration; and *śraddhā*, faith.

37. Rāmānuja, *Vedārthasaṅgraha,* 93: *nāmarūpavibhāgavibhaktasthūlacidacidvastuśarīraṃ brahma kāryāvastham / brahmaṇaḥ tathāvidhasthūlabhāva eva sṛṣṭiḥ ityucyate /. Vedārthasaṅgraha of Śrī Rāmānujācārya,* Mysore, 1956.

means."[38] In other words, Brahman is the foundation of the apparent, visible universe, the multifold attributes of which are only temporarily 'superimposed' upon its being. The ontological status of the phenomenal world, which is produced by *māyā,* is intermediary and essentially indefinable. Only the reality of *jīva* can be spoken about without reservation; only the soul, being initially identical with the higher Brahman, can be called *sat* (real). The soul is omnipresent (*vibhu*) and universally diffused (*sarva-gata*) like Brahman, though, of course, these characteristics should not be interpreted in a literal sense, since *jīva* in Advaita cannot be regarded as substance.

According to Śaṅkara, the notion of a multitude of souls is valid only at the level of the empirical world; it is connected with a preceding evolution *(pariṇāma)* which took place entirely in the sphere of *avidyā* and which endowed the soul with individuality as a concise history of its former transmigrations. While *ātman* stays within the limits of the body, emotions and intellect, there cannot be any dissolution, any absolute unity *(sarvathā-aikyam)* with Brahman; there is only similarity, resemblance—just as between the reflection or image *(pratibimba)* and the reflected prototype *(bimba).* In Śaṅkara's Commentary on *Brahmasūtra* it is clearly said: "And the soul is only the reflection of the higher *ātman*."[39]

However, besides this conception, which in later Advaita (in particular, in the systems of Prakāśātman, Sarvajñātman and Vidyāraṇya) got the name of *bimba-pratibimba-vāda,* or, the teaching about the reflection and the prototype, Śaṅkara suggested yet another view of the multitude of souls. In his Commentary on *Brahmasūtra* (II.3.17, etc.) he gives the example of ether *(ākāśa),* which

---

38. Śaṅkara, *Upadeśasāhasrī, Gadya-bandha,* I.18: *svāmavilakṣaṇayoḥ nāmarūpayoḥ jagadbījabhūtayoḥ svātmasthayoḥ tattvānyatvābhyāmanirvacanīyayoḥ svayaṃvedyayoḥ śadbhāvamātreṇācintyaśaktitvād vyākartā avyākṛtayoḥ* /.

39. Śaṅkara, Commentary on *Brahmasūtra,* II.3.50: *ābhāsa eva caiṣa jīvaḥ parasyātmano ...* /.

seems to be divided because of the earthen pots that appear to contain it. After the pots are removed, the initial unity of *ākāśa* is reinstated. In the same way, the soul, now interpreted not as a reflection of the pure consciousness in *avidyā* but as this very consciousness itself, realizes its nature as Brahman, as soon as all the temporary limitations and adjuncts *(upādhi)* of *avidyā* are removed. "All the cause of the disjunction /of the souls/," says the Advaitist, "lies in the adjunctive limitations, /originating/ from *buddhi* and the like, just as the cause of the dividing of clear ether /lies/ in its connection with earthen pots."[40] This theory, later formulated by Vācaspatimiśra as the 'teaching about disjunction' *(avaccheda-vāda),* was slightly less popular in Advaita.

Since both these conceptions are given by Śaṅkara one after the other, without pointing out possible inconsistencies and contradictions, they should probably be regarded as metaphors, useful for approaching Brahman, but not in their literal *(mukhya)* senses. One might add that if *bimba-pratibimba-vāda* correlates better with the state of similarity with the higher *ātman,* that can be attained during one's life,[41] *avaccheda-vāda,* which stresses the dissolution of the soul in Brahman, corresponds rather to the

---

40. Śaṅkara, Commentary on *Brahmasūtra,* II.3.17: *buddhyādy-upādhinimittaṃ tvasya pravibhāgapratibhānākāśasyena ghaṭādisaṃbandhanimittam* /.

41. The notion concerning the possibility of liberation in one's life time (*jīvamukti*) was one of the specific traits of Śaṅkara's Advaita. According to it, liberation *(mokṣa)* cancels the action of all *karma* that binds this individual soul—with the exception of the *karma* which has already started to bear fruits (it is usually called *prārabdha-karma*). Therefore the liberated one, who has attained identity with the higher Brahma, still preserves his body up to the time of his natural death. Of course, he does not particularly care any more about subjugating his actions to moral and religious duties: his compassion and kindness spontaneously pour down on all the world. Other schools of Vedanta maintained that ultimate liberation could be possible only after shedding the body after death (the concept of *videha-mukti,* or liberation without the body). About this vide: S. K. Ramachandra Rao, *Jīvanmukti in Advaita,* Gandhinagar, 1979.

liberation accomplished after death, when the inertia of former *karma* has been exhausted.

The very identity of *jīva* and the higher Brahman is postulated by Śaṅkara owing to their common nature. Answering the arguments of the Vaiśeṣikas, the followers of Kaṇāda, who regarded consciousness as an adventitious *(āgantuka),* accidental attribute of the soul, Śaṅkara supports the opinion of the Sāṃkhyayikas, according to which *jīva* is conscious by its very nature. Therefore consciousness *(caitanya, vidyā)* is considered in Advaita as the eternally existing, independent reality which is self-evident. It manifests all the objets, 'illuminating them as a lamp', but does not need any other entity for its own manifestation; that is, it is understood as self-luminous *(svayaṃprakāśa).* Finally, it is immutable, united, none other than the higher Brahman itself.

The consciousness which is usually related to the distinguishing of knowledge *(jñāna),* the knowing subject *(jñātṛ)* and the objects of cognition, is placed by Śaṅkara on the level of *aparavidyā* and is regarded as merely convenient *(vyāvahārika).* It is not by chance that one of the Bādarāyaṇa *sūtras* (II.3.18)[42] is presented by Śaṅkara in the following form: "So /the soul is/ only knowledge / or cognition/."[43] That is, he is reading in it the word *jñaḥ* used by Bādarāyaṇa as *jñāna,* or, knowledge, cognition. According to Pāṇini's grammar (III.1.135), *jñaḥ* means *jnātṛ,* or the knower, the subject of cognition. That is how this *sūtra* is actually interpreted by Rāmānuja, as well as by the other commentator of *Brahmasūtra,* Niṃbarka (*ca.* eleventh century), the follower of a Vedantic school called Dvaita-Vedanta. In this way the latter Vedantists—primarily Rāmānuja—posit knowledge as an essential, inalienable attribute, belonging to *ātman* (both to Īśvara and the souls) in contrast to inanimate things *(jaḍa).*

---

42. *jño 'ta eva* /.

43. Śaṅkara, Commentary on *Brahmasūtra,* II.3.18: *jñānamata eva* /.

For Śaṅkara himself the above-mentioned *sūtra* represents a separate *adhikaraṇa;* that is, it is supposed to introduce its own independent topic for consideration. Regarding consciousness as the inner nature of the soul, Śaṅkara, as we remember, likens consciousness to light and heat, which represent not essential attributes or function of fire, but are its very own nature. An indirect corroboration for this thesis is, to his mind, provided by the fact that this nature is invariably manifested in all states of the soul. Even in deep sleep *(suṣupti)*, notes Śaṅkara after Gauḍapāda, *jīva* returns to consciousness as if to some folded-up inner core. "There was not a time," says the Advaitist, "when the soul was not one with Brahman, because its nature is immutable; but in dreaming, as well as in the waking state, it appears to assume a different form owing to the influence of adjunctive limitations, while in deep sleep, during their fading away, one can speak about the attainment of one's own nature."[44] Then even liberation is regarded as the ultimate realization of this inner nature of the soul, that is, not as the collecting of data or cognitive methods, not as a cognitive act, but as *knowledge* itself, being the pure and unmixed initial entity. Probably because of this view in some schools of Sāṃkhya and Yoga, where *ātman* is represented as pure consciousness devoid of any attributes, one finds the concept of 'liberation during one's life' *(jīvamukti),* similar to that in Advaita.

In contrast to that, for Rāmānuja the Advaitist notion of knowledge as pure identity of the soul and Brahman, where there was no differentiations or attributes, seems absolutely absurd. Indeed, this identity is as if balancing on the very brink of non-being, its reality is only postulated, introuduced arbitrarily, owing to the reference to

---

44. Śaṅkara, Commentary on *Brahmasūtra,* III.2.7: *api ca na kadācijjīvasya brahmaṇā saṃpattirnāsti svarūpasyānupāyitvāt / svapnajagaritayostu upādhisaṃparkavaśātpararūpāpattimivāpekṣya tadupaśamāt suṣupteḥ svarūpāpattirvakṣyate ... /.*

śruti texts. One might remember that it was because of this dangerous trick on the edge of Śūnyavāda that the later Vedantins—starting form Rāmānuja (and prompted by Bhāskara)—called Śaṅkara a crypto-Buddhist *(pracchanna-bauddha).*

I have already drawn attention to the fact that the sphere of lower, or profane knowledge *(aparavidyā)* in Śaṅkara's system includes not only sense experience and logical inference, but also ordinary religious practice, where the object of worship *(upāsanā)* is the personified God the creator, or Īśvara, having numerous merits and accomplishments. Owing to its interpretation of the higher Brahman, Advaita occupies quite a unique place among other Vedanta schools, since for them the higher reality is Saguṇa-Brahman (most often this role is assigned to Nārāyaṇa-Viṣṇu). The accumulation of merits *(puṇya)* is just a preliminary condition, which is necessary but not sufficient for attaining liberation. One who is paying for it by ascetics, piety or love, only gets good share *(bhāga)* in a subsequent trasmigration. All these ways and means are nothing but methods of orientation within the world of *karma*, which cannot ever lead an adept beyond their limits. "These rites and means, the adorning with a sacred thread and the like," says the Advaitist, "are separated from realization of unity with the higher *ātman*."[45] Or, as Śaṅkara explains in his Commentary on *Bṛhadāraṇyakopaniṣad,* "all ordinary /rites/ prescribed by the sacred texts for the lifetime of a man, that is, similar /in this respect/ to specialized /rites/, also cannot have their fruit in liberation."[46] The same argumentation is applied in Advaita to any moral norms or duties that regulate the life

---

45. Śaṅkara, *Upadeśasāhasrī, Gadyabandha,* I.30: *karmaṇāṃ tatsādhanānāṃ ca yajñopavītādīnāṃ paramātmābhedapratipattiviru-dhatvāt.*

46. Śaṅkara, Commentary on *Bṛhadāraṇyakopaniṣad,* III.3.1 (introduction): ... *taiścāviśeṣānnaimittikatvena jīvanādinimitte ca śravaṇāt tathā nityānāmapi na mokṣaḥ phalam* /.

of people. "In its base," says Śaṅkara, "every injunction is an erroneous concept that exists only for somebody who cannot see that his *ātman* is no more connected with the body than ether with earthen pots."[47]

In general, according to Advaita, the soul by its inner nature is alien to any kind of action, since from the acceptance of its activity there would necessarily follow the impossibility of *mokṣa.*Unlike the adherents of the greater part of other religious and philosophical schools, Śaṅkara maintains that any ability to act could not just remain unused, folded-up in a sort of a potency—even should the man who had already attained liberation try to avoid any connection with worldly activity. Indeed, were the possibility of liberation dependent upon some outward circumstances and means, it could not be regarded as absolutely self-contained. Therefore, one has to admit that the soul, being identical with the higher Brahman, cannot act and cannot enjoy the fruits of action, and the state of activity is brought about by its adjunctive, 'body' instruments. "In this world a carpenter is unhappy," argues the Advaitist, "when he has in his hands the instruments of his work—a small axe and the like—and only having returned home, having put down the instruments, being self-contained, inactive and non-engaged, /this carpenter/ is happy. And similarly, the *ātman* connected wih duality, which is brought about by *avidyā,* staying in dreaming or waking state, /this *ātman*/ is an agent and /therefore/ unhappy. But the same /*ātman*/, having returned to its own being, that is, to the higher Brahman, for the sake of the destruction of tiredness, free from /the chain of/ cause and effects, inactive, is happy and stays self-luminous, clear."[48]

---

47. Śaṅkara, Commentary on *Brahmasūtra,* II.3.48: *satyaṃ vyatirekādarśino niyojyatvaṃ tathāpi vyomādighaṭavadehādyasaṃhatatvamapaśyata evātmano niyojyatvābhimānaḥ* /.

48. Śaṅkara, Commentary on *Brahmasūra,* II.3.40: *tathā tu takṣā loke vāsyādikaraṇahastaḥ kartā duḥkhī bhavati sa eva svagṛhaṃ*

Having examined the Advaita notion of the individual soul, let us try to distinguish the concepts of this system from those of its closest counterparts, that is, from the ideas of Sāṃkhya and Viśiṣṭa-Advaita. It is well-known that according to Rāmānuja's teaching, *jīva,* being united with Brahman, is still endowed with many specific features: it has a specific (minimal) size and is capable of knowing and acting. And Sāṃkhya has a striking likeness with Advaita in is notion of *ātman:* in both systems it is considered as pure consciousness, as inactive reality devoid of any attributes. Still, Sāṃkhya, in contrast with Advaita, defends the thesis that there is a multitude of *ātmans.* In the words of the Advaitist from the first *adhyāya* of his Commentary on *Brahmasūtra,* "this text called *śārīraka* /that is, telling about the embodied soul/ is started against all these who refute the notion that *ātman* is only one".[49]

First of all, I would like to remind the reader that in Śaṅkara's system *avidyā* might be linked to the concept of shaping future incarnations of the soul by its actions in the past. In other words, the world of *avidyā,* that is, the phenomenal world, which is not endowed with independent reality, is just the world where the soul is bound by its *sāṃsāric* transmigrations which obey the law of *karma.* But this kind of attitude brings us to the following line of inference.

Firstly, beyond the act of play, or creation, Brahman is in no way related to the universe, where only changeability reigns (this changeability of phenomena is produced by *karma)*; it can be comprehended only as something essentially opposed to *karma.*

---

prāpto vimuktavāsyādiarṇaḥ svastho nirvṛto nirvyāpāraḥ sukhī bhavatyevamavidyāpratyupasthāpitadvaitasaṃpṛkta ātmā svapnajāgaritāvasthayoḥ kartā duḥkhī bhavati sa tacchramāpanuttaye svamātmānaṃ paraṃ brahma praviśya vimuktakāryakaraṇasaṃghāto 'kartā sukhī bhavati saṃprasādāvasthāyām /.

49. Śaṅkara, Commentary on *Brahmasūtra,* I.3.19: *teṣām sarveṣāmāmaikatvasamyagdarśanapratipakṣabhūtānāṃ pratibodhāyedaṃ śārīrakamārabdham* /.

Secondly, *karma*, or active, evolving *avidyā* in its turn represents something outer or external in relation to Brahman. As a result of specific actions, emotions and volitions of the individual soul in the past, *karma* incessantly and unavoidably produces the no-less-definite sense organs, and personal features of the subsequent incarnation. *Karma* creates for the *jīva* its future methods and ways of perception, thus outlining its future destiny, but only for as long as this destiny is under its power and is exhausted by the interlinking of the phenomena. Actually, one might say that only *karma* is ever creating the world of empirical events. On the universal scale this process is, as we have already seen, beginningless—just as there is no beginning for *avidyā* or *jīva* itself.

Hopefully, this approach does not seem to be an arbitrary identification of Śaṅkara's views with, say, the position of Vijñānavāda. Still, let us not forget that Śaṅkara does not distinguish between *māyā* and *avidyā*, that is, between the universal aspect of the illusory cosmic play of becoming and subjectively obscured perception, or ignorance. Finally, do not let us forget—and this is yet another corroboration of the ultimate 'single-layer' structure of the world in Śaṅkara's system, since it is not divided into a reflection and its prototype, but rather they are ultimately merged together—that all the psychic traits of the soul are mere productions of *avidyā*. By analogy with Sāṃkhya one might say that they are natural *(prakṛta)* formations.

On the level of the reality of *māyā*, the relation of reflection and its prototype exists only between Brahman and *jīva*. From the standpoint of the ultimate truth, *jīva* itself has nothing to reflect; it is only looking[50] through the

50. As it is said in *Bṛhadāraṇyakopaniṣad*, IV.3.23: "If he does not see /anything in deep sleep, it is like this because/ the seer does not see. There is no destruction for the seer and seeing, because /they / cannot perish. There is nothing different from him that he could have seen." *(yadvai tanna paśyati paśyanvai tanna paśyati na hi draṣṭurdṛṣṭerviparilopo vidyate 'vināśitva / na tu taddvitīyamasti tato 'nyadvibhaktaṃ yatpaśyet / .)* In his commentary on this passage

veil or, rather, through the colored glass of *avidyā*. Hence—the deep-rooted comprehension of *ātman* as *sākṣin* (witness). It is important to take into account that one is not holding this piece of glass against the light: the illuminating ray of light is emanating from the side of the onlooker, and still, the world of *avidyā* is not really a stable and dependable picture. The image is vague and translucent, since light goes through it and continues to spread farther. While this ray of light is still passing through the layer of glass, it seems colored itself, but moving farther and further away, it becomes colorless.

Of cource, the world in Advaita is determined not by subjective attributes of a concrete consciousness, but rather by *avidyā,* which is common for everybody; this *avidyā* is one and only one, just as Brahman is only one. "It is impossible," maintains Śaṅkara, "that the individual soul, /that is/ knowledge, would be different from this Brahman, and /it is impossible/ that there would exist numerous effects/ or separate souls."[51]

Thirdly, there is yet another argument in favor of likening *avidyā* and *karma*: both of them are only preliminary steps in the ascent. One cannot omit them, but one cannot rely on them alone for attaining the goal. Rational knowledge (for instance, logical inference) in Advaita is not just a lower kind of knowledge which has a transition, a bridge, to the higher knowledge. In exactly the same way, all moral and religious merits, quite rightful within

---

Śaṅkara explains that deep sleep *(suṣupti)* is here a metaphor of liberation, while the seer, the subject who perceives— in spite of the suffix determining the agent of action *(tṛc)*—is absolutely identical with seeing. A similar interpretation can be found in *Upadeśasāhasrī* "Since the perceiver himself is only eternal perception, because /here/ it cannot be as it is in logical doctrines, that perception is one thing, while the perceiver is something different." (*nityopalabdhimātra eva hi upalabdhā na tu tārkikasamaya iva anyā upalabdhiḥ anya upalabdhā ca* /. *(Gadyabandha,* I.79).

51. Śaṅkara, Commentary on *Brahmasūtra,* II.1.23: *naivam ekasyāpi brahmano jīvaprājñapṛthaktvaṃ kāryavaicitryaṃ copapadyata iti* ... /

the limits of *karma*, cannot become true means or a bridge leading to the realization of the identity of *jīva* and Brahman. As soon as liberation dawns, they become useless; moreover, liberation is possible only through their destruction.

In Sāṃkhya, since *ātman* (*puruṣa*) is pure consciousness, which cannot be defined further, and *prakṛti* is responsible for the creation of the empirical world, *puruṣa* is regarded as essentially inactive. But, while in Advaita, the multitude of souls (of course, the karmic chain of transmigration might hold together one and the same soul, but there are supposed to be innumerable chains, representing different souls) is valid only on the empirical, lower stage of reality, staying within the limits of *aparavidyā*, in Sāṃkhya, as mentioned before, the ultimate reality includes a multitude of *ātmans*. It can probably be explained by the fact that *prakṛti* formations do not depend upon *puruṣas*, while *māyā-avidyā* in Advaita is the creative potency, or power (*śakti*) of Brahman itself. It is, so to speak, its own reverse side, (which cannot be defined either as identical or as different from it). Being essentially independent from consciousness, different modifications of *prakṛti* can shape and define a multitude of pure *ātmans*. In other words, the multitude of *ātmans* in Sāṃkhya correlates in a certain respect with the reality of nature *(prakṛti)*, since beyond the relationship with *prakṛti* all the *puruṣas* are equally indefinable and, therefore, essentially indistinguishable.

For further corroboration we might return now to the analytics of consciousness, which perfectly reflects the main points of dispute between Sāṃkhya and Śaṅkara's teaching. The most important shifting of emphasis can be seen in the following circumstance. Advaita, which denies the existence of any ultimate entity except *ātman* (and therefore rejects any notion of real 'nature' or 'matter'), refused to regard even *antaḥkaraṇa* (internal organ) as a kind of substance. Since all psychic states are regarded here as different from *ātman* but still dependent upon it, the 'inner organ' is represented as a sequence of functions or mental acts (*vṛtti)* that are illusively superimposed on pure consciousness. Accordingly, *ahaṅkāra* (ego-consciousness, the notion of 'I') ceases to be just an intermediate link between *buddhi* and *manas*, but each of these elements—components of *antaḥkaraṇa*—is now regarded as function, as a movement of thought which is responsible for a confusion of *ātman* with specific manifestations of psychic life. This movement may be repeated incessantly and in different combinations, which creates the necessary prerequisites for the temporary, illusory dividing of *ātman* into a multitude of *jīvas*.

The process of formation of *antaḥkaraṇa* is minutely examined by Śaṅkara's disciple Padmapāda in *Pañcapādikā.* According to him, in the first superimposition of *avidyā* upon *ātman* it is as if the pure consciousness assumes intentionality, becomes directed outwards, positing itself as *sākṣin,* or witness. In the second stage *avidyā* produces *ahaṅkāra,* which is again superimposed upon *ātman*, so that the latter becomes posited as *ahaṅkārin,* or the foundation of the notion of ego. Regarding itself as an individual 'I', *ātman* is evolved into the inner organ, or *antaḥkaraṇa.* So, in the third stage there begins a superimposition of this *antaḥkaraṇa* on *ātman,* and the latter becomes posited as *pramātṛ*, or cognizing subject. In the fourth stage *antaḥkaraṇa* evolves into several *indriyas,* or sense organs; after the superimposition of these *indriyas* upon the cognizing subject, there appears *bhoktṛ,* or the subject of enjoyment. The fifth superimposition—that of the body together with sense organs—upon this subject creates the prerequisites for the appearance of *prāṇin* (breathing, alive one), or *śārīrin* (embodied being); while the sixth one, that is, the superimposition of specific external conditions, contributes to the forming of *saṃsārin,* or the subject of transmigrations.

It seems that because of the inevitable correlation between the multitude of consciousnesses and the reality of the 'natural', inanimate world, the inner balance of Viśiṣṭa-Advaita (the core of which is the doctrine of *bhakti,* or love, 'participation', which calls for relationship at least between two irreducibly separate and real *ātmans*) seems to imply, and even demand, the admission of the real existence of the world. The same goes for a much more serious attitude towards activity, which, together with the faculty of cognition, is regarded by Rāmānuja as an essential and inalienable attribute of the soul, potentially preserved even in its liberated state. And these irreducible attributes *(viśeṣaṇa)* effectively guard the individuality of each *jīva,* which cannot be dissolved in Brahman even after liberation. Finally, owing to this indestructible reality of the external world—it could only be folded up into a subtle *(sūkṣma)* state—*karma* plays a much more essential role in Viśiṣṭa-Advaita than in Śaṅkara's teaching.

In Advaita, the ultimate liberation from *saṃsāra* is regarded as the event which is stipulated and actually brought about by the very essence of the human soul: "since *buddhi* and *ātman* are different /in their nature/, their combination must necessarily come to an end."[52] Meanwhile, in Rāmānuja's system liberation from *karma* seems rather an arbitrary ending, an event that takes place thanks to God's mercy alone: it is interpreted as a kind of *gift* or *favor (prasāda),* and is essentially deliverance from suffering only but not from all personal characteristics as well. Owing to this unavoidable reality of the world, even the faculty of cognition is understood by Rāmānuja as differing according to its scope: it is regarded primarily as reflection, and therefore the grade of its truth or accuracy depends mainly upon the range of the perceived objects.

Still, though it might sound a bit paradoxical, Śaṅkara's Advaita relies much more on human freedom, if we interpret the latter primarily as a right to risk and a consent to take endless responsibility for one's own destiny. It certainly makes the adept transcend the narrow limits of a relationship based on act and retribution, and demands

52. Śaṅkara, Commentary on *Brahmasūtra,* II.3.29: *tato buddhyātmanorbhinnayoḥ saṃyogāvaśādamavaśyaṃ bhavatīti ... /.*

the utmost exertion of his forces, never really promising success. In comparison with Śaṅkara's teaching, Viśiṣṭa-Advaita of Rāmānuja seems much more 'gentle' and tolerant: liberation is ultimately guaranteed by the endless mercy of Īśvara, and each good deed and auspicious thought is also taken into account. One might pay particular attention to the serious attitude of Viśiṣṭa-Advaita towards all religious injunctions; the path walked by a *jīva* in accordance with these prescriptions is regarded as something auspicious even after liberation. And even the most dependable means of liberation—the adept's love of Īśvara, growing out of meditation—is regarded by Rāmānuja as a sort of indispensable demand addressed to the person and entailing a reward.

CHAPTER VII

Conclusion

1. *SUMMARY*

The investigation is almost accomplished, and it is now time to sum up the main points. Aside from the retrospective history of Vedanta, and the sketch of Śaṅkara's life and creative activity, I have tried to provide a consistent exposition and interpretation of the Advaitist's teaching. The order of investigation followed (with only minor deviations) the line of classification into gnoseology; ontology; and ethics and soteriology. On the whole, this sequence is rather closely correlated with the well-known Vedanta definition of Brahman as *saccidānanda (sat-cit-ānanda);* that is, of Brahman as reality, consciousness and bliss. It was more convenient for my purpose to switch the two first components of the sequence. Perhaps it may be excused, since the formula itself does not appear in Śaṅkara's works in any precise way—it was invented by later Vedanta. As for the ideas and crucial problems of Advaita, they were examined from the viewpoint of this definition of higher reality.

From the formal point of view, the presentation of Śaṅkara's teaching began by comparing its tenets with the concepts of those systems most distant and alien in spirit, that is with the ideas of his heterodox opponents. The examination ended with the analysis of the closest systems—Pūrva-Mīmāṃsā, as well as Sāṃkhya and Viśiṣṭa-Advaita. The development of problematics was simultaneously traced in opposite direction: starting with the highest conceptions of apophatic theology related to Nirguṇa-

Brahman, and their down to the bottom of the pyramid of notions, exploring the relationship to ritual, ethical duties and the personified Īśvara. Actually, though, we've made a full circle, since the previous chaper of the book offers an exposition of appropriate ways of reading sacred text and of deliberation on the higher Brahman.

Hopefully, the main conclusion of the present work is more or less clear from the very process of argumentation. It is the polemics of Śaṅkara with his most hostile adversaries or, as in the case with Rāmānuja, the collision of Advaita ideas with the concepts of his later opponents, that clearly demonstrates the role of *śruti* in this orthodox system. The texts of the sacred scripture do not represent any unnecessary addition to Advaita; they cannot be regarded as a tribute to time or, in the words of P. Deussen, a tribute to 'national prejudices'. The constant reference to these texts, and the deep-rooted reliance upon the language of *śruti* ultimately sprang from the inner regularities of Śaṅkara's teaching, from its main theoretical tenets.

Finally, one should say at least a few words concerning Śaṅkara's significance for the present-day philosophical situation, since I believe that his ideas are of quite considerable interest, not only from the historical point of view, but also from a more immediate theoretical one. Of course, scholars examining his system do not always take into consideration the most important sides of Advaita; to be more precise, they do not often choose the traits and features specific to the teaching of Śaṅkara. For instance, many published works deal with the *practical* attitude of Advaita towards the goal of philosophizing, in contrast with the speculative argumentation characteristic of Western philosophical systems. One might mention, for instance, the book by an American scholar J. Taber,[1] in which the author examines the teaching of Śaṅkara,

1. John A. Taber, *Transformative Philosophy: A Study of Śaṅkara, Fichte, and Heidegger,* Honolulu, 1983. One might note, incidentally, that this is one of those rare comparativist philosophical works, where

Fitchte and Heidegger from the angle of their ability to radically change the very outlook of man and his general orientations to life.

However, to my mind, the quest for a possible correlation between Advaita ideas and some notions of present-day versions of hermeneutics and semiotics could prove to be much more fruitful. It is interesting that some similar problems, though related primarily to Buddhist material, are now being investigated by quite a number of scholars specializing in the philosophy of language.[2]

The possibility of a serious comparative analysis of Advaita and present-day philosophical trends is to a great extent facilitated by the specialized investigations into Śaṅkara's system, as well as by the existing translations of his main works. Of course, eastern mysticism—including the religious and philosophical currents within the fold of Vedanta—seems to be in vogue right now; and of course, like any fashion, it can be regarded as an indicator of deeply ingrained social and spiritual need. Whether Śaṅkara will prove useful for the further evolution of philosophical trends, will become clear only in due time.

Generally speaking, any little-known philosophical school or trend comes to the foreground not by mere chance but in its own opportune time. For instance, the radical turn of Western philosophy, accomplished primarily by Arthur Schopenhauer—the turn which made it face a new sphere of problems, and which ultimately prepared the way for Husserl's phenomenology and the 'philosophy of

---

Indian material is taken, so to speak, at first hand: from original Sanskrit sources.

2. One of the graphic examples is presented by the conceptual argumentation of a French semiotic Roland Barthes, presented in his book on Japanese culture, which is entitled *The Empire of Signs* (Roland Barthes, *L'empire des signes,* Genève, 1970). One of his articles deals with the analysis of works by P. Sollers; it is accompanied by some rather apt observations concerning the language operations peculiar to Zen Buddhism.

life'—had been maturing in its own inmost recesses and had grown in response to its own problems. The texts of the Upaniṣads, as well as the Buddhist notions, were rather handy, but had the first scholarly translations from Sanskrit and Pali not appeared, something else would have probably turned up that would have become a suitable pretext and source for Schopenhauer's teaching. Accordingly, if a miracle had happened and Śaṅkara's works had become known in Europe by the 13th century (just as Arab aristotelians become known), Thomas Aquinas would have found some points of contact—and dispute—with the Advaitist. But the list of problems would have been entirely different: probably they would have included questions about the source of the world, the cosmological proof of the existence of God and the hierarchical organization of being.

Now the cutting edge in Western philosophy (except, of course, its scientological and positivist currents) is in a completely different place. In the foreground one can see the problem of correlation between philosophy and language, the question concerning 'pure' consciousness and the possibility of its auto-reflection, the need for 'indirect' (usually literary and poetic) means of philosophical exposition and the like. For instance, the greatest among living Western philosophers, Paul Ricoeur, considers the most important task of present-day philosophy to be "la greffe du probléme herméneutique sur la méthode phénoménologique" ("the grafting of the hermeneutical problem upon the phenomenological method.")[3] Here a serious acquaintance with Advaita may prove helpful, since in its own historical and cultural framework it was exactly that: the

3. Paul Ricoeur, *Le conflit des interprétations. Essai d'herméneutique,* Paris, 1969, p. 7. Ricoeur says in this work that he fully shares the conclusions of the later Heidegger, though to his mind the German philosopher somewhat simplified his task, only slightly skriting some important problems and often superseding a consistent philosophical analysis by poeticized descriptions.

grafting of the hermeneutical attitude of grammarians and, partly, Mīmāṃsakas to some aspects of Buddhist phenomenology. The viability of the newly formed teaching is amply demonstrated by the evolution of Vedanta in India, which has successfully continued up to these days.

2. *VEDANTA AFTER ŚAṄKARA*

The divergence in views of the later adherents of Advaita-Vedanta concerned mainly the problems that had not had a uniform interpretation from Śaṅkara, namely the problem of the source and foundation ('refuge', *āśraya*) of *avidyā*, as well as that of the nature of Īśvara and *jīva*. While Śaṅkara practically identified *māyā* and *avidyā*, his followers were mostly inclined towards the notion according to which *māyā* displayed primarily creative, generating (*vikṣepa*—lit.: dividing, splitting up) functions, and *avidyā* was manifested as an obscuring, covering, concealing *(āvaraṇa)* force.

On the whole, Advaita after Śaṅkara continued to develop along three main lines. The first one originates in the ideas of Śaṅkara's closest disciple, Padmapāda, the author of *Pañcapādikā*. In the12th century Prakāśātman wrote a commentary on *Pañcapādikā,* and the title of this work, *Vivaraṇa,* (or, clarification, sub-commentary) was widely used as a name of a new Advaita school. The adherents of this Vivaraṇa school—Śrīharṣa (*ca.* 12th century), Citsukha (12th century) and others—were laying stress on the 'positive' character of *māyā,* so that this entity was acquiring a certain independence and was more and more resembling something like Sāṃkhya *prakṛti.* In their solution of the problem of the notion of *jīva* the followers of Vivaraṇa were tending towards *bimba-pratibimba-vāda*, since it presupposed the reflection of Brahman in a relatively independent *māyā.*

The second trend within Advaita had its foundation in the works of another of Śaṅkara's pupil, Sureśvara (*ca.* 8th to 9th century), *Naiṣkarmya-siddhi* and *Vārttika,* a sub-commentary on Śaṅkara's Commentary on *Bṛhadāraṇya-*

kopaniṣad. In his polemics with the followers of Pūrva-Mīmāṃsā, Sureśvara notes that while the knowledge of Vedic texts, being verbalized and rationally organized, cannot in itself directly lead to the realization of Brahman, a constant and uninterrupted repetition of sacred sayings (somewhat similar to the Byzantine school of hesychast Christian mystics with its concept of 'constant inner prayer'—'ησυχία) contributes to an adept's gradual advancement towards liberation. According to Sureśvara, the base of *avidyā* is not a single *jīva* but pure consciousness itself. This latter notion supplied a pretext for the critique of Advaita on the part of Viṣṇuite followers within the Vedanta fold: their main argument boiled down to the observation that if it were so, the liberation of any *jīva,* that is, the destruction of its *avidyā,* would automatically lead to the liberation of all souls temporarily bound by *saṃsāra.* Some ideas of Sureśvara and his adherent Sarvajñātman (*ca.* 10th to 11th century) found their later development in the notion of *dṛṣṭi-sṛṣṭi* 'seeing, equal to creation', or, a sort of a solipsistic interpretation of being), the most prominent advocate of which was Prakāśānanda (16th and beginning of the 17th century), the author of the treatise *Siddhāntamuktāvalī.* Considering *māyā* to be absolutely illusory, Prakāśānanda pointed out that one could hardly speak about causality in Advaita, since the existence of the objects there might be reduced to their perception. Marking another extreme point in the development of Advaita, the concept of *dṛṣṭi-sṛṣṭi* is connected most closely to the ideas of Buddhist Vijñānavāda.

Elaboration of the third trend within Advaita was connected with the creative activity of Maṇḍanamiśra (the author of *Brahmasiddhi*) and Vācaspatimiśra (the author of *Bhāmatī*). Vācaspatimiśra distinguished between two kinds of *avidyā*: the subjective and the universal, or 'root' one *(mūlāvidyā);* the latter was supposed to subsist even after the end of the universal cycle. The followers of Vācaspatimiśra gave their preference to the doctrine of *avaccheda-vāda,* since, in their opinion, *avidyā* was rooted in separate *jīvas* and not in the higher Brahman. This Advaita school might be regarded as a sort of a compromise between the quasi-Sāṃkhyaic Vivaraṇa and the almost solipsistic notions of Sureśvara's adherents.

Unlike Advaita, which emphasized the identity of Brahman and the human soul, the followers of the Bhedābheda school maintained that Brahman simultaneously exists in two aspects: as transcendent entity, absolutely different from the world, and as immanently residing in the world and living souls, forming an indissoluble unity with this world. Some scholars look for the sources of the doctrine in *Puruṣa-sūkta* of the *Ṛgveda* corpus. And the first attempt to interpret *Brahmasūtra* along Bhedābheda lines—namely, recognizing as equally valid both the *śruti* sayings concerning the identity of Brahman and the world, and the texts on their ultimate difference—was made by Śaṅkara's younger contemporary, Bhāskara: Bhāskara is also considered to be one of the founders of the Viṣṇuite trend inside Vedanta. Bhedābheda denied the higher reality of Brahman devoid of attributes *(nirguṇa)* and upheld the view according to which Brahman, as the cause of the world, also emanated into the manifoldness of the universe, regarded as its effect.

Early Bhedābheda still closely approached some notions of Advaita: in spite of all his bitter dispute with Śaṅkara, Bhāskara maintained that Brahman is endowed with a sort of inseparable, indivisible nature *(ekī-bhāva),* while its dissolution in the world is caused by actually existing transient limitations *(upādhi).* Insisting upon the absolute reality of Brahman endowed with attributes *(saguṇa),* he thought that in its ultimate manifestation this Brahman was devoid of form, in particular, that it was not affected by worldly manifoldness (*niṣprapañca*) and did not have any parts or 'limbs' *(niravayava),* and only as such could be regarded as the object of worship.

Another eminent follower of Bhedābheda doctrine, Yādava (early 11th century), taught that through its energy of emanation *(pariṇāma-śakti)* Brahman was really evolving into its own personified form (Īśvara), as well as into numerous souls *(cit)* and inanimate nature *(acit).* The equality of the aspects of identity and difference and the admission of the relative reality of a separate soul bring this school of thought closer to Viśiṣṭa-Advaita. It was no mere chance that Yādava's favorite image of the unity of the sea and its waves—the image that depicts the indissoluble interconnection between the higher Brahman endowed with forms and attributes, and the souls that it had given rise to—was an image readily used by Rāmānuja in his commentary on *Brahmasūtra.*

Besides the ideas of Bhedābheda that made a significant impact on the formation of *Viśiṣṭa-Advaita* (lit.: non-duality, defined by differentiations), this Viṣṇuite school was deeply influenced by the doctrine of *bhakti*, expressed in the texts of *Pāñcarātra,* as well as in religious and erotic hymns composed by the Alvaras. The main concept of Viśiṣṭa-Advaita were shaped in the works of Yāmuna, the author of *Siddhitraya* (*ca.* 11th century) and, primarily, those of Rāmānuja (the treatises *Vedārthasaṅgraha, Vedāntasāra, Vedāntadīpa,* the celebrated commentary on *Brahmasūtra*, known as *Śrībhāṣya,* etc., written in the 11th and the beginning of the 12th century).

For Rāmānuja, the Advaita notion of Brahman as pure consciousness devoid of any attributes too dangerously resembles the Mādhyamika concept of *śūnya* and therefore seems to be virtually balancing on the verge of non-being, non-existence. According to Viśiṣṭa-Advaita, the higher Brahman is "the supreme *puruṣa* which is free from any imperfections and endowed with innumerable virtues of unsurpassable excellence" (*Śrībhāṣya,* I.1.2). In other words, it is Īśvara, or God the Creator, Nārāyaṇa-Viṣṇu, worshiped by orthodox believers. It is no wonder that the notion of *māyā* gets a new interpretation in Rāmānuja's system, entirely different from that suggested by Advaita. The very word *māyā* beyond the context of polemics is used with reference to *Śvetāśvataropaniṣad* (IV.9), where *māyā* is supposed to define 'wonderful things'. One can easily see that here it does not mean the illusory nature of the world but rather its manifoldness and variety.

In Rāmānuja's opinion, Īśvara is both the 'instrumental' *(nimitta)* and the 'material' *(upādāna)* cause of the world, since the universe as a whole is its own actual evolution *(pariṇāma)*. But the *satkāryavāda* doctrine, peculiar to Viśiṣṭa-Advaita, is much closer in its essence to the analogous doctrine of Sāṃkhya than to the causality theory of Śaṅkara. The manifested world of inanimate objects and living souls that has its source in Brahman had already existed in a 'subtle' from (*kāraṇāvasthā,* lit.: the state of the cause) before the very act of creation. Unlike Bhāskara, Rāmānuja believes that Brahman cannot be even thought of without its manifestations; in other words, the reality is recognized not only for Īśvara but also for numerous souls *(jīva)* and inanimate objects *(jaḍa)*.

Rāmānuja's doctrine of causality finds its linguistic expression in the notion of *samānādhikaraṇa,* that is, the 'universal foundation': one and the same object, to which you can ascribe various predicates (or one and the same source of various effects). But if for Advaita the existence of the 'universal foundation' of the world is explained through its initial identity with Brahman and the illusory nature of any definitions or attributes, while for Bhedābheda the stress is laid upon the recognition of simultaneous and equal existence of different aspects inherent in one and the same reality, Viśiṣṭa-Advaita is virtually coming back to a more literal and more immediate interpretation: namely, to the notion of the relation that binds together an attribute and its substrate *(dharma-dharmin-bhāva)*.

An atomic soul, whose individuality is preserved even in liberation, is an extremely small unit of substance; because of its minimal size, it can also be regarded as an attribute or definition of some substance of the higher plane. Innumerable *jīvas* are functioning as different modi, or forms of manifestation *(prakāra)* of Īśvara, and as such, are forming its 'body'. (Their own bodies are, in their turn, formed by inanimate 'material' elements, or *jaḍa)*. At the same time they are attributes, inalienable characteristics *(viśeṣaṇa),* of God. Brahman, defined *(viśeṣya)* by these attributes, is a living, changeable whole *(kṛtsnatva)* that is ever subject to the process of transformation, ever undergoing internal evolution; this attitude towards eternal *pariṇāma* allows Visiṣṭa-Advaita—in spite of its obvious inclination to Sāṃkhya ideas—to dispense with the assumption of *prakṛti* as a separate, independent origin, or initial source of the universe. It is just the way Rāmānuja elaborates the central thesis of Vedanta concerning the unity of *ātman* and Brahman: Īśvara, unsurpassed in his power and glory, could not be identical with dependent souls (while each of them, in its turn, is essentially different both from him and from other *jīvas*), but, being an infinitely perfect and infinitely determined substance, he is connected with his attributes by an inseparable *(apṛthaksiddha)* relationship.

The famous 'seven objections' *(sapta-anupapatti),* offered by Rāmānuja against Advaita (vide: *Śrībhāṣya,* I.1.1.) spring from the difficulty of explaining the transition from the attributeless and self-identical Brahman to the variety and changeability of the empirical world. His polemical arguments are concentrated mainly on two problems: the problem of the source and foundation of *avidyā,* responsible for the evolving of the universe, and that of the essential ineffability of *ātman* as pure consciousness, as well as the problem of indescribability *(anirvacanīyatva)* of nescience (that is, the concept according to which the world is regarded not only as 'Anderssein', but primarily as an allegory, or metaphor of the higher Brahman).

Arguing with Advaita, Rāmānuja brings forward his own peculiar concept of knowledge and nescience. Consciousness (or cognition) is always directed towards the object, and because of this intentionality it is always given *together with* the object; being filled up by its contents, it inevitably carries within itself some differentiating characteristics. This qualitatively heterogeneous, attributive cognition *(dharmabhūta-jñāna)* is not a self-sufficient essence, but rather an attribute of some substrate, or—what is practically the same for Viśiṣṭa-Advaita—an ability or faculty of some definite subject. Therefore, 'knowledge-light', or 'cognition-light', suggested by Advaita, within the frame of Viśiṣṭa-Advaita is being transformed into an ability, a capacity to illuminate—or a sort of luminosity, encircling a source of light, that is, a separate *ātman* or even Iśvara. And while the *jīvas,* forming the parts of God's 'body', somewhat resemble pin-pointed sources of light, everyone of which is surrounded by a more or less extended luminous halo, Īśvara is completely illuminated by his own being, absolutely transparent for himself, since his every part or attribute is simultaneously an object for his divine omniscience. In other words, the concept of knowledge and congnition in Rāmānuja's system presupposes a counter-positing of a subject and an object, as well as a multiplicity of cognizing souls *(cit)* and cognized inanimate objects *(acit).* Both the former and the latter are ever existing (only being transformed from their 'subtle' into 'gross' state and back in the alternation of universal cycles) and ever relating to each other, constituting the modi *(prakāra)* of one and the sole God.

Considering the Advaita notion of *māyā-avidyā* and its concept of the grades of reality and knowledge to be an impermissible concession to Buddhist views, Rāmānuja opposes to it the thesis of 'correctness' (*yāthārthatva*—lit.: conformity, accordance with reality) of any knowledge or cognition. Since cognition in Viśiṣṭa-Advaita is reduced just to the ability to illuminate (that is, to reflect passively) independent objects, it differs only by the fullness of the grasping of its object-field, contracting or extending according to the abilities of the subject, but always painstakingly reflecting something that stands opposite it.

That is why Viśiṣṭa-Advaita does not know the opposition of true knowledge *(pramā)* and illusion, mistaken cognition *(bhrama)* in the absolute sense: all the worldly phenomena, in Rāmānuja's opinion, are tightly interconnected, linked with each other, participating in the unity of Brahman. Therefore, even the conch-shell, which from a distance could be taken for a piece of silver, must necessarily contain, if only in minute quantities, real particles of silver. And the preferability of some perceptions, which are regarded as more 'correct' than the others, could be accounted for by their wider pragmatic validity *(vyavahāra-guṇa),* just like the importance of distinguishing silver from mother-of-pearl is primarily called for by the requirements of practice. Viśiṣṭa-Advaita is the only system of Indian philosophy where the theory of 'discrimination of errors' *(vibhrama-viveka)* is devoid of any ontological and gnoseological significance and is interpreted on a purely psychological basis; all perception errors are considered to be a kind of a pathological aberration and are derived from specific defects of sense organs, intellectual qualities and other attributes of the soul. In Rāmānuja's system logic is subordinated to psychology and through its medium to religious speculation, since the cognition abilities of every particular *jīva* are caused by its previous *karma.*

Rāmānuja recognizes the existence of three sources of valid knowledge *(pramāṇa)*: *pratyakṣa,* or sense perception, including the so-called 'perception of absence' *(abhāva); anumāna,* or inference, which includes also comparison and conditional assumption; and *āgama,* that is, the evidence of authority. While discussing the concept of *nirvikalpaka-jñāna* and *savikalpaka-jñāna* (that is, knowledge 'with' or 'without' inventing attributes), which was more or less traditional for the greater part of Indian philosophical schools, he maintains that both these kinds of cognition should be regarded as 'attributive' *(saviśeṣa),* though the former provides only immediate perception of an object, while the latter includes it within the scope of earlier associations belonging to this particular subject. All the *pramāṇas* lead to the rise of specific and qualitatively heterogenous knowledge *(dharmabhūta-jñāna),* and any knowledge or cognition which is devoid of characteristics cannot exist—neither as the higher knowledge taught by Advaita, nor as an initial stage of a cognitive process (for instance, as a homogenous perception recognized by Nyāya). Logical inference deals only with objects and relations presented by sense perception; it transforms these sensations, re-arranging them in accordance with formal rules of syllogistics (*vyāpti*, lit.: the relationship of penetration); the evidence of authority, which also conforms to the data of perception, depends for its correctness upon the person or text providing the necessary evidence. The validity of sacred scripture is based on the evidence of Īśvara; injunctions (*vidhi*) supplied by these texts should be regarded as direct instructions of God, who makes known what he expects from people.

Brahman in Viśiṣṭa-Advaita is not only the support *(adhāra)* of all living beings, he is also the ruler *(niyantṛ),* secretly staying inside them *(antaryāmin)* and directing his subjects towards liberation. The idea of the world and the souls as constituting the body *(śarīra)* of Īśvara finds a new emphasis in the ethical and religious views of Rāmānuja. In his words, "the body is a substance which can be fully controlled by *ātman,* and which *ātman* might support in order to achieve its goals; it is totally dependent upon *ātman*" (*Śrībhāsya,* II.1.9). Viṣṇu, entering into all beings as their inner soul *(śarīrin),* determines himself their rewards and punishments, while simultaneously acting as their only protector *(rakṣaka).*

Fully accepting the notions of traditional religious beliefs concerning the incarnations of Īśvara (and besides the higher, or *para* form of God, they include his main emanations, *vyūha, avatāra,* or widely known embodiments of Viṣṇu; inner rulers of separate *jīvas—antaryāmin;* and *arcā*, or some minute portions of divine nature, contained within the temple objects of worship), Rāmānuja emphasizes that God condescends to step down and enter them owing to his infinite mercy *(kṛpā)* towards all living beings. In its turn, *jīva*—if it does not belong to the number of eternally liberated *(nitya-mukta)* or already liberated (*mukta*) souls, staying with Brahman in the divine world—Vaikuṇṭha, but for the time being remains bound by *saṃsāra*—should give Īśvara an occasion to manifest this mercy. Warning the adepts against the extremes of Advaita and Pūrva-Mīmāṃsā, Rāmānuja calls for the combination of knowledge and actions based on religious injunctions. The possibility of their harmonization he sees in *bhakti*, where the knowledge of Brahman and religious worship *(upāsana)* are merged together. *Bhakti*, being a kind of participation in Brahman, calls for constant inner concentration on the part of the adept. However, if one does not feel prepared for strenuous effort and is rather oppressed by observing preliminary conditions, there is a somewhat easier or roundabout way to the same goal—*prapatti* (lit.: falling down at somebody's feet), or the way of self-resignation and passionate devotional love.

Rāmānuja opposes the Advaita idea of an independent and free advancement of an adept to liberation: in his opinion, the relationship between Īśvara and the separate *jīva* is always that of a master and a servant; that is why liberation is duly regarded as a gift, as a merciful act *(prasāda)* of God. The soul, which in Viśiṣṭa-Advaita is understood as *ātman* endowed with attributes, as cognizing and acting agent, preserves its individuality even after its union with Brahman. Along with the recognition of the reality of the world and the continuous ascending steps of knowledge, which differ only by the scope or range of grasping peculiar to different *ātmans*—starting with lower *jīvas* and going up to Īśvara himself—Viśiṣṭa-Advaita also insists upon the continuous gradation of merits *(puṇya)*, which influences the status of *jīva* even after its liberation.

In the later mediaeval period the ideas of Viśiṣṭa-Advaita became much more popular than Śaṅkara's teaching; it may be explained by the acceptance of the doctrine of *bhakti*, by a tolerant attitude towards traditional local cults, and by the relatively more simple philosophical views expressed by Viśiṣṭa-Advaita. The followers of Rāmānuja tried to substantiate their ideas not only through the famous 'triple canon' *(prasthānatraya)* of Vedanta, but also through notions derived from *Prabandham*, the Tamil corpus of texts known for its strong mystic tinge. The most prominent Viśiṣṭa adherent after Rāmānuja—and simultaneously a staunch advocate of 'both Vedantas' *(ubhaya-vedānta)*, that is the two above-mentioned canonic traditions—was Veṅkaṭanātha (13th through the middle of the

14th century), the founder of the so-called Northern school (Vadagalai) of Viśiṣṭa-Advaita. Another of Rāmānuja's followers was Pillai Lokācārya (13th century), who laid the foundation for a Viṣṇuite sect known as Tengalai, or Southern school; he defended the leading position of the Tamil canon. The adherents of Viśiṣṭa-Advaita after Rāmānuja were mainly occupied with gnoseological, as well as ethical and religious problems (the correlation between *karma* and divine mercy, etc.).

The chronological as well as semantic bridge between the school of Rāmānuja and that of Madhva was supplied by the ideas of the 'second Bhedābheda', suggested by Nimbārka (*ca.* 11th century). Nimbārka managed to introduce the notion of changeability into the very core of the concept of Brahman. In his system, usually called Dvaitādvaita (duality and non-duality), he distinguishes between the static, or self-identical aspect of Brahman *(abheda)* and its dynamic, or differentiating aspect *(bheda),* manifested as a potency, or energy *(śakti).* Nimbārka's notion concerning the real separate existence of *jīva,* which receives its form from Brahman and is dependent upon it, directly leads us to the main notions of the Dvaita school.

Dvaita-Vedānta (from *dvaita*, or duality) was formed within the fold of a Viṣṇuite trend in Vedanta. To an even greater extent than Viśiṣṭa-Advaita, it tried to deepen the theistic motifs of this religious and philosophical system. However, in the purely philosophical constructions of Dvaita one can easily trace the influence not only of Sāṃkhya (as was true for Rāmānuja's ideas) but also of Nyāya-Vaiśeṣika. Among the works of the Vedanta 'triple canon' Dvaita lays particular stress upon the *Bhagavadgītā* (and on other epic texts as well) and theistically interpreted *Brahmasūtra;* besides, Dvaita can be characterized by its clear orientation towards the Purāṇas. The most noted Dvaita adherent was Madhva (13th through possibly the beginning of the 14th century), the author of the commentary on *Brahmasūtra (Anuvyākhyāna)* and the commentary on *Bhagavata-purāṇa,* ten treatises on logic and metaphysics *(Daśaprakaraṇa),* a metrical treatise *Mahābhārata-tātparyanirṇaya,* among other works.

According to Dvaita, the world should not be regarded as an illusion (suggested by Śaṅkara) or a kind of emanation of Brahman (maintained by Viśiṣṭa-Advaita or Bhedābheda): Brahman is not a material *(upādāna),* but only instrumental *(nimitta)* cause of the universe. However, unlike Vaiśeṣika, Dvaita would not reduce the role of Brahman to something like a primal act: it defends the concept of 'permanent creation' *(parādhīnaviśeṣāpti),* understood as the acquisition of new differentiating attributes, entirely dependent upon the will of another (that is, Brahman). This creation, leading to the emergence of new attributes, actually boils down to the constant intervention of Brahman, who can at will reshape even the very structure of the initial material. Producing its impact upon attributes, Brahman can change the very nature of worldly things.

Fully acknowledging the danger of certain pantheistic tendencies within Viśiṣṭa-Advaita, Madhva insists upon the entirely transcendent character of Brahman, which directs the process of the evolving universe but by no means exists in its foundation. Deriving the very word *śarīra,* or body, from *śara* (understood as perishable, decaying), Madhva contends that the world and souls cannot be regarded as a 'body' of Brahman, since it would lead to the lessening and reducing of its perfection. In his opinion, all corresponding texts should be interpreted as indicating the 'spiritual' body of Īśvara. The material cause of the universe is (just as in Sāṃkhya) *prakṛti* (primordial nature, material substance).

To Madhva's mind, all *śruti* sayings concerning the one and the sole Brahman are trying to convey the idea that there is no other being which could rival Brahman in merits and perfections. The difference between Brahman and the rest of the world, created from *prakṛti,* is rooted not in the level of reality, but only in the degree of independence. According to Dvaita, there are three real and eternal entities: God, souls *(jīva)* and inanimate objects (*jaḍa*). The first one is independent *(svatantra);* it is Lord Kṛṣṇa. The two latter (*jīva* and *jaḍa*) are considered to be dependent *(paratantra).* The name given to the system refers to the absolute difference which divides every pair of these entities; in other words, the name 'duality' indicates the initial opposition and non-similarity between the parts of each dual relationship: that of God and *jīva, jīva* and *jaḍa,* God and *jaḍa,* any two *jīvas* and finally any two *jaḍas*, or particles of the inanimate world.

The world emerges into being at the beginning of every universal cycle through the energy *(śakti)* of Īśvara. This energy or potency, often personified in the image of Viṣṇu's consort, Lakṣmī, begins the evolution of matter, or *prakṛti,* "similar to light and transparent fabric." *Prakṛti* represents the immediate source and foundation for the three *guṇas: sattva, rajas* and *tamas,* which are ruled by the three aspects and embodiments of Lakṣmī (respectively, Śrī, Bhū and Durgā). Through the medium of the *guṇas, prakṛti* gives birth to the 24 main elements of nature; the scheme of their emergence closely follows that of Sāṃkhya. Innumerable and varied *jīvas,* being connected with the instruments of cognition supplied by *prakṛti,* animate all the minutest atoms in the universe; they are harmoniously ruled by Īśvara.

In Madhva's opinion, all the *jīvas* are pinpoint bearers of cognition (or consciousness), organized in a hierarchy of cognizant subjects. The relationship between the *jīvas* and Brahman is determined by the doctrine of 'image and proto-image' *('bimba-pratibimba-vāda).* However, in contrast to Śaṅkara's teaching, *jīva* is regarded here as a reflection of God not because of the limiting adjuncts, which are eliminated during liberation, but by its very nature. In Madhva's words, just as a rainbow is not only a reflection but also a refraction of sunbeams, different *jīvas* are differently colored by the light of Brahman penetrating their nature (vide: *Anuvyākhyāna*, II.3.50).

Though Brahman's attributes are undoubtedly transcendent, they are defined by the same terms as corresponding empirical qualities owing to the internal resemblance *(sādṛśya)* between God and the world (vide: *Anuvyākhyāna,* III.2.32-34). But that also means that Brahman in Dvaita is in principle (even if not completely) attainable through cognition and knowledge. There are so-called 'pure' means of valid knowledge *(kevalapramāṇa),* that serve as intuitive and clairvoyant perceptions of Kṛṣṇa, Lakṣmī and some chosen *yogins,* but for the souls that are included in the wheel of *saṃsāra,* there are usually only three valid sources of knowledge *(aṇupramāṇa): pratyakṣa* (sense perception), *anumāna* (inference) and *āgama* (evidence of sacred scripture). All these *pramāṇas* 'correspond to the reality' *(yathārtha),* and, revealing their objects, supply the material for the intuitive knowledge of the inner witness *(sākṣin),* which forms the base of every *jīva.* All errors and faults of perception mean that the *sākṣin* is temporarily not functioning, so that *manas* (a product of *prakṛti*) is acting without any control; in other words they are explained away on a purely psychological basis. The most important of the *pramāṇas* is *āgama,* because, according to Dvaita, the Vedas are absolutely authoritative, 'uncreated by people' *(apauruṣeya)* and are the only means of knowing Brahman.

Gradation *(tāratamya)* in Dvaita is peculiar not only for the souls' capacity of knowledge, but also for their other qualities. Depending upon former actions, as well as upon predominance of *sattva* (bright, clear, intelligent), *rajas* (passionate) or *tamas* (dull, obscure) *guṇas,* souls are divided into three categories: eternally free *(nityamukta),* liberated *(mukta)* and bound *(baddha).* The latter, in their turn, might be *muktiyogya* (chosen for liberation), *tamoyogya* (predestined for hell) and *nityasṃsāriṇaḥ,* or destined to stay in *saṃsāra* forever. The concept of rigid predestination of souls distinguishes Dvaita from other religious and philosophical schools; some scholars were even of the opinion that here one could find traces of Islamic influence.

Dvaita insists upon absolute implementation of all Vedic injunctions, stressing the validity of religious merits *(puṇya),* In Madhva's system an extremely important part is played by the spiritual teacher *(guru),* whose task was to lead the disciple from ritual worship *(upāsana)* to meditation on the nature of Brahman, and, finally to the immediate realization of this nature *(satkarṣaṇa)* (vide: *Anuvyākhyāna,* III. 3.44-46). However, the greatest spiritual effort available to an adept is *bhakti,* which is interpreted as an uninterrupted flow of love *(sneha)* to Kṛṣṇa. When a soul serves God in this way,God bestows on it his mercy *(prasāda),* as well as, eventually, liberation. The growth of *bhakti* in the heart of the adept is a clear sign that this person is undoubtedly chosen for liberation, while his way to Kṛṣṇa is somewhat eased through the mediation of Kṛṣṇa's son Vāyu.

Having reached liberation, soul does not dissolve in God but acquires various means of bliss and 'participation' in the divine nature. Madhva mentions four main kinds of *mokṣa: sayujya,* or entering the 'spiritual body' of Brahman (with a version of *sṛṣṭi,* or acquisition of divine powers); *salokya* staying in heaven where one can see Brahman; *samīpya,* constant closeness to God, bestowed upon wise yogins; and *sarūpya,* or resembling the divine form, peculiar to the servants and escorts of Kṛṣṇa.

The most prominent Dvaita adherents after Madhva were Jayatīrtha (14th century) and Vyāsatīrtha (15th through 16th century). The former is mostly known as an astute commentator on Madhva's works. Vyāsatīrtha, in his turn, was quite a brilliant logician, dealing mainly with epistemological problems. In his treatises he disputed with the followers of Nyāya, Vaiśeṣika, as well as Viśiṣṭa-Advaita (primarily with Veṅkaṭanātha) and other Vedanta schools. The immediate impact of Dvaita ideas, as well as some notions of Nimbārka's Bhedābheda, shaped quite a number of teachings inside the Kṛṣṇaite trend of Vedanta. One might mention here Viśuddha-Advaita of Vallabha (*ca.* 15th and 16th centuries) and the school of Caitanya (*ca.* 15th century) among others.

Later developments within the fold of Vedanta, especially its Neo-Vedantic currents and the like, generally fall outside the scope of this book. However, some observations concerning the role of *śruti* in this system might prove useful in explaining the quite unusual persistence and vitality manifested by the sacred tradition of India up to these days. Actually, the survival of this tradition cannot be satisfactorily understood if one is tempted to account for it by profusely elaborating on the 'conservatism' of the traditional mind, the 'stability' of cultural tradition and the 'rigidity' of theistic dogmas.

Bibliography

ŚAṄKARA'S WORKS

Brahmasūtra Commentary

Brahmasūtrabhāṣyam. Ed. by Ānandajñāna. Poona, 1900-1903.

The Brahmasūtrabhāṣya. Ed. by R.A.K. Narayan. Bombay, 1904.

Brahmasūtra Śaṅkarabhāṣya. Translated by V.M. Apte. Bombay, 1960.

Brahmasūtrabhāṣya. Translated by Swami Gambhirananda. Calcutta, 1965.

"Brahmasūtrabhāṣya," I.I.I (Russian translation and notes by N.Isayeva) *Narody Azii i Afriki,* 1983, no. 4.

"Brahmasūtrabhāṣya," I.I.4 (Russian translation and notes by N. Isayeva) *Narody Azii i Afriki,* 1985, no 5.

"Brahmasūtrabhāṣya," II. III.17-18, 29. 40-41 (Russian translation and notes by N. Isayeva): In: *Drevnyaya Indiya. Yazyk, kultura, tekst.* Moscow, 1985.

"Brahmasūtrabhāṣya", II.II.18-27 (Russian translation and notes by N. Isayeva) In: *Buddizm: istoriya i kultura.* Moscow, 1989.

Date, V.H. *Vedānta Explained. Śaṅkara's Commentary on the Brahmasūtra.* Vols. 1-2. New Delhi, 1973.

Die Sūtra's des Vedānta oder die Çārīraka-Mīmāṃsā des Bādarāyaṇa nebst dem vollständigen Kommentare des Çankara aus dem Sanskrit übersetzt von Paul Deussen. Leipzig, 1887.

Prolégomènes au Vedānta, traduction avec annotations par L. Rénou (1-4 *sūtra*). Paris, 1951.

The Vedānta sūtras of Bādarāyaṇa with the Commentary by Śancara. Translated by George Thibaut. Oxford, 1890-1896. Reprint: *Sacred Books of the East*, vols. 34, 38. Delhi, 1968.

Works of Śaṅkarācārya. Vol. 3. *Brahmasūtra* with Śaṅkarabhāṣya. Delhi, 1964.

Commentary on the Upaniṣads

Bṛhadāraṇyaka Upaniṣad. With the Commentary of Śaṅkarācārya and the Gloss of Ānanda Giri. Ed by E. Röer. Calcutta, 1849-56.

The Bṛhadāraṇyaka Upaniṣad. The Commentary of Śaṅkarācārya. Translated into English by Swami Madhavananda. Calcutta, 1965.

Chāndogya Upaniṣad. With the Commentary of Śaṅkarācārya and the Gloss of Ānanda Giri. Ed. by E. Röer. Calcutta, 1850.

The Chāndogya-Upaniṣad, a Treatise on Vedānta Philosophy. Translated into English with the Commentary of Śaṅkara by Ganganath Jha. Poona, 1942.

Eight Upaniṣads. With the Commentary of Śaṅkara. Translated into English by Swami Gambhirananda *(Īśā, Kena, Kaṭha, Taittirīya, Aitareya, Muṇḍaka, Māṇḍūkya* and *Praśna).* Calcutta, 1956.

Īśā, Kena, Kaṭha, Praśna, Muṇḍaka, Māṇḍūkya Upaniṣads. With the Commentary of Śaṅkarācārya and the Gloss of Ānanda Giri. Ed. by E. Röer. Calcutta, 1850.

Īśā and Kena Upaniṣads. With the Commentary of Śaṅkara. Edited and translated into English by S. Gosvamin. Calcutta, 1964.

Māṇḍūkyopaniṣad. With the Commentary of Śaṅkara. Translated into English by Swami Nikhilananda. Mysore, 1944.

Taittirīya and Aitareya Upaniṣads. With the Commentary of Śaṅkarācārya and the Gloss of Ānanda Giri. Ed. by E. Röer. Calcutta, 1850.

The Works of Śrī Śaṅkarācārya. Vol. 1. *Ten Principal Upaniṣads.* Delhi, 1964 (Reprint from the Edition of T.K. Balasubramanyam Iyer Gurubhaktasikhamani, 1910).

Bhagavadgītā Commentary

The Bhagavadgītā. With the Commentary of Śrī Śaṅkarācārya. Translated into English by A.Mahadeva Sastri. Madras, 1897.

Gītā in Śaṅkara's Own Words. Translated into English by V. Panoli. Vols. 1-4. Madras, 1979.

Śrīmadbhagavadgītā. With the Commentary of Śaṅkara. Ed. by D.V. Gokhale. Poona, 1950.

Śrīmadbhagavadgītā. With the Commentary of Śaṅkara and the Gloss of Ānandagiri. Ed. by K. Sastri Agase. Poona, 1927.

The Works of Śaṅkarācārya. Vol. 2. *Bhagavadgītā* with Śaṅkarabhāṣya. Delhi, 1964 (Reprint from the Edition of T.K. Balasubramanyam Iyer Gurubhaktasikhamani, 1910).

Other Works by Śaṅkara

Ānandalaharī. Edited with English Translation by Arthur Avalon. London, 1917.

Aparokṣānubhūti, Ātmabodha, Daśaślokī, Śataślokī, Upadeśasāhasrī. Minor Works of Śaṅkarācārya. Edited by H. R. Bhagavat. Poona, 1925.

"Aparokṣānubhūti" (Russian translation with notes by E.Zilberman) *Voprosy filosofii,* Moscow, 1972, no. 5.

"Ātmabodha." Traduit en Français par F. Néve. *Journal Asiatique,* Paris, 1866, no. 7.

Ātmabodha. With Fourteen Stotras in Appendix. Edited and Translated into English by Svami Nikhilananda. Madras, 1947.

"Ātmabodha" (Russian translation and notes by A. Syrkin). *Antologiya mirovoy filosofii.* T.I. Moscow, 1969.

Ātmabodhah. Self-knowledge of Śrī Śaṅkarācārya. Madras, 1978.

Daśaślokī. Edited with English Translation by T.M.P. Mahadevan and N.Veezhainatham. Madras, 1965.

Encyclopedia of Indian Philosophies: Advaita Vedānta up to Śaṅkara and his Pupils. Edited by Karl H. Potter. Princeton, 1981.

Hymns to the Goddess. By Śaṅkara and Others. Edited and Translated into English by Arthur Avalon. Madras, 1964.

The Hymns of Śaṅkara. Edited and Translated into English by T.M.P. Mahadevan. Madras, 1970.

Lalitātriśatīstotra. With Śaṅkara's bhāṣya. Translated into English by C. Suryanarayana Murti. Madras, 1967.

Lalitātriśatīstotram. With Śaṅkarācārya's Commentary. Edited by C. Sankararama Sastri. Madras, 1949.

The Pinnacle of Indian Thought (Vivekacūḍāmaṇi). Translated into English by E. Wood. Madras, 1967 (ritradotto in italiano, Roma, 1973).

Pañcīkaraṇam. Translated into English. Madras, 1947.

Śaṅkara's Upadeśasāhasrī. Critically Edited with Introduction and Indices by Sengaku Mayeda. Tokyo, 1973.

Śaṅkarācārya. Śrī Śaṅkara's Teachings in His Own Words. Edited by Atmananda. Bombay, 1960.

Sarvasiddhāntasaṅgraha. Edited with an English Translation by M. Rangacarya. Madras, 1909.

"Sarva-darśana-siddhānta-saṅgraha," chapter 1 (Russian translation with notes by N. Isayeva) *Ucheniye zapiski Tartuskogo universiteta. Trudy po vostokovedeniyu.* Tartu, 1981.

Sarvasiddhāntasaṅgraha. Translated by P.S. Bose. Calcutta, 1929.

Saundaryalaharī (Vol. 1, *Ānandalaharī*). Srirangam, 1953.

Saundaryalaharī. Edited and Translated by W. Norman Brown. Cambridge (Mass.) 1958.

Shankara Acharya. The Crest Jewel of Wisdom. Vivekachudamani. Attributed to Shankaracharya. Translated by Ch. Johnston. London, 1964.

Shankara. Das Kleinod der Unterscheidung. Viveka-chudamani. Mit einer Einleitung von Swami Prabhavananda und C. Isherwood. München, 1957.

Śivānandalaharī. Edited with English Translation by T.M.P. Mahadevan. Madras, 1963.

Upadeśasāhasrī von Meister Śaṅkara (Gadyaprabandha), übersetzt und erläutert von P. Hacker. Bonn, 1949.

Upadeśasāhasrī. With the Commentary Padayojanikā by Śrīmad Rāmatīrtha. Edited by V.L. Sastri Pansikar. Bombay, 1930.

Vivekacūḍāmaṇi, Edited with English Translation by Svami Madhavacaraya. Mayavati, 1921 (Traduit en Français par M. Sauton. Paris, 1946).

Vivekacūḍāmaṇi. Edited by S. Ramayya Bharati. Bangalore, 1902.

Viṣṇusahasranāmastotra. With Śaṅkarācārya Commentary and English Translation by R. Anantakrsna Sastri. Adyar, 1927.

Viṣṇusahasranāma. With the Commentary of Śaṅkarācārya. Edited by Arthur Avalon. Calcutta, 1928.

OTHER SANSKRIT SOURCES

Amarakośa. Edited with Commentary of Bhanujadīkṣita, by Sivadattakovida. Bombay, 1889.

Apta-mīmāṃsā by Samāntabhadra. Edited by J. Mukhtar. Benares, 1967.

The Bhāmatī of Vācaspati on the Śaṅkarabhāṣya on the Brahmasūtra. Edited with English Translation by S.S. Suryanarayana Sastri and C. Kunhan Raja. Adyar, 1933.

Brahmasiddhi by Ācārya Maṇḍanamiśra. Commentary by Śaṅkhapāṇi. Edited by S.Kuppuswamy Sastri. Madras, 1937.

Bṛhati by Prabhākara. Edited with 'Ṛjuvimala' of Śalikanatha Miśra by Chinnaswami Sastri. Chowkhambha Sanskrit Series, 69. Benares, 1929-33.

Iṣṭasiddhi by Vimuktātman. With Extracts from the Commentary Vivaraṇa of Jñānottama. Edited by M. Hiriyanna. Baroda, 1933.

Mādhyamikā-kārikā. Nagārjuna's Mādhyamikaśāstra. Edited with Candrakīrti's 'Prasannapāda' by P.L. Vaidya. Buddhist Sanskrit Texts Series, 10. Mithila, 1960.

Nyāya-sūtra-bhāṣya by Vātsyāyana. Edited by Anantalal Thakur. Mithila Institute Series, 20. Darbhanga, 1967.

Nyāya-pariśuddhi by Veṅkaṭanātha. Chowkhambha Sanskrit Series. Benares, 1931.

Naiṣkārmyasiddhi by Sureśvara. Edited by G.A. Jacob and Revised by M. Hiriyanna. Poona, 1925.

Pañcadaśī by Vidyāraṇya. A Treatise on Advaita Metaphysics. Translated from the Sanskrit by H.P. Shastri. London, 1954.

Pañcapādikā by Padmapāda. Edited with Citsukha's 'Tatparyadīpikā', Prakāśatman's 'Vivaraṇa', Nṛsiṃhāśrama's 'Bhāvaprakāśikā', Ātmasvarūpa's 'Prabodhapariṣodhini', and Vijñānātman's 'Tatparyārthadyotinī'. Edited by Srirama Sastri and S. R. Krsnamurti Sastri. Madras Government Oriental Series, 155. Madras, 1958.

Śabarabhāṣya. Edited by Ratnagopalabhatta. Benares, 1910.

Saddarśanasamuccaya by Haribhadra. Tenali, a.o.

Śaṅkaravijaya vyasacāla-viracitāya. Edited by T. Candrasekharan. Madras, 1954.

Sāṃkhya-tattva-kaumudī by Vācaspati Miśra. Edited with Raghunātha's *Sāṃkhyatattvavilāsa* by Rameshcandra. Calcutta Sanskrit Series, 15. Calcutta, 1935.

Ślokavārttika by Kumārila. Edited by Ramasastri Tailanga. Chowkhambha Sanskrit Series, 11. Benares, 1898.

Śrībhāṣya by Rāmānuja. Edited by V. S. Abhyankar. Poona, 1904.

Tattva-saṅgraha by Śāntarakṣita. With Kamalaśīla's Pañjikā. Gaekwad's Oriental Series, no. 30. Baroda, 1926.

Tattvopaplavasiṃha of Jayaraśibhaṭṭa. Edited by Sukhlaji Sanghavi and R.C. Parikh. Gaekwad's Oriental Series, no. 87. Baroda, 1940.

Triṃśika by Vasubandhu. With Sthīramati's Commentary. Poona, 1965.

Vākyapadīya of Bhartṛhari. Edited by Prof. K.V. Abhyankar and Acarya V.P. Limaye. Poona, 1965.

The Vedāntasāra. A Manual of Hindu Pantheism. Translated with Copious Annotations by G. A. Jacob. Varanasi, 1972.

Vedārthasaṃgraha of Rāmānuja. Critically Edited and Annotated. Translated by J.A.B. van Buitenen. Poona, 1956.

Critical Literature

Antarkar, W.R. "Saṅksepa Śaṅkara Jaya of Śrī Mādhavācārya or Śaṅkara Digvijaya of Śri Vidyāraṇyamuni." *Journal of the University of Bombay.* November 1972, vol. 61, no. 77.

Averintsev, S.S., *Poetika rannevizantiyskoy literatury.* Moscow, 1977.

Ayyar, K.A.K. *Vedanta or the Science of Reality.* Holenarsipur, 1965.

Bahadur, K.P. *The Wisdom of Vedanta.* New Delhi, 1983.

Barthes, R. *L' émpire des signes.* Genévea, 1970.

Basham, A.L. *History and Doctrines of the Ājīvikas: A Vanished Indian Religion.* London, 1951.

Bauer, F. "Advaita Vedanta and Contemporary Western Ethics." *Philosophy East & West,* January 1987, vol. 37, no. 1.

Belvalkar, S.K. *Śrī Gopal Basu Mallik Lectures on Vedanta Philosophy.* Part 1. Poona, 1929.

Belvalkar, S.K., and Ranade R.D., *History of Indian Philosophy: The Creative Period.* New Delhi, 1974.

Betty, Stafford L. *Vadirāja's Refutation of Śaṅkara's Non-Dualism. Clearing the Way for Theism.* Delhi, 1978.

Bhattacharya, V. *The Āgamaśāstra of Gauḍapāda.* Calcutta, 1943.

Bhattacharya, V. "Śaṃkara and Diṅnāga". *Indian Historical Quarterly.* January 1952, vol. 6.

Bhikshu, S. *A Survey of Buddhism.* Bangalore, 1976.

Biardeau, M. *Quelques réflexions sur l'apophatisme de Śaṅkara. Indo-Iranian Journal,* 1959.

Biardeau, M. *Théorie de la connaissance et philosophie de la parole dans le brahmanisme classique.* Paris, 1964.

Kar, Bijayananda. *The Theories of Error in Indian Philosophy. An Analytical Study.* Delhi, 1978.

Brown, Norman W. *The Creative Role of the Goddess Vāc in the Rig-veda.* The Hague, 1968.

Bronkhorst, J. *The Two Traditions of Meditation in Ancient India.* Stuttgart, 1986.

Brückner, H. *Zum Beweisverfahren Śaṃkaras: Eine Beobachtung der Form und Funktion von dṛṣṭānta im Bṛhadāraṇyakopaniṣadbhāṣya und Chāndogyopaniṣadbhāṣya des Śaṃkara Bhagavatpāda.* Berlin, 1979.

Bugault, Guy. *La notion de "prajñā" ou de sapience selon les perspectives du "Mahāyāna": Part de la connaissance et de l'inconnaissance dans l'anagogie bouddhique.* Paris, 1968.

Cammann, K. *Das System des Advaita nach der Lehre Prakāśātmans.* Wiesbaden, 1965.

Carman, J.B. *The Theology of Rāmānuja: An Essay in Interreligious Understanding.* New Haven, 1974.

Conze, E. *Buddhist Thought in India.* Michigan, 1967.

Damrell, J. *Seeking Spiritual Meaning: The World of Vedanta.* London, 1977.

Dasgupta, S. *A History of Indian Philosophy.* Vols. 1-4. Cambridge, 1921-22.

Dasgupta, S. *A History of Indian Philosophy*. Vol. 5. Cambridge, 1955.

Dasgupta, S. *Introduction to Tantric Buddhism,* Calcutta, 1950.

Denifle, H.S. *Die deutschen Mystiker des 14. Jahrahunderts*. Beitrag zur Deutung ihrer Lehre. (Herausgeben von O. Speiss). Freiburg, 1951.

Deshpande, Bani. *The Universe of Vedānta*. Bombay, 1974.

Deussen, P. *Das System des Vedānta*. Leipzig, 1883.

Deussen, P. *Vedanta und Platonismus im Lichte der Kantischen Philosophie*. Berlin, 1922.

Deussen, P. *The Philosophy of the Vedānta. The Vedāntasāra* of Sadānanda Yogendra. Calcutta, 1957.

Deussen, P. *The System of the Vedanta*. London, 1972.

Deutsch, E. *Advaita Vedānta: A Philosophical Reconstruction*. London, 1969.

D'Sa, F. *Śabdaprāmāṇyam in Śabara and Kumārila*. Vienna, 1980.

Durell, D. *Aquinas: God and Action*. London, 1979.

Ebeling, H. *Meister Eckharts Mystik: Studien zu den Geisteskämpfen um die Wende des 13. Jahrhunderts*. Neudruck. Aalen, 1966.

Eckhart, Meister. *Deutsche Werke*. Stuttgart.

Eckhart, Meister. *Lateinische Werke*. Stuttgart.

Edgerton, F. *Mīmāṃsā Nyāya Prakāśa*. New Haven, 1929.

Eco, U. *Il nome della rosa*. Roma, 1978.

Eikhenbaum, B. *O poezii*. Leningrad, 1969.

Eliot, C. *Hinduism and Buddhism*. Vols. 1-3. New York, 1954.

Encyclopedia of Indian Philosophies: Advaita Vedānta up to Śaṅkara and His Pupils. Edited by Karl H. Potter. Princeton, 1981.

Freidenberg, O.M. *Mif i literatury drevnosti.* Moscow, 1978.

Cardona, G. "On Reasoning from Anvaya and Vyatireka in Early Advaita." *Studies in Indian Philosophy.* Ahmedabad, 1981.

Gerow, E. *A Glossary of Indian Figures of Speech.* The Hague-Paris, 1971.

Giri, Swami Mahadevananda. *Vedic Culture.* Calcutta, 1947.

Glasenapp, Helmuth von. *Der Stufenweg zum Göttliche: Śaṅkaras Philosophie der All-Einheit.* Baden-Baden, 1948.

Glasenapp, Helmuth von. *Vedānta and Buddhismus.* Wiesbaden, 1950.

Gnoli, R. *The Aesthetic Experience According to Abhinavagupta.* Roma, 1956.

Gonda, J. *Remarks on Similes in Sanskrit Literature.* Leiden, 1949.

Gonda, J. *Stylistic Repetition in the Veda.* Amsterdam, 1959.

Gonda, J. *Triads in the Veda.* Amsterdam, 1976.

Granoff, P. *Philosophy and Argument in Late Vedānta. Śrī Harṣa's Khaṇḍanakhaṇḍakhādya.* Dordrecht, 1978.

Grimes, J.A. *Quest for Certainty: A Comparative Study of Heidegger and Śaṅkara.* New York, 1989.

Ghurye, G.S. *Indian Sadhus.* Bombay, 1953.

Günther, H.V. *The Tantric View of Life.* London, 1973.

Hacker, P. Śaṅkarācārya and Śaṅkarabhagavatpāda. "Preliminary Remarks Concerning the Authorship Problem." *New Indian Antiquary* 1947, vol. 9. (Revised version: P. Hacker. Kleine Schriften, S. 41-58. Wiesbaden, 1978).

Hacker, P. "Vedānta Studien, 1. Bemerkungen zum Idealismus Śaṅkaras." *Die Welt des Orients,* Bd. 3, Wuppertal, 1948.

Hacker, P. *Upadeśasāhasrī von Meister Shankara.* Aus dem Sanskrit übersetzt und erläutert von Paul Hacker. Religionsgeschichtliche Texte. Herausgeben von Gustav Mensching. Heft 2. Bonn, 1949.

Hacker, P. "Eigentümlichkeiten der Lehre und Terminologie Saṅkaras: Avidyā, Nāmarūpa, Māyā, Īśvara." *Zeitschrift der Deutschen Morgenländischen Gesellschaft*. Bd. 100, 1950.

Hacker, P. *Untersuchungen über Texte des frühen Advaitavāda. 1. Die Schüler Śaṅkaras*. Mainz. Akademie der Wissenschaften und der Literature. Abhandlungen. Geistes-und Sozialwissenschaftliche Klasse. Jg. 1950, no 26. Wiesbaden, 1951.

Hacker, P. "Jayantabhaṭṭa und Vācaspatimiśra, ihre Zeit und ihre Bedeuting für die Chronologie des Vedānta. Beitriäge zur indischen Philologie und Altertumskunde. Alt-.und Neu-Indische Studien, 7. Hamburg, 1951.

Hacker, P. "Die Lehre von den Realitätsgraden im Advaita-Vedānta." *Zetschrift für Missionswissenschaft und Religionswissenschaft*. Münster/Westfallen. Bd. 36, 1952.

Hacker, P. *Vivarta. Studien zur Geschichte der illusionistischen Kosmologie und Erkenntnistheorie der Inder*. Mainz. Akademie der Wissenschaften und der Literatur. Abhandlungen Geistes und Sozialiwissenschaftliche Klasse. Jg. 1953, no 26, Wiesbaden.

Hacker, P. "Relations of Early Advaitins to Vaiṣṇavism." *Wiener Zeitschrift für die Kunde Süd-und Ostasiens*. Bd. 9, 1965.

Hacker, P. "Śaṅkara der Yogin und Śaṅkara der Advaitin. Einige Beobachtungen." *Beiträge zur Geistesgeschichte Indiens*. Festschrift für Erich Frauwallner. Wien, 1968 .

Hacker, P. "Notes on the Māṇḍūkyopaniṣad and Śaṅkara's Āgamaśāstra-vivaraṇa". *India Maior*. Congratulation Volume Presented to J. Gonda. Leiden, 1972.

Hacker, P. Rez.: Rudolf Otto. *Westöstliche Mystik*. 3. Auflage, München, 1971. "Zeitschrift für Missionswissenschaft und Religionswissenschaft". Münster/Westfallen. Bd. 58, 1974.

Hacker, P. Kleine Schriften. Herausgegeben von L. Schmithausen. Wiesbaden, 1978.

Halbfass, W. *Studies in Kumārila and Śaṅkara*. Reinbek, 1983.

Heidegger, M. *Unterwegs zur Sprache*. Pfullingen, 1959.

Heinrich, W. *Verklärung und Erlösung in Vedanta*. Salzburg, 1956.

Hiriyanna, M. *Outlines of Indian Philosophy*. Bombay, 1976.

I-Tsing, *A Record of the Buddhist Religion* (AD 671-95). Oxford, 1896.

Ingalls, D.H.H. "Saṃkara's Arguments against the Buddhists." *Philosophy East and West*, January 1954, vol. 3, no. 4.

Inklusivismus. *Eine indische Denkform*. Herausgeben von G. Oberhammer. Wien, 1983.

Ivānka, E. von. *Plato Christianus. Übernahme und Umgestaltung des Plationismus durch die Väter*. Einsiedeln, 1964.

Ivanov, V. *Ocherki po istorii semiotiki v SSSR*. Moscow, 1976.

Jha, R. Ch. *The Vedic and the Buddhist Concept of Reality As Interpreted by Śaṅkara and Nāgārjuna*. Calcutta, 1973.

Kane, P.V. *History of Dharmaśāstra*. Vol. 2. Part 1. Poona, 1941.

Keith, A.B. "The Karma-Mīmāṃsā." *Journal of the Royal Asiatic* Society, 1907.

Keith, A.B. *The Karma-Mīmāṃsā*. London, 1921.

Kierkegaard, Søren. *Afsluttende uvidenskabelig Efterskrift til de philosophiske Smuler. Mimisk-pathetisk-dialektisk Sammenskrift, Existentielt Indlaeg af Johannes Climacus. S. Kierkegaards Samlede Vaerker*. Bind 10 (Andet halvbind). København, 1962.

Kunjunni, Raja K. *Indian Theories of Meaning*. Madras, 1963.

Kunjunni, Raja K. "On the Data of Śaṃkarācārya and Allied Problems." *Adyar Library Bulletin*. Vol. 24, pts. 3-4, 1960.

Kuppuswamy, Sastri S. *Introduction to Maṇḍanamiśra's Brahmasiddhi*. Madras, 1937.

Lacombe, O. *L'absolu selon le Vedānta*. Paris, 1937.

Levy, John. *Immediate Knowledge and Happiness (Sadhyomukti): The Vedāntic Doctrine of Non-Duality*. London, 1970.

Le Saux, H. *Sagesse hindou, mystique chrétienne: du védanta à la Trinitè*. Paris, 1965.

Lossky, V. *A l'image et à la resemblance de Dieu*. Paris, 1967.

Lott, E.J. *Vedantic Approaches to God.* London,1980.

Mahadevan, T.M.P. *The Philosophy of Advaita.* London, 1938.

Mahadevan, T.M.P. *Gauḍapāda: A Study in Early Advaita.* Madras, 1952.

Mahadevan, T.M.P. *The Study of Advaita.* London, 1957.

Mahadevan, T.M.P. "The Sage of Kañchi." *Preceptors of Advaita.* Edited by T.M.P. Mahadevan. Madras, 1968.

Mahadevan, T.M.P. *The Hymns of Śaṅkara.* Madras, 1970.

Mainkar, T.G. *The Making of the Vedānta.* Delhi, 1980.

Martin-Dubost, P. *Çankara et le Vedanta.* Paris, 1973.

Matilal, B.K. *Epistemology, Logic and Grammar in Indian Philosophical Analysis.* Paris, 1971.

Matilal, B.K. Foreword. Granoff Ph. *Philosophy and Argument in Late Vedānta.* London. 1978.

Max Müller, F. *Three Lectures on the Vedānta Philosophy.* London, 1984.

Max Müller, F. *The Six Systems of Indian Philosophy.* New Delhi, 1973.

Mayeda, Sengaku. "The Authenticity of the Bhagavadgītābhāṣya Ascribed to Śaṅkara." *Wiener Zeitschrift für die Kunde Süd-und Ostasiens.* 1965, t. 9.

Mayeda, Sengaku. *Śaṅkara's Upadeśasāhasrī.* Critically edited with Introduction and Indices. Tokyo, 1973.

Mehta, J.L. "Heidegger and Vedanta: Reflections on a Questionable Theme." *International Philosophical Quarterly.* New York, 1978, vol. 18,no 2.

Menon, Y. Keśhava and Allen F.R. *The Pure Principle. An Introduction to the Philosophy of Śaṅkara.* Ann Arbor (Mich.), 1960.

Moeller, V. *Die Mythologie der vedischen Religion und das Hinduismus.* Stuttgart, 1966.

Morichini, G. "History of Early Vedanta". *East and West*. IsMEO. Rome, 1960.

Morretta, A. *Il pensiero Vedanta*. Roma, 1968.

Mudgal, S. *Advaita of Śaṅkarà: a Reappraisal*. Delhi, 1975.

Murti, T.R.V. "Saṃvṛti and Paramārtha in Mādhyamika and Advaita Vedānta." *The Problem of Two Truths in Buddhism and Vedanta*. Boston, 1973.

Nakamura, Hajime. "The Vedānta As Noticed in Mediaeval Jain Literature." *Indological Studies in Honor of W. Norman Brown*. New Haven, 1962.

Nakamura, Hajime. "Bhāskara, the Vedāntin, in Buddhist Literature." *Annals of the Bhandarkar Oriental Research Institute*. Golden Jubilee Volume. Vols. 68-69. Poona, 1968.

Nakamura, Hajime. *A History of Early Vedānta Philosophy*. Delhi, 1983.

O'Flaherty, W.D. *Asceticism and Eroticism in the Mythology of Siva*. London, 1973.

Oberhammer, G. *Parasarabhaṭṭas Tattvaratnakaraḥ*. (Österreichische Akademie der Wissenschaften. Philosophisch-historische Klasse. Bd. 346. Veröffentlichen der Kommission für Sprachen und Kulturen Südasiens. H. 14. Materialen zur Geschichte der Rāmānuja-Schule, 1). Wien, 1979.

Otto, R. *West-östliche Mystik: Vergleich und Unterscheidung zur Wesendeutung*. Gotha, 1926.

Padmarajiah, Y.J. *Jaina Theories of Reality and Knowledge*, Bombay, 1963.

Panikkar, R. *The Vedic Experience*. Poona, 1958.

Pathak, K.B. "The Data of Śaṅkarācāraya." *Indian Antiquary*. Vol. 2. London, 1892.

Pathak, K.B. "Bhartṛhari and Kumārila." *Journal of the Bombay Branch of the Royal Asiatic Society*. Bombay, 1912, vol. 18.

Piantelli, M. *Śaṅkara e la rinascita del brāhmanesimo*. Fossano, 1974.

Potebnia, A.A. *Iz zapisok po teorii slovesnosti.* Kharkov, 1905.

Puri, B.N. *India under the Kushanas.* Bombay, 1964.

Radhakrishna, Sastri S.V. *Śrī Śaṅkaravijayamakaranda.* Tiruchy, 1978.

Radhakrishna, S. *Indian Philosophy.* London, 1951.

Ramachandra Rao, S.K. *Jīvanmukti in Advaita.* Gandhinagar, 1979.

Ramachandra Rao, S.K. *Consciousness in Advaita: Source Material and Methodological Considerations.* Bangalore, 1989.

Rénou, L. "Les povoirs de la parole dans les hymnes védiques." *Edudes védoques et paninénnes.* T. 1. Paris, 1955.

Ricoeur, P. *Le conflict des interprétations. Essai d'herméneutique.* Paris, 1969.

Rhys-Davids, T.W. *Dialogues of the Buddha.* Vol. 1. Oxford, 1899.

Rozenberg, O.O. *Problemy buddiyskoy filosofii.* Petrograd, 1918.

Rüping, K. *Studien zur Frühgeschichte der Vedānta-Philosophie.* Teil 1. *Philogische üntersuchungen zu den Brahmasūtra-Kommentaren des Śaṅkara und des Bhāskara,* Wiesbaden, 1977.

Sartre, J.P. *L'imaginaire.* Paris, 1940.

Sartre, J.P. *Un théâtre de situations.* Paris, 1973.

Satchidananda Murty K. *Revelation and Reason in Advaita Vedānta.* New York, 1959.

Schmithausen, Lambert. *Maṇḍanamiśra's Vibhramavivekah. Mit einer Studie zur Entwicklung der indischen Irrtumslehre.* Wien, 1965.

Sengupta, Anima. *Sāṃkhya and Advaita Vedānta: A Comparative Study.* Patna, 1973.

Sengupta, B.K. *A Critique on the Vivaraṇa School.* Studies in Some Fundamental Advaitist Theories. Calcutta, 1959.

Sharma, C.D. *A Critical Survey of Indian Philosophy.* London, 1960.

Silburn, L. *Le Vijñāna Bhairava*. Paris, 1961.

Silburn, L. *La Mahārthamañjarī de Maheśvarānanda. Avec des extraits du Parimāla*. Paris, 1968.

Singh, S. *Consciousness As Ultimate Principle*. New Delhi, 1985.

Sinha, D. *The Idealist Standpoint: A Study in the Vedāntic Metaphysics of Experience*. Santiniketan, 1965.

Sinha, Jadunath. *Problems of Post-Śaṃkara Advaita Vedānta*. Calcutta, 1971.

Saussure, F. de. *Cours de linguistique générale*. Paris, 1972.

Smart, Ninian. *Doctrine and Argument in Indian Philosophy*. London, 1964.

Sprung, M., ed. *The Problem of Two Truths in Buddhism and Vedānta*. Boston, 1973.

Srinivasacari, D.N. *Śaṅkara and Rāmānuja*. Madras, 1913.

Srinivasachari, P.N. *Advaita and Viśiṣṭādvaita*. Bombay, 1961.

Stcherbatsky, T. *Buddhist Logic*. Vols. 1-2. Leningrad, 1930.

Stcherbatsky, T. *The Central Conception of Buddhism*. Calcutta, 1956.

Taber, J. A. *Transformative Philosophy: A Sudy of Śaṅkara, Fichte, and Heidegger*. Honolulu, 1983.

Tatia, N. *Studies in Jaina Philosophy*. Benaras, 1951.

Telang, K.T. "The Data of Śaṃkarācārya." *New Indian Antiquary*, Vol. 13, 1929.

Thapar, R. *Aśoka and the Decline of the Mauryas*. Oxford, 1961.

Tripathi, M.S. *A Sketch of the Vedānta Philosophy*. New Delhi, 1982.

Tucci, G. *A Sketch of Indian Materialism: Proceedings of the First Indian Philosophical Congress*. Delhi, 1925.

Tucci, G. *Minor Buddhist Texts*. Part 2. IsMEO. Rome, 1958.

Tucci, G. *Linee di una storia del materialismo indiano: Opera minora. P.* 1. Roma, 1971.

Vetter, T. *Maṇḍanamiśra's Brahmasiddhiḥ Brahmakāṇḍaḥ.* Übersetzung, Einleitung und Anmerkungen. Wien, 1969.

Vetter, T. *Sarvajñātman's Saṃkṣepaśārīrakam.* Wien, 1972.

Vetter, T. *Studien zur Lehre und Entwicklung Śaṅkaras.* Wien, 1979.

Walleser, Max von. *Der ältere Vedānta. Geschichte, Kritik und Lehre.* Heidelberg, 1910.

Warder, A.K. *Indian Buddhism.* Delhi, 1970.

Wayman, A. *The Buddhist Tantras: Light on Indo-Tibetan Esotericism.* New York, 1973.

Weisgerber, L. *Von den Kräften der deutschen Sprache III. Die Muttersprache im Aufbau unserer Kultur.* 2. Auflage. Düsseldorf, 1957.

Weisgerber, L. *Zweimal Sprache.* Düsseldorf, 1973.

Whaling F., "Śaṅkara and Buddhism." *Journal of Indian Philosophy,* Dordrecht, 1979, vol. 7, no 1.

Winternitz, M. *Geschichte der indischen Literatur.* Bd. 2. Leipzig, 1913.

Wood, E.E. *The Glorious Presence: A Study of the Vedanta Philosophy and Its Relation to Modern Thought.* New York, 1951.

Wood, E.E. *The Vedānta Dictionary.* New York, 1964.

Yelizarenkova, T. Ya., Toporov V.N. "Drevneindiyskaya poetika i yeyo indoyevropeyskiye istoki". *Literatura i kultura drevney i srednevekovoy Indii.* Moscow, 1979.

Yelizarenkova, T.Ta., Toporov V.N. "O vediyskoy zagadke tipa 'brahmodya," *Paremiologicheskiye issledovaniya.* Moscow, 1984.

Zilberman, D. "Priblizhayushchiye rassuzhdeniya o modalnoy metodologii i summe metafizik." *Rossiya (Russia). Studi e ricerche a cura di Vittorio Strada.* Roma, 1980, no. 4.

Zilberman, D.B. *The Birth of Meaning in Hindu Thought.* Edited by Robert S. Cohen. Dordrecht, 1988.

Index